EXPOSING VIOLENCE

Leonardo

Seán Cubitt, Editor-in-Chief

Making Sense: Cognition, Computing, Art, and Embodiment, Simon Penny, 2017

Weather as Medium: Toward a Meteorological Art, Janine Randerson, 2018

Laboratory Lifestyles: The Construction of Scientific Fictions, edited by Sandra Kaji-O'Grady, Chris L. Smith, and Russell Hughes, 2019

Invisible Colors: The Arts of the Atomic Age, Gabrielle Decamous, 2019

Virtual Menageries: Animals as Mediators in Network Cultures, Jody Berland, 2019

From Fingers to Digits: An Artificial Aesthetic, Margaret A. Boden and Ernest A. Edmonds, 2019

MATERIAL WITNESS: Media, Forensics, Evidence, Susan Schuppli, 2020

Tactics of Interfacing: Encoding Affect in Art and Technology, Ksenia Fedorova, 2020

Giving Bodies Back to Data: Image Makers, Bricolage, and Reinvention in Magnetic Resonance Technology, Silvia Casini, 2021

A Biography of the Pixel, Alvy Ray Smith, 2021

Living Books: Experiments in the Posthumanities, Janneke Adema, 2021

Art in the Age of Machine Learning, Sofian Audry, 2021

Northern Sparks: Innovation, Technology Policy, and the Arts in Canada from Expo 67 to the Internet Age, Michael Century, 2022

Design in Motion: Film Experiments at the Bauhaus, Laura A. Frahm, 2022

Christa Sommerer & Laurent Mignonneau: The Artwork as a Living System 1992–2022, edited by Karin Ohlenschläger, Peter Weibel, and Alfred Weidinger, 2023

Computational Formalism: Art History and Machine Learning, Amanda Wasielewski, 2023

Art + DIY Electronics, Garnet Hertz, 2023

Picture Research: The Work of Intermediation from Pre-Photography to Post-Digitization, Nina Lager Vestberg, 2023

Voidopolis, Kat Mustatea, 2023

After Eating: Metabolizing the Arts, Lindsay Kelley, 2023

Tactical Publishing: Using Senses, Software, and Archives in the Twenty-First Century, Alessandro Ludovico, 2024

The Future Is Present: Art, Technology, and the Work of Mobile Image, Philip Glahn and Cary Levine, 2024

Living Surfaces: Images, Plants, and Environments of Media, Abelardo Gil-Fournier and Jussi Parikka, 2024

Heartbeat Art, Claudia Arozqueta, 2025

Ecologies of Artistic Practice: Rethinking Cultural Economies through Art and Technology, Ashley Lee Wong, 2025

Proxistant Vision: Motion, Navigation, Scale, Synne Tollerud Bull and Dragan Miletic, 2025

The Cory Arcangel Hack: Digital Culture and Aesthetic Practice, Eivind Røssaak, 2025

Exposing Violence: Media Practices and Aesthetics of Radical Truth, Agnieszka Jelewska and Michał Krawczak, 2026

See http://mitpress.mit.edu for complete list of titles in this series

EXPOSING VIOLENCE

MEDIA PRACTICES AND AESTHETICS OF RADICAL TRUTH

AGNIESZKA JELEWSKA AND
MICHAŁ KRAWCZAK

THE MIT PRESS
CAMBRIDGE, MASSACHUSETTS
LONDON, ENGLAND

The MIT Press
Massachusetts Institute of Technology
77 Massachusetts Avenue
Cambridge, MA 02139
mitpress.mit.edu

The MIT Press would like to thank the anonymous peer reviewers who provided comments on drafts of this book. The generous work of academic experts is essential for establishing the authority and quality of our publications. We acknowledge with gratitude the contributions of these otherwise uncredited readers.

This book was set in Arnhem Pro and New Frank by New Best-set Typesetters Ltd. Printed and bound in the United States of America.

Library of Congress Cataloging-in-Publication Data

Names: Jelewska, Agnieszka author | Krawczak, Michał author
Title: Exposing violence : media practices and aesthetics of radical truth / Agnieszka Jelewska and Michał Krawczak.
Description: Cambridge : The MIT Press, 2026. | Series: Leonardo | Includes bibliographical references and index.
Identifiers: LCCN 2025027775 (print) | LCCN 2025027776 (ebook) | ISBN 9780262053464 paperback | ISBN 9780262053471 epub | ISBN 9780262053488 pdf
Subjects: LCSH: Mass media--Philosophy | Truthfulness and falsehood--Social aspects | Mass media--Aesthetics
Classification: LCC P90 .J34525 2026 (print) | LCC P90 (ebook)
LC record available at https://lccn.loc.gov/2025027775
LC ebook record available at https://lccn.loc.gov/2025027776

10 9 8 7 6 5 4 3 2 1

EU Authorised Representative: Easy Access System Europe, Mustamäe tee 50, 10621 Tallinn, Estonia | Email: gpsr.requests@easproject.com

CONTENTS

SERIES FOREWORD

Leonardo, the International Society for the Arts, Sciences, and Technology, fosters transformation at the nexus of art, science, and technology because complex problems require creative solutions. The Leonardo book series shares these aims of artistic and scientific experimentation and publishes books to define problems and discover solutions, to critique old knowledge and create the new.

In the early twentieth century, the arts and sciences seemed to interact instinctively. Modern art and modern poetry were automatically associated with relativity and quantum physics, as if the two were expressions of a single zeitgeist. At the end of the Second World War, once again it seemed perfectly clear that avant-garde artists, architects, and social planners would join cyberneticists and information theorists to address the problems of the new world order and to create new ways of depicting and understanding its complexity through shared experiences of elegance and experiment. Throughout the twentieth century, the modern constantly mixed art and science.

In the twenty-first century, though, we are no longer modern but contemporary, and now the wedge between art and science that C. P. Snow saw emerging in the 1950s has turned into a culture war. Governments prefer science to arts education yet stand accused of ignoring or manipulating science. The arts struggle to justify themselves in terms of economic or communicative efficiency that devalues their highest aspirations. And yet never before have artists, scientists, and technologists worked together so closely to create individual and collective works of cultural power and intellectual grace. Leonardo looks beyond predicting dangers and challenges, beyond even planning for the unpredictable. The series publishes books that are both timely and of enduring value—books that address the perils of our time while also exploring new forms of beauty and understanding.

Seán Cubitt, Editor-in-Chief, Leonardo Book Series

PREFACE

We began researching and compiling material for this book several years ago. In 2014, we received a grant for this research carried out at the Humanities/Art/Technology Research Center, which we had established at Adam Mickiewicz University, Poznań, Poland. Committed to interdisciplinary studies, the Center has developed collective experimental practices involving the use of critical theories and technological tools. These practices are components of the research methods and methodologies developed in, and situated between, the fields of media studies, critical media design, posthuman studies, environmental humanities, social justice, and critical anthropology. As part of the Center's activities, we have held workshops with international artists, designers, researchers of various disciplines, and activists. The principal objective of these meetings has always been to solve a problem related to the place where we worked. We use the same open and collective working model in our curatorial practices when we collaborate with artists and jointly create exhibitions that engage critical media practices. All the above experiences have taught us various group work methodologies. They have also demonstrated to us the importance of teamwork and the necessity of interdisciplinary dialogue.

While conducting the research that informs this book, we focused on new forms of experimental media practices in relation to social transformations. The developments in science and technology in the transgression of the post-technological turn into the entanglements or agglomerations between the digital and the material. Initially, we analyzed the various experimental media art practices of the late twentieth and twenty-first centuries that became a laboratory for new forms and strategies of knowledge production in relation to cultural and social transformations. Subsequently, we narrowed down our studies to the most recent trends, practices, and activities dealing with the development of new forms and strategies of tracing and exposing violence and the social dissemination of the tools and processes inherent in these practices.

Pursuing the research objectives of the grant, we held many study tours and visited numerous media art festivals, conferences, and workshops. The presence of such practices at festivals of media art and digital culture is a major point of reference for our book. For many of these phenomena, exhibitions socialize and disseminate knowledge produced in interaction with an audience. Instrumental for our work were, among others, projects held by the Zentrum für Kunst und Medien (ZKM) (Center for Art and Media) in Karlsruhe, the Transmediale festival in Berlin, and the Ars Electronica festival in Linz.

The exhibitions and projects held at the ZKM are based on comprehensive and substantive curatorial practices. Several of its exhibitions—including *Making Things Public: Atmospheres of Democracy* (2005), *Global Activism* (2013), the *Globale* series (2015), *Open Codes: Digital Culture Techniques* (2018), and *Critical Zones: Observatories for Earthly Politics* (2020)—provide a reference framework for this book. The shows were major contributors to our thinking about epistemic and aesthetic relations in the context of media practices. The exhibition strategies of these shows presented art in relation to significant phenomena of digital culture but also erased the boundaries between many types of artistic, scientific, cultural, social, and political creativity. Since its launch, Transmediale has provided a critical platform for modern art and media practices that transform digital societies in the context of political and civil agency. Frequently discussed at this festival in recent years have been strategies of resistance—new forms of network activism and digital solidarity with those who, through top-down technopolitics, are excluded from the networked culture. The festivals' topics include the increasing radicalization of net culture, the threats of digital capitalism, datafication, and new forms of digital populism. Some of the groups we analyze in the book have received awards at the Ars Electronica festival.[1] Of particular importance in generating a forum for discussion of the phenomena we were investigating were the projects recognized and awarded in the digital communities category.

Furthermore, our interest in the transformations brought about by technological advances and the bottom-up construction of media practices has an autoethnographic aspect. We were both born in a divided Europe. In Poland, part of the Eastern Bloc, there was censorship, propaganda, and disinformation, and as children and teenagers, we both were eyewitnesses to political transformations. Our research has previously dealt with the processes of media democratization in relation to strategies of resistance and the emergence of grassroots forms of participatory culture. In the introduction to the book *Art and Technology in Poland: From Cybercommunism to the Culture of Makers* (Jelewska and Krawczak 2014), we discuss the significance of grassroots developments of the media system. The practices it produced were resistant to the Polish political situation in the 1980s, which was, on one hand, strongly marked by the violence of the totalitarian regime and, on the other, generated a cultural fear of technology that was then identified with military systems. We also examine the consequences of this fear in the 1990s after the transformation of Poland's political and economic systems. Our earlier research project focused on the then Eastern Bloc countries, but this location allowed us to understand and explain, using concrete examples, the patterns of operation of the media and related cultural practices in a situation of political and social transgression. These experiences have helped us avoid generalizations resulting from technoglobalization.

Many of the issues and case studies described in this book have been part of our recent university teaching practice. The activities of groups and individual artists, case studies, research methodologies and their technical aspects, and social and political contexts have been analyzed with students of interactive media and critical design. They also have been discussed at numerous workshops and practical events outside the university. In this way, the method of working with these problems has assumed a theoretical, didactic, and practical character. We believe that this is also one of the features of agglomerative aesthetics addressed in this book. Our classes and workshops have resulted in many prototypes, analyses, and projects, and the content of this book was instrumental for the development of students' academic and practical competence.

The book does not summarize a media practice trend that has come to an end and can therefore be analyzed from a historical perspective. Our identifications of these phenomena are not definitive as they continue to develop their internal strategies and to affect each another. We also believe that they will have long-term implications. Therefore, in the material gathered in this book, we are looking for signs and manifestations of new paradigms of practicing knowledge based on a transparent process of truth seeking, forms of opening it up to social debate, new strategies of tool sharing, and practices of mutual learning.

Yet another consequence of the phenomena addressed in this book is the overlap of strategies, methodologies, tools, and certain aesthetic elements of new art forms with more traditional art forms. While media art has always featured currents linked to artivism (direct social and political engagement), in recent years increasing numbers of such projects have been featured at festivals like Ars Electronica and Transmediale and also at fairly traditional visual art festivals, such as the Twelfth Berlin Biennale for Contemporary Art (curated by Kader Attia in 2022) and the Sixtieth Venice Biennale (curated by Adriano Pedrosa in 2024).

We hope that the book describes only the beginning of important developments within "open justice"—the creation of new archives that collect data on violence, interactive environments that activate new comprehension through the affective experience of violence, and the bottom-up production of tools that enable the tracking and disclosure of violence. We also hope that this book will help to disseminate knowledge about antiviolence strategies in the material and digital environments. Finally, we hope that it will be seen as a tribute to those who dedicate their time to reveal the truth about human and environmental injustice—civil journalists, creators of archives documenting the crimes and violence of wars, committed media artists, media designers, researchers, activists, and all who are willing (and sometimes even obliged because of the social or political situation they find themselves in) to engage in tracking, recording, and publicizing acts of violence.

ACKNOWLEDGMENTS

This book has provided us with the opportunity to share the ideas and practices of many of the artists, creators, designers, investigators, researchers, activists, theoreticians, and practitioners who are fighting to reclaim the truth about violence. Each of the projects evoked in the book is important. Each brings new tools, approaches, and ways of creating an aesthetic of radical truth. In our opinion, these practices will become increasingly important in the near future because the more we want to learn about the truth—both historical and everyday—the more brutal the resistance tends to become from those who benefit from spreading disinformation and capitalizing on human and environmental harm. The projects we discuss counteract this by working on new ways of acquiring knowledge about violence and sharing methods of exposing it.

This book would not have been possible without many people to whom we owe enormous support. Above all, during this intensive period of several years of collecting materials and writing the book, our families—our parents and our other loved ones—supported us with conversations and helped us by devoting their time to us. We would also like to express our heartfelt thanks to our daughter, Zofia Gaja, who has heard countless times that we were working on an important book. It was not always easy for her to understand why our time was divided between her and this project, yet she showed patience and a desire to see us succeed. We hope that one day, when she is a little older, she will want to read this book herself.

We are grateful to our many colleagues and friends from different places in the world—the researchers, academics, and artists who debated and argued with us for hours at a time. They were invaluable to us. We would like to thank Harshavardhan Bhat, Adela Goldbard, Paweł Janicki, Peter Kahn, Jacek Łuminski, Anna Nacher, Julian Reid, Jens Schröter, Wojciech Sowa, Brett Zehner, and, above all, our colleagues and friends at the Humanities/Art/Technology Research Center, who were always willing to support us and help with many little research tasks that sometimes became overwhelming: Jakub Alejski, Elżbieta Kowalska, Patryk Lichota, Miłosz Markiewicz, Oliwia Olesiejuk, Anna Paprzycka, Aleksy Szymkiewicz, and Jacek Zydorowicz.

For their support and unwavering faith in this project, we would like to thank the academics, directors, deans, and rectors at Adam Mickewicz University, especially Ewa Guderian-Czaplińska, Bogumiła Kaniewska, Rafał Koschany, Alina Mądry, Bogusław Mróz, Jacek Sójka, and Rafał Witkowski.

Also, our thanks to the artists, designers, and curators we collaborated with on various projects and learned a lot from: Michał Cichy, Anna Galas-Kosil, Przemysław Jasielski, Raman Tratsiuk, Rafał Zapała, and Edyta Zielnik.

We are grateful to all those who recently gave us the opportunity to share publicly and discuss these complex topics at lectures and open seminars: first and foremost, Magda Romańska, Rob Sabal, Jan Skorupa, and Aleksandra Skowrońska, but also Małgorzata Jankowska and Jakub Jernańczyk.

We would also like to express our special thanks to our master's and doctoral students in interactive media and critical design. They attended our classes on these topics, assisted us in teaching, and later created their own projects inspired by what we have written about here. Together we were able to discuss and practice the aesthetics of radical truth openly.

Working on this book also involved countless hours of conversations with each other. These conversations were often provoked by music that became inseparable from our research background. The music we listened to during the conversations generated a field of additional reflection by asking questions and often provoking us to adopt new perspectives. We would like to thank the artists whose work is an invisible yet significant layer of this book: Fatima AlQuadiri, Black Monument Ensemble, DeForest Brown Jr., DAM (Da Arab MCs), Lonnie Holley, Shabaka Hutchings, Damon Locks, Moor Mother, Sons of Kemet, Duval Timothy, and Adrien Younge.

Additional thanks also go to this book's proofreader, Marcin Turski, for his careful attention to the detail and support in refining the manuscript.[1] We would also like to thank Stephen Dersley, who collaborated with us and provided linguistic advice on many texts related to the book.

We conducted research for this book under a grant awarded to us by the Polish National Science Center in 2014.[2] One of the research tasks was to conduct in-depth interviews with three people who were important in developing media art and theory—Roy Ascott, Jill Scott, and Peter Weibel. In every discussion, our interviewees highlighted in detail the epistemic and social functions of media. In conversation with Jill Scott, cognition was primarily sensorial. Roy Ascott has continued to pursue cognition in experimental projects of shared pedagogy that create ecosystemic qualities between process participants and the environment. In Peter Weibel's artistic and curatorial projects, cognition was meant to analyze, understand, and publicly present by using media as social and scientific devices. The conversations with Weibel inspired us to include the concept of "radical" in the book's title. When we asked him how it was possible that he once practiced extreme forms of performance art, later became fascinated by hard sciences, and eventually became a curator of exhibitions in which digital art had deep social and political functions, Weibel replied that he always was radical—meaning engaged, searching, explaining, and including the audience in each of his projects.

Many thanks to Seán Cubitt, editor of the Leonardo book series, for supporting this project and providing the necessary encouragement. He not only published a book that served as a vital inspiration for us, *Truth: Aesthetic Politics*, but also wholeheartedly believed in the project and offered tremendous support at every stage of the publishing process. We also thank Gabriela Bueno Gibbs for her hospitality and valuable assistance throughout the editorial journey. Special thanks are extended to Rosemary Winfield and Deborah Cantor-Adams for their very thorough and insightful comments on the text, which helped shape its final form.

INTRODUCTION

This book describes contemporary media practices that expose the violence inflicted on human beings and the environment. The aesthetics of radical truth (AeRT) in our book sets out a *modus operandi* for practices that emerged in the second decade of the twenty-first century and that have used media as tools to trace violence and to coproduce traces, signs, evidence, and images that help expose, visualize, and publicize that violence. The most recent socially engaged media projects—launched by independent groups of artists and researchers, interdisciplinary teams emerging at universities, and small laboratory groups—have increasingly revealed the potential to produce new relational and open paradigms of knowledge based on strategies of intertwining studio, laboratory, research, design, activist, and media practices. Within this vast landscape, special attention is paid here to projects situated at the crossroads of art, science, activism, and engaged journalism, their main goal being the development of experimental, innovative, and shared forms of recording, revealing, tracing, identifying, and especially publicizing and critically analyzing various forms of violence. These forms include structural violence, direct violence (which targets individuals, groups, or the environment), and the latest forms of tracking and digital surveillance. It is these practices that this book addresses.

Because the practices and groups we write about began to emerge primarily in the second decade of the twenty-first century, the aesthetics of radical truth they pursue must be learned and analyzed in correlation with what was happening in that decade in various parts of the world. The Arab Spring and other forms of protest against oppressive authorities offered fleeting hope for the possible prosocial, activist, and civic use of technological tools. Armed conflicts and wars in Syria and other Arab countries, ISIS terrorism, waves of migration, the climate crisis, and the wars in Ukraine and in Gaza were taking place as we finished writing this book. First, then, these practices stem from opposing the proliferation of new forms of violence against people and the environment. Second, they function in a manner that fuses digital and material realities. Third, they operate in a context of novel potential uses of technological tools as epistemic media, which help disclose and appropriately and ethically visualize this violence. The contemporary forms of violence are extremely varied and heterogeneous in structure and may be directed against social groups, individuals, or parts of the natural environment.

When we started to delve deeper into the new strategies and tendencies that emerged as grassroots modalities of exposing violence, we found that they are a major tendency in social, scientific, and artistic practices. While this tendency is not composed of homogeneous phenomena, just as situations of violence are not homogeneous and each time require a different research approach, it can be described by means of a set of characteristics.

First, the distinguishing features of the practices for exposing violence include openness and the creation of knowledge based on coparticipation. Depending on the group type and the situation of violence, coparticipation has two semantic tiers. It means being open to the active engagement of coparticipants or working with the communities and individuals who have experienced violence. Both the above meanings often overlap in the examples we evoke.

Second, it involves the ethics of care (Held 2006; Latour 2004; Puig de la Bellacasa 2017), which is not a prescriptive set of tenets but a process of establishing them in relation to victimized groups, persons, and the environment. This process is invariably relational and situated (Haraway 1988; 2016). We refer to it in the book as more-than-human care. The situations we write about call for the involvement of more-than-human ethics and sensitivity. More-than-human here does not describe nonhuman beings (the way the term is used by posthumanism scholars) but denotes a more-than-human-rights concept. Thus, acting above and beyond the structures set by specific states and global organizations, it also marks a need to deconstruct the concept of human rights.

Third, the principal elements of this tendency are the shared tools and transparent practices of data acquisition and their methodologies of analysis. The ethics of care is important here, as the groups we discuss often work in traumatized environments that have been affected by various forms of violence. Hence, the launch of the research process and the sharing of tools have an ethical significance for the formation of new forms of collaborative creation of knowledge about violence.

Fourth, most of the projects discussed here share the creation of experimental forms and tools of violence-related data acquisition. These tools often involve epistemic media that capture and store data providing evidence of violence.

Fifth, characteristic of these practices is the development of unique setups and interfaces for presenting data and evidence and their acquisition process. Dissemination of violence via independent strategies helps introduce the subject matter into public debate.

Sixth, these are most often grassroots projects in the tradition of resistance, activism, engaged media art, and institutional critique. As such, they often emerge and grow outside the major knowledge-production hubs.

Seventh, all the projects appear within a situation where the material and the digital are intertwined—where real (physical) crime is recorded, forwarded, commented on, and disseminated in digital format. When addressing the essence of the digital and the material in reference to photographs and recordings made during the war in Syria, Donatella Della Ratta, the author of the book *Shooting a Revolution: Visual Media and Warfare in Syria* (2018), uses the term "networked images." The photos and recordings are not in themselves signs of crimes. Rather, they exist in circulation and relation to other images, to the crime scene, and to the people who made, shared, and described them. Crime and violence are invariably committed in a particular place and affect particular people or elements of the environment, but their images, data, and online dissemination (in recordings from satellites, cell phones, and video cameras) are essential components in the documentation and verification process. We indicate the emergence of new forms of violence in which oppressive digital actions have consequences in the physical world and vice versa. This coupling of physical and digital violence is often structurally exploited, especially when cyber regimes of states use methods of datafication and dataveillance.

In this book, media are any objects capable of recording data or its traces. They do not have to be purely technical objects. They can be any form of organic or inorganic matter in which traces of an event or a process have been, intentionally or otherwise, recorded. Such a comprehensive definition is used by many of the theorists and practitioners cited in this book, including Eyal Weizman, who uses the concept of media dense environments (2017); Susan Schuppli, who employs material witness theory (2020); and materialist concepts of geological media and medianatures by Jussi Parikka (2015). The above definitions help understand and identify relationships between events and their material or digital media traces.

To fully explain the processes discussed here, the above definitions must be extended even more in order to expose the relationships between different media or objects that act in the function of media. In media studies, we might point to media ecologies, developed by Matthew Fuller (2005), Seán Cubitt (2005, 2015), and Cajetan Iheka (2021), as well as to the critical infrastructural theories developed by Lisa Parks and Nicole Starosielski (2015). All of them highlighted the interrelational character of media and their social, political, and technological corporate state. However, we believe that something else is emerging in the practices we address that previously has not been directly identified in media studies. The resulting media traces can clump together into larger formations of varied tissue and morphology. We call the resulting entities *agglomerates*, a term we borrow from geological sciences, where it stands for conglomerates with impermanent, temporal structure and diverse morphology. The distinguishing mark of agglomerates, however, is the root cause of their emergence—that is, an external pressure and a dynamic or slow internal force that interact and lead to the compression and unstable fusion of elements that would not naturally come together.

Therefore, in our methodological concept, the object of study is not so much the media themselves but their morphological interdependence in the agglomerate. A critical analysis of this interdependence makes it possible to identify forms of interacting pressure (violence). To study these processes, we need new perspectives, new tools, and even whole environments in which to collect and analytically reconstruct the agglomeration process. The groups and artists we write about deliberately and methodologically collect, extract, elaborate, and exploit media traces by placing them in the media environments of their design.

Whether or not we analyze media evidence juxtaposed in digital environments for the purpose of event reconstructions (as practiced by SITU Research, by Forensic Architecture with its Timemap, or by Arab archives built with the use of the Pad.ma platform), we invariably deal with open-source software. The sharing, cocreation, and transparency of the software code is equally agglomerative here. It is tied to the openness of joining others in collaborative labor and is also ethical, based on the transparency of information and software code. Media tools enable the creation of an ecosystem for collaborative labor *in situ* at the point of violence. Minor tools and the auxiliary strategies generate entire systems of support and resistance policies. These are the kinds of phenomena we address when we discuss practices such as the use of drones in the creation of collective indigenous maps in the Amazon and Indonesia or multifaceted media support in migration and refugee processes in Europe.

In organized ecotechnological environments, even the tiniest things can acquire significance and agency. They depict the real world with its problems and violence. Here, however, we talk about performing the work of exposing violence and not about a mediatized reality. Things and objects produce knowledge of violence through a process that Bruno Latour called the process of "how to make things public" (Latour 2004) and via systems he dubbed the "parliament of things" (Latour 1993), which we discuss in detail in the following chapters. Within the agglomerate, even the tiniest possible elements start to signify and have significance, and collaborative labor generates a policy of community, resistance, and justice.

The aesthetics of radical truth, a term defining the strategies used within engaged media practices, is a constituent of two major cognitive fields. The first part of the term introduces the discourse and practice of seeing aesthetics as a social representation and arrangement of things, objects, facts, data, people (Latour and Halsall 2012), aesthetics as an "aesthetic regime of politics" (Rancière 2004), aesthetics as the sharing with the recipients the process of establishing evidence of violence (Weizman 2017), and "relational aesthetics" as the production of objects with political agency (Bourriaud 1998). This meaning of aesthetics provides a significant force that binds the policy of objects and their representation with the cognitive, scientific, forensic, and archival process (Biber and Luker 2017; Hyde and Rezek 2014). We discuss the aesthetics of radical truth further in chapter 1. The second part of the term introduces the notion of radical truth as the essential cognitive basis underlying all these practices. This may seem surprising to many. Can truth be radical? Is not all truth simply truth? Today, amid considerations of post-truth (Mcintyre 2018) in a reality marked by emerging speculative movements and flourishing online conspiracy theories, using the word *truth* itself can be perceived as a radical gesture. Through analyses of new practices, we try to demonstrate in the book that in the era of post-truth and "dark epistemic" (Weizman 2019), truth must be radically reintroduced into social and political debate. Since not every fact, image, or data can be considered true, truth requires novel infrastructures, methods, and ways through which it can be realized. These methods are novel also because the ways of publicizing and disseminating truth are changing under the influence of the development of data and image storage technologies, as well as online communication modes. As Eyal Weizman, a contemporary theorist and practitioner of truth relating to situations of violence, puts it in an interview: "Though propaganda has always existed, . . . we are entering a dark new era in which there is an attack on the very possibility of truth" (Bazalgette and Weizman 2018).

The projects we discuss in this book are a contradiction of these processes. The truth they work on is not merely a state of affairs or a process of recording a situation or phenomenon. It is also a procedure of reconstruction, of including others (human and nonhuman) in cognition, and of sharing tools for verifying the entire cognitive process. The practices we write about are ways of reestablishing truth defined in this way as a social value and also the attendant notion of radical as yielding new forms of resistance, activism, and grassroots engagement.

In 1984, Michel Foucault delivered one of his last lectures, *The Courage of Truth* (Foucault 2011). In it, the French philosopher reintroduces the category of truth as a radically open way of communicating, understanding, and accepting it by its recipients. This approach and practice of truth is meant to allow individuals and groups to break free from top-down regimes appropriating the concept. In the lectures, he examines significant epistemic transitions and shifts towards truth. Moving from the initial lectures on the construction of truth in Euripides and Thucydides as forms of self-governance, to the later emphasis on the perception of truth as articulated by Socrates and the Cynics, or unwavering truth-tellers. Foucault uses references to the formation of the foundations of Greek democracy and the forum as a vehicle for its practice to reestablish radical truth as a tool and a means for the modern formation of knowledge as well as relationships and communication based on trust, openness, and transparency.

Describing the radicality of truth as nonconcealment and its straightforward, clear communication using discourse, Foucault points to strategies of direct inquiry, sharing, and social truth telling. As Bernard E. Harcourt (2016) puts it in the introduction to the English-language edition of the essays, these strategies were to proceed from so-called risk to courage and from political to ethical *parrhesia*. The courage of truth as *parrhesia* is realized by "the person who speaks and who, regardless of everything, takes the risk of telling the whole truth that he thinks, but it is also the interlocutor's courage in agreeing to accept the hurtful truth that he hears" (Foucault 2011, 13). The truth becomes a process of arriving at it and of including the interlocutors through its communication, which is honest and direct (it does not conceal but reveals). The goal of these practices is to convince the interlocutors of the rightness of the arguments and to affectively attune them to understanding through radical transparency and openness. Thus, Foucault's notion transcended the political and rhetorical uses of *parrhesia*, focusing on the fact that it opens the way to an entire ethical modality in a sense of existence as oeuvre, which he called an "aesthetics of existence" (Foucault 2011, 163).

The fusion of the radicality of truth with the aesthetics of being is a key recognition we find in Foucault's writings. An aesthetics of radical truth amalgamates these spheres of being and cognition, truth, openness, radicality, and responsibility. Foucault's last lectures demonstrate the need for a contemporary turn to truth as openness in its practice. When speaking of this, Foucault referred mainly to the notion of discourse as "the revolutionary discourse plays the role of parrhesiastic discourse when it takes the form of a critique of existing society. Philosophical discourse as analysis, as reflection on human finitude and criticism of everything which may exceed the limits of human finitude. . . . And when scientific discourse is deployed as criticism of prejudices, of existing forms of knowledge, of dominant institutions, of current ways of doing things . . . it plays this parrhesiastic role" (Foucault 2011, 30). However, referring in his *The Courage of Truth* to Socrates, Foucault seemed to transcend the notion of truth ascribed only to discourse. After all, Socrates was known not for teaching his own wisdom but for pursuing truth throughout his life. He was not a self-proclaimed sage or expert but a person constantly striving to know and discuss with interlocutors as partners in this path. In Foucault's essays, it is Socrates—much more than the Cynics, who thought they had access to the truth—who is a figure-sign of the emerging notion of radical truth as a continuous process of its unveiling, establishing, communicating, telling, and sharing.

Foucault believed that individuals, rather than solely the institutions and systems responsible for power development, reveal or extract truth using specific cognitive tools. Thus, truth is not given top-down and solely maintained by an elite system but must be developed, discussed, demonstrated, and proved to be socially acceptable.

Foucault's concept is in a way continued by Seán Cubitt in his book *Truth: Aesthetic Politics* (Cubitt 2023). However, Cubitt makes another major transgression as he ties the discovery and demonstration of truth with its profound location and work of engaged persons and the participation in this process of nonhuman entities and subjects (Cubitt 2023, 12). In his own words, "there is no fixed truth to return to. Nor can we return to or recreate neutrality—scientific, political or philosophical. Truth was always ecological—always situated, always relational, always caught up in who was saying what to whom, about what, how, for what purposes and with what effects" (2023, 10–11). Understanding the ecological nature of truth offers a new opportunity to reclaim this notion as the core of a newly conceived epistemology of modernity based on the truth "we produce, in common and as commons, together with our nonhuman partners" (2023, 11). Cubitt indicates that the first thing we must do to remake the truth is to recognize that it is neither given nor an object of faith or even veneration; it is simply "a job of work" (2023, 12). Ideally, the work of truth is "the cultural work that the dispersed members of a commons undertake in order to become a commons" (2023, 12).

Following the directives from the last works of Foucault as well as the concept of ecological truth proposed by Cubitt, we use the notion of radical truth in the context of the project we analyze in the book, one that is based on practices that are discursive and also related to *techne* and *praxis* (that is, capacities for pursuing, making available, communicating, and sharing the truth). Its engaged and transparent ontology is realized somewhat differently today with new tools and practices. Therefore, the notion of radical truth used in this book is understood in multiple ways:

- We evoke the Latin etymology of the term *radical* (*radix*) (a "root"). We then focus on the foundations and ways of reaching down to the very bottom of things. The fundamental fact calls for a radical perspective of treating things, objects, the media matter, infrastructures, data, and people as knowledge-producing elements, even if traditionally we do not see them as participating in the process. Furthermore, there is no one single strategy of knowledge production. They are many and varied, the way roots are. Roots make up diverse and morphologically complex systems responsible for the development and maintenance of life and for communication.
- Equally important in this dimension is the need to reclaim the term *radical* in the context of truth and a transparent process of exposing and countering violence. The term *radical* ceases to describe the political division into right or left and instead becomes a feature of nonsystemic, grassroots practices and actions on behalf of those affected by violence. The traditions of the notion of radical can be found in a great number of critical research projects redefining philosophy (Kautzer 2015) and legislation (Douzinas 2019) from the perspective of the need for openness and a turn toward the issues of violence and exclusion affecting specific communities. A focus on reclaiming the right to a political voice can be found in the current of radical feminism (Atkinson 1969; Koedt et al. 1973) or in the concept of radical care expressed in the feminist spirit (Hobart et al. 2020) as a critique of institutional perceptions of state aid and support toward citizens. Another important reference is radical indigenous and decolonial projects and studies

(Basdeo 1997; Rabaka 2010; Singh and Singh 2010; Smith 1999), which draw attention to historical aspects and long-term systemic traumas that surface in very different situations and circumstances. These are just a few examples that renew and reestablish the notion of radical as empowering a critical approach to various forms of pointing out and analyzing exclusions and violence in modern state, economic, and social systems.

- The notion of the radical may in historical terms be linked, for example, to engaged practices of media art that hark back to the 1970s. Today, their consequences are located in art itself and in such media discourse as new media studies, software studies, and postdigital studies. In the context of media art, the term *radical* has referred primarily to phenomena and practices that have used media as tools for critical theories, activism, and social actions. Starting with video art in the 1970s, one of the platforms of exchanging experience was *Radical Software*, a magazine established in 1970 in New York by Phyllis Gershuny and Beryl Korot. The journal, published over a four-year period, became a social generator and platform for sharing experiences and practices aimed at radically transforming the media system in relation to ecological, informational, social, and cultural theories. As David A. Ross noted in 2003 when referring to the founders of the organization, what warranted change "was not the machines, but the instructions used to operate them. The social implications were evident: radical hardware was fine but what was critically needed was *Radical Software*" (Ross 2003). Subsequently, the term *radical* was repeatedly applied to media practices directly linked to activism, such as hacktivism, tactical media (Lovink 2002, Raley 2009), e-activism, and cyberactivism.
- Radical truth is invariably situated (Haraway 1988, 2016) in the social, political, economic, cultural, and historical context. Each example discussed in this book is shown in this radically positioned context.
- In a reality where images representing disasters and aberrations are repeatedly used online (disassociated from their tangible aspect to sow disinformation) or are frequently reprocessed (through media recycling, meme culture, and the commercialization of the visual aspect of culture), there is a radical significance to perceiving the digital artefact in relation to matter and to its location and to pinning it down to the actual fact and to reality. This helps verify its actual nature. The process of pursuing this feedback is the process of collective engagement and knowledge production. The founder

of Bellingcat, Eliot Higgins, describes this process in reference to his group: "Paradoxically, in this age of online disinformation, facts are easier to come by than ever. . . . Evidence exists and falsehoods exist, and people still care about the difference" (Higgins 2021, 5–6).

- The practices we discuss and the tools we examine call for change through action and engagement. The processes of cocreation and sharing result in the emergence of epistemic communities and epistemic cultures. Eyal Weizman describes the process as establishing "an unlikely but fundamental commons in which the production facts constitute the foundation of an expanded epistemic community of practice built around a shared perception and understanding of the world" (Weizman 2019, n.p.).
- Radical truth thus becomes a public and common truth, shared and jointly accepted in the course of collective knowledge production. Radical truth is an inclusive process based on transparent, open, and overtly disseminated data. The process aims at introducing long-term change and "community of inquiry," which is a concept "developed to describe scientific modes of inquiry and how reality, facts, and truth are settled on through collective processes" (Gabrys 2019, 76). The work of truth practices needs to be collective and social practices. Thus, new forms of pedagogy emerge, based on sharing and joint production of tools, practices, and study processes. They become a common truth.
- Radicalness relates to the fact that the groups and collectives we discuss side with the vulnerable, the excluded, the absent, the politically and socially misappropriated, and the economically exploited. They side with those who have no voice of their own.
- Radical means resistance. Toolmaking, archive building, and evidence gathering are practices of resistance and countersurveillance. In this respect, we can learn a lot from activist movements, do-it-yourself projects, and indigenous studies and practices (Simpson 2017). The radicality of truth from the perspective of the phenomena we study has its contexts in practices and discourses that are socially engaged, critical, and rooted in collective knowledge creation.
- Radical truth is ecological (Cubitt 2023) and multisensorial. Ecological, which means the truth is shared in the community that has developed it and by those who have at different stages and in variable degrees participated in its creation. Truth is multisensorial, which means that it is created from

discourse, stimuli, and affects and is shared by language, images, data, and collective affects and experience.

Radical truth results from the agglomerative collaboration of vulnerable subjects who in earlier social, legal, and cultural systems had no privilege to record traces, collect data, verify facts, or generate knowledge and evidence. Historically, truth has been produced by those with access to technical and expert tools. Truth was in large measure generated by diverse socially, culturally, and religiously sanctioned institutions. This was how the dominant discourse was born, which was a tool for political dominance. The historical perspective of this process was aptly defined by the Haitian historian Michel-Rolph Trouillot in his book *Silencing the Past: Power and the Production of History* (Trouillot 2015). So-called historical truth has invariably been the tool of structures of power, which is why in the past it went hand in hand with colonialism, racism, and extractivism. In the past, this kind of truth codetermined archives and documents and was a tool subordinated to the interests of the majority or a more powerful and technologized minority. The contemporary concept of truth we address in this book is the result of a process of democratization of technology, as well as the collective work of human and nonhuman subjects applying the ethics of care (Puig de la Bellacasa 2017), sharing data and tools through media practices. Thus, those who were previously denied access to the system of truth production have gained opportunities for communal emancipation and acquired tools to fight for justice. These processes represent the flip side of everything associated with contemporary issues of post-truth, such as conspiracy theories, "dark epistemology" (Weizman 2019), and "anti-epistemology" (Fuller and Weizman 2021). In this situation, post-truth is a tool for wielding political dominance by those who fear losing the privilege of exclusive determination of reality. This is what distinguishes the projects we write about from practices that ostensibly point to the truth but are in fact either conspiracy movements or promote dark epistemology. It is an essential distinction occurring at the level of epistemology and ontology of truth. As Cubitt aptly indicates, "truth is a practice, but so is untruth, and they cannot be distinguished by the fact that they are successful, by whatever measure we apply. The natural, social and human sciences no longer pretend to possess absolute truth. It is in general a hallmark of neo-populist, not to say neo-fascist, politicians and political movements to claim that they do. They proclaim their one true God, the alternative fact, to trump the collective wisdom that says there is no single truth and no single place to interpret it from" (Cubitt 2023, 11–12).

We divide the material collected in this book into five main sections. Each examines slightly different practices and tools for tracking and combating violence in today's world.

In chapter 1, "Aesthetics as Labor for Reclaiming Truth," we introduce the concept of the aesthetics of radical truth in the context of aesthetics as environment, politics, forensics, and sensibility. We propose to refer to agglomerate formation for AeRT processes to define the labor done to reveal violence. Agglomerate processes are set among others in relation to geological, physical, and chemical sciences. At the same time, we see the agglomerate as a "traveling concept" (Bal 2002) that helps us reveal the relationship between violence, its physical and digital traces, and the processes of mediatization and dissemination in communication networks. We describe features of AeRT as agglomerative and dynamic—that is, as an open, inclusive way of shaping grassroots practices for tracing, pinpointing, and reconstructing violence in the nexus of the material and the digital. This is aesthetics as a labor against violence. An agglomerative research approach is a way of describing phenomena, facts, stories, and events as joining and producing unstable and dynamic morphological structures. It enables an analysis of structurally discontinuous phenomena and examines phenomena in motion and in their continuance, during the processes of formation.

Chapter 2, "Radical Investigators of Military Violence," analyzes the production and social sharing of object agglomerates as new mediatized witnesses to violence. The starting point are the critical concepts of Bruno Latour concerning "object-oriented democracy" (Latour 2005), "intermediarity" (Simondon 2017), "intra-actions" (Barad 2007), care (Puig de la Bellacasa 2017), and theories of feminist science and technology studies (feminist STS). In this chapter, we discuss examples of counterviolence as strategies for conducting experimental research, investigations performed by groups such as Forensic Architecture and SITU Research, and collaborative open-source intelligence techniques (OSINT) used by

Bellingcat (2017, 2022). In the second chapter, we take a closer look at Bellingcat's projects, including the 2017 investigation concerning mass executions committed near Benghazi, Libya, by units subordinate to Mahmoud Mustafa Al-Werfalli and the collaborative digital platform Mapping Civilian Harm in Ukraine from 2022. We look at the investigation by SITU Research between 2015 and 2018 under the Euromaidan Event Reconstruction, resulting in producing evidence for a trial taking place in Ukraine of Berkut officers charged with using violence against protesters. We scrutinize here projects such as The Use of White Phosphorus Munitions in Urban Environments, carried out jointly by SITU Research and Forensic Architecture, offering evidence for the use by the Israeli army of controversial weapons against Palestinian civilians during a conflict in late 2008 and early 2009, and The Bombing of Rafah, carried out by the Forensic Architecture and Amnesty International, meant to identify the type of weapons used and to reveal systemic military violence by Israeli forces against Palestinian civilians in the bombing of Rafah in 2014. A major element of the analyses in this chapter is the consideration of proprietary digital tools designed by groups that enable collaborative action and produce agglomerative potential, adding further participants to the processes of proving the truth. Showing the processes of agglomerative object formation makes it possible to indicate that an agglomerate is not a finite object but a conglomerate and amalgamate. This means that in the case of the practices we address here, it is possible to attach certain elements and include people and things via successive mediations. These include adding material through data collection and joining in its social forms of distribution and circulation.

Chapter 3, "Slow Violence and Data Resistance," evokes two major methodological concepts. One is "slow violence," defined by Rob Nixon (2011) as merging the experience of abuse of humans, nonhumans, and environments. The other concept is the perspectives arising from critical data studies and practices of radical situated data, consisting in resistance to normativizing and averaging forces of digital algorithmization (Loukissas 2019) and in embodying the demands of data justice. In this chapter, we look into collaborative practices that are carried out in tandem with local communities and that employ media tools made for specific conditions of violence data collection and preservation. We discuss examples of such practices carried out by members of local communities and use new do-it-yourself ways to self-collect data, monitor the environment, and stand up against illegal practices that devastate the environment. Using examples of the activities of Safecast and of the Public Laboratory for Open Technology and Science (Public Lab), we define media practices related to citizen and community science in relation to disaster studies (Fortun and Morgan 2015), and by describing projects using drones by indigenous communities in Indonesia and Amazonian forests, we identify processes of bottom-up decolonization of mapping technologies and practices in relation to traditional ecological knowledge (TEK) (Posey and Balick 2006). Throughout this chapter, the critique of top-down models of knowledge production indicates the potential for simple media practices to be applied to bottom-up data acquisition and environmental strategy design.

In chapter 4, "The Liquid Violence of Borderization Regimes," we focus on the EU borders and border zones, which in the last decade have become sites of new forms of violence, cyber regimes, and practices of radical solidarity opposed to them. This direct and systemic violence is fed by complex historical, political, and cultural prejudices and regulations. When combined with processes of digitization of national borders, they generate implicit procedures of exclusion and segregation. In this chapter, we further define collective practices of countersurveillance, countertracking, and new forms of cooperation between volunteers, activists, and refugees aimed at documenting and combating this violence. We examine the concept of the border, which is becoming a strategically important site for new forms of violence and for the practices of deconstructing and combating it. We juxtapose contemporary discourses related to the development of digital and smart borders and the processes related to refugees and migrants. We describe here organized support practices for those forced to leave their homes and seek refuge in foreign countries, and we cite Forensic Oceanography investigations that offer evidence of abuse of authority and strategies of liquid violence. In the second part of the chapter, we focus on analyzing the process of weaponization of migrants, observed during the 2021–2022 humanitarian crisis on the border between Poland and Belarus. From the perspective of an aesthetics of radical truth, this chapter shows grassroots practices and forms of counterviolence during the formation of the agglomerate, its media morphological structures, and the conglomeration of its successive elements.

Chapter 5, "Digital Archives for Epistemic Justice," identifies the agglomerative creation of grassroots archives, documents, and narratives, which are practices of resistance to "regimes of invisibility" (Attia 2022). We agglomerate research perspectives from deconstruction, decolonization, and archive critiques within the discourses of living archives (Dekker 2017), mediascapes (Appadurai 2003), and media archaeology (Ernst 2016, 2021). The examples we analyze are new types of digital collaborative archives and experimental tools for collecting testimonies and memories, forms of open repositories, and documentaries that reveal the interdependencies between historical and environmental memories. In this chapter, we examine examples of recent Arab archives documenting different forms of protest and resistance to state regimes, including the first protests of the 2010 Arab Spring in Egypt, the documentation of repression and military violence in the Syrian war, and the most recent archives creating a visual history of resistance in Lebanon. We discuss archives such as the 858: An Archive of Resistance (established in 2011), the Syrian Archive (active since 2014), and the Alsaha Archive (active since 2019). We also analyze the Police Brutality at the Black Lives Matter protest project, carried out by Forensic Architecture in collaboration with Bellingcat as of 2020, a kind of living archive documenting systemic culture of violence against protesters. The final section of this chapter discusses experimental forms that combine features of open and living archives with interactive online documentary and forensic investigation, which are directly linked to mediated forms of memory of violence against indigenous people, refugees, and migrants. The chapter discusses the 2015 Quipu Project, which collect testimonies of witnesses and victims of government-imposed sterilizations that affected indigenous inhabitants of Peru.

The epilogue, "Toward an Agglomerative Aesthetics of Radical Truth," introduces a new field of research that aims at identifying and analyzing the shifts in collaborative media practices. In reference to the notions of "communities of sense" (Rancière 2009), we point to an aesthetics of radical truth as a consistent tendency of building practices of resistance in the twenty-first century. The critical text we refer to is *The Specters of Marx: The*

State of the Debt, the Work of Mourning and the New International by Jacques Derrida (2011). In the lectures of the French philosopher, we find a critique that even in the 1990s foreshadowed the threats of new forms of violence arising from contemporary forms of colonialism and covert apartheid. Derrida proposed to leave the comfortable positions of academic criticism and adopt that of a migrant, which redefines in practice concepts such as justice, community, hospitality, and care. Derrida's idea ties in with that of Edward Said, who focuses on practices in the possibility of postcolonial democratic field (Said 2003) and in the "methodology of the oppressed" introduced by Chela Sandoval (2000). Grassroots media practices have enabled a resurgence of political agency and the building up of resistance to violence against human beings and the environment. This resistance, however, is already firmly embedded in postcolonial critique and concepts of radical situatedness. The media have a cohesive function in these projects as they produce counterinfrastructures that help reveal the truth about covert forms of violence. The coupling of artistic, media, scientific, activist, journalistic, social, and creative practices with the critical and materialistic approaches to technology that we write about in this book has confirmed our conviction that we deal with the production of AeRT. In this respect, truth is more than a fact. It is a set of facts and data collected and presented in a coherent environment (both via traditional exhibitions and digital platforms). It is highly likely that the bottom-up use of media and the social turn toward radical truth will become one of the elements of new open paradigms of knowledge production in societies for which global equilibria and equally situated and local strategies of social and environmental justice will be relevant.

The way we wrote this book is also agglomeratively part of the concept of AeRT. It is its continuation in research, an extension in the text-narrative, and a record of the joints and structures that produce practices against violence. In our analyses, descriptions, and interpretations, we followed in the footsteps of many critics of both theorists and practitioners of contemporary culture and oppressive models of society (such as Michel Foucault, Jacques Rancière, Jacques Derrida, Nicholas De Genova, Bruno Latour, and Donna Haraway), capitalism and colonialism (such as Achille Mbembe, Eyal Weizman, and Chela Sandoval), and the technosocial conditions of modernity (like Seán Cubitt, Jussi Parikka, Matthew

Fuller, Wolfgang Ernst, Jenifer Gabrys, Karen Barad, and Susan Schuppli). These are just a few of the authors referred to in the book who point out new avenues for critical research within contemporary social, cultural, economic, and environmental issues in terms of evolving technological infrastructures.

However, like an aesthetics of radical truth, our book is heterogeneous, dynamic, and open-ended. We reach out to the ideas of philosophers and critics of media, society, and culture and to a variety of documents. These include reports, press and media coverage, data from social networks (such as posts, photos, and videos posted on Telegram, Twitter, X, YouTube, and other platforms), stories and eyewitness accounts, and studies by activists and grassroots groups working against violence. All these documents are agglomeratively incorporated into the research framework and described in this book. Each chapter follows a slightly different narrative structure, depending on the issue at hand. Sometimes we are guided by the critical thinking of specific researchers. Sometimes we are driven by our own experiences gained during the workshops conducted by the groups we write about. The agglomerative nature of this book is likewise evident in the transversal use of perspectives and methods originally appropriated by various scholarly disciplines. In the individual chapters, we group various concepts, research approaches, and analytical tools, only to then let them disintegrate like an impermanent agglomerate. In this way, we do not generate stable inter- or transdisciplinary connections. Rather, we test how, from the perspective of scholarly discourse and media practice, we can talk about strategies to counter contemporary violence in the plethora of its cultural, political, and geographical forms? How can we understand and destabilize the privileged position of violence in the contemporary world? In chapter 1, we combine tools from aesthetics, philosophy, critical media studies, and critical theory. In chapter 2, we apply theories of infrastructural media studies as well as discourse on engaged journalism, anthropology, sociology, and meteorology. Chapter 3 makes use of critical data science, environmental humanities, human geography, critical cartography, and experimental anthropology, while chapter 4, we merge legal discourse with countersurveillance theories, tactical media, social activism, and the deconstruction of human rights by the processes of digital dividuation. Chapter 5 combines discourse on media archives with critical decolonial studies and media archeology. In the epilogue, we revisit the fundamental and radical questions and, applying philosophy, propose an overt theory of engagement in the work for the sake of truth and justice, a theory that is open to new additions. Each book chapter has a distinct discursive character and can stand on its own as an independent part, while the aforementioned disciplines and subdisciplines of science do not exhaust the scholarly apparatus used. The common denominators of all the sections of the book are the processes of agglomerating concepts, theories, recognitions, tools, and methodologies. They are also the pasting together and disintegrating that pave way for new knowledge construction experiments. The structure of each chapter reflects the complex dynamics of the questions we cover to integrate the discourse into the framework of an aesthetics of radical truth.

1

AESTHETICS AS LABOR FOR RECLAIMING TRUTH

The phenomena we address in the book within the aesthetics of radical truth (AeRT) chronologically belong to the second and third decades of the twenty-first century. Most of the projects included here resulted from a reaction to violence and injustice occurring in the last dozen or so years. A few address issues related to the current consequences of long-term structural violence whose root causes have accumulated over many decades. What helps us see the formally diverse grassroots phenomena as a shared trend are the strategies of technological media use and the processes of designed openness and social inclusivity that have emerged as the main tools for demonstrating the truth about violence. Bottom-up media strategies, proprietary tools, systems, and methodologies for collecting data about crimes, offenses, and abuses against people and the environment are also coupled with the changing image of violence in the twenty-first century. As have many other areas of life, violence has become mediatized, technologized, and digitalized. The practices we report on in this book have emerged in response to the changing and increasingly veiled landscape of violence. From the perspective of the research material we have accumulated, the second and third decades of the twenty-first century have been a rough time—a period of wars, conflicts, terrorism, refugee crises, environmental disasters, and global pandemic. However, the 2010s and 2020s have also been a time of revolt against social and environmental injustice, totalitarian regimes, and corporate and state violence.

MODERN VIOLENCE IN MEDIA DENSE ENVIRONMENTS

The second decade of the twenty-first century began with the Arab Spring in 2010 in Tunisia. Often referred to as the first smartphone revolution, the movement quickly spread to many other countries like Bahrain, Egypt, Libya, Syria, and Yemen. Street demonstrations took place across Algeria, Iraq, Jordan, Khuzestan province (Iran), Kuwait, Lebanon, Morocco, Oman, and Sudan. Minor demonstrations occurred in Djibouti, Mauritania, Moroccan-occupied Western Sahara, Palestine, and Saudi Arabia. Initially, the Arab Spring promised to be a true revolution and inspired high hopes. Unfortunately, its ideals were never achieved in full, and some unforeseen consequences led to conflicts and wars that have continued to this day, with special cruelty in Syria and Palestine. During the Arab Spring, there was an unprecedented, massive use of telephones as tools of communication as protesters documented the course of the demonstrations and the violence committed against them. Also during the Arab Spring, the internet became a battlefield for democratic rights as governments imposed unprecedented censorship and restrictions on free access to the internet, including attempts to cut off citizens from the web (Egypt, Libya, and Syria) and attempts to hack and steal passwords to citizens' private social media accounts (Tunisia). These restrictions on access and control of civic activity online triggered a debate about treating internet access and freedom of communication as fundamental human rights.

The 2010s also were marked by the rise of global terrorism, including the emergence of the self-proclaimed ISIS (Islamic State of Iraq and Syria) in 2014. Its followers established footholds in Middle East states like Syria and Iraq, and some chapters, like those in Afghanistan and Pakistan, gained numerous allies in African countries. During this time, terrorists seized new media tools to disseminate their propaganda on social media, record their own crimes, and make the videos available online to instill fear. Atrocious examples include video recordings of executions.

Terrorism, intrastate wars and conflicts, and various forms of apartheid unleashed massive waves of refugees. A report by the United Nations High Commissioner for Refugees (UNHCR) (2021) estimates that the global number of forcibly internally displaced individuals in mid-2021 was 48 million. As much as 68 percent of these refugees came from just five countries—Afghanistan (2.6 million), Myanmar (1.1 million), South Sudan (2.3 million), Syrian Arab Republic (6.8 million), and Venezuela (4.1 million). At the same time, the United Nations Relief and Works Agency for Palestine Refugees in the Near East (UNRWA) estimated the number of refugees from Palestine at 5.7 million (UNHCR 2021). For thousands, the voyage from Africa to Europe across the Mediterranean Sea proved deadly. Many of these tragedies were recorded and documented. Refugees use their smartphones to take photos, shoot videos, and contact their relatives and various organizations that offer such help. In every such case, a trace remains to identify violence.

The second decade of the twenty-first century also saw a global discussion on the climate crisis, alarming data published by scientists on the pollution of the planet, and demonstrations and climate strikes that have involved more and more activists and people concerned with the problems of the planet. The climate problem has incalculable consequences, including forced climate migration, the degradation of sustainable agricultural policies, and the prospect of global famine. With the rise of climate denialism (Norgaard 2011), the politicization of denialist tendencies by populist politicians, and a widening consensus gap, a strategy for bottom-up environmental data mining has emerged. The rise of concepts such as citizen science and community science is symbolic of the need to redefine the problem, not only in scholarly terms but also in its environmental tangibility and materiality, which directly affect local communities. This redefinition involves transformations within the acquisition of, access to, and rights to environmental data, creating a separate system for identifying and understanding climate change in relation to local knowledge, culture, and economics. Local communities' data ownership involves the production of a discrete bottom-up infrastructure for monitoring the state of the environment, prototyping sensors and measuring devices, and integrating environmental problems into local politics and culture. This became evident in 2011 when a tsunami-induced disaster occurred in the nuclear power plant in Fukushima, Japan. It brought back memories of the 1986 Chernobyl power plant blast in the Ukrainian Soviet Socialist Republic and the atomic bombs dropped on Hiroshima and Nagasaki in Japan in 1945. The Fukushima disaster sparked further top-down discussions on radioactivity and climate responsibility. However, in the face of underreporting and a lack of transparent information about the actual levels of radioactivity, grassroots initiatives emerged that began to develop an organized system of citizen measurements and to use experimental media to generate a cultural narrative independent of official media coverage (Jelewska and Krawczak 2025).

In the 2010s and 2020s, new forms of resistance to political regimes have been seen across the world, including in Ukraine (Euromaidan in 2013–2014), Belarus (protests in 2020–2021), and Russia (antigovernment protests in 2011–2012, student protests in 2019, protests over election results in 2021, and protests by supporters of Alexei Navalny in 2021). Civic protest movements have also been driven by new forms of social organization (following the principle of collective distributed leadership) in Hong Kong (with the slogan "Be Water" in 2019–2020) and in Barcelona (with the slogan "Tsunami Democratic" in 2019). In addition, women's strikes—in Argentina (2015); Chile, Colombia, El Salvador, and Mexico (2019–2021); and Poland (2016, 2020–2021)—have been vociferous statements against femicide laws tightening antiabortion laws and restricting access to medical care. These protests were largely held in a hybrid space that combined traditional forms of demonstrating with digital tools and used social media to self-organize and broadcast events. Unique grassroots practices emerged within some of these phenomena. Protesters in Hong Kong and Barcelona designed smartphone apps that could not be infiltrated by the authorities, while in Belarus, citizens resorted to digital strategies such as doxing to reveal the identities of officers in the OMON (Special Purpose Police Detachment)[1] who brutally attacked the protesters.

The 2010s witnessed the rise of populist movements and the radicalization of state policies in countries in Europe, the United States, Latin America, and India. Equally noticeable was the influence on global politics of hacking movements and whistleblowers, with Julian Assange and Edward Snowden emerging as icons of the movement.[2]

Finally, it was a time of an accelerated platformization of capitalism as networks, social platforms, and instant messaging were developed that hybridized the physical and the digital. These processes were also accelerated by the COVID-19 pandemic, which made online communication the primary form of interaction; at the same time, there was rapid development of digital communication tools, disinformation and new forms of AI. All of this has its implications in the transformation of nearly every aspect of reality, including changes in communication paradigms in social relations, the algorithmization and dividuation of individuals in economic and administrative systems, and new ways of conducting and managing armed conflict.

Many of the ongoing war conflicts in the twenty-first century seem to be long-lasting "states of war" (Virilio 2002; Virilio and Bertrand 2012). These conflicts have resulted from earlier US interventions in Afghanistan (2001) and Iraq (2003); the Israeli–Palestinian conflict, which has continued for nearly a hundred years (claiming ever-new casualties and new wars, as in 2023); and the reemerging Russian imperial policy, which regularly attempts to destabilize the former Eastern Bloc countries. The Russian Federation's armed aggression against part of the territory of Ukraine began in February 2014, turned into a long-lasting hybrid war, and transformed into regular warfare throughout Ukraine in February 2022.

Recent decades have seen continuing structural violence, which has persisted for hundreds of years. The deep roots of such violence (Galtung 1969; Vorobej 2008)—such as racism, apartheid, and cultural and economic segregation—take different forms at different points in history. They also continue in new forms the political and systemic paradigms of sovereignty and control of individuals and groups (Mbembe 2003). Responding to systemic racism and to continued colonialism and cultural segregation in the US and UK, global protests after the 2012 murder of Trayvon Martin, a seventeen-year-old African American, by a Hispanic, civilian member of a Florida neighborhood watch association and after the 2020 murder of George Floyd, a black citizen, by a white police officer in Minneapolis, Minnesota, was captured by CCTV cameras and recorded by witnesses' phones. The video of the murder of George Floyd became a symbol of media evidence of structural violence. In the Black Lives Matter (BLM) protests that swept across the United States, Australia, South Africa, Canada, South America, UK and European countries, demonstrators recorded many acts of police violence against protesters.

In the projects we write about, which deal with structurally rooted forms of violence, it is necessary to take a broad spatial and historical view. The occurrence of these forms of violence in a specific place and at a given time is relevant to the amassed traces and evidence of crime, yet understanding and learning about them are long-term endeavors. Many of the symptoms of structural violence continue to present themselves and have spilled over into the 2020s.

Our goal is not to provide a description of the violence-related phenomena that have occurred in the past decade. Nor do we attempt to map them, which would exceed the scope of this chapter and book. Many of these phenomena are adequately covered in the literature in international relations, political science, sociology, media studies, anthropology, and critical humanities. Instead, we want to identify groups, phenomena, and syndromes whose activities can be seen as trends of the 2010s and 2020s and to record these crimes in a bottom-up manner—using experimental technological tools, tracking the violence generated by these conflicts, showing the different faces of these conflicts, and giving voice to the excluded and overlooked witnesses and victims of crime and abuse.

When we talk about tracking, studying, showing, and sharing violence-related data acquired through various media, we realize that as participants in these projects, we come to know them through various forms of mediation. This relates to the broader perspectives and consequences that have emerged as communicative, social, economic, political, and cultural realities have been integrated with digital technologies, as seen in the above phenomena and situations of violence generation and recording. This is not a mere hybridization of phenomena and practices but an entirely new paradigm in which these elements—digital and analogue, digital and physical, digital and material, and digital and social—become inseparable. The integration of the digital and other areas of reality has equally transformed the digital and the other areas that integrate with it. Along with these transformations, the forms of violence against people and the environment—various practices of resistance, the reclaiming of political agency through media technologies (socially and culturally), the presentation of data and images of facts, and the involvement of audiences in the process of understanding and learning about them—have changed. At the same time, some concepts and categories—like participation, complicity, collective action, witnessing, documenting—have undergone semantic shifts and redefinitions. They have incorporated technological causality into their scope of meaning and opened in the process of argument formation to the disclosure of nonhuman actants.

The processes of mediatization, remediatization, digitalization, and hybridization of reality have led to the emergence of a need to stabilize the concept of truth, evidence, and testimony through socially accepted mechanisms for their production and authentication.

In media studies and digital media studies, the hybridization process is defined to indicate a new ontology of medial reality as, for example, "medianatures" (Parikka 2018). It is analyzed in terms of consequences for social structures in the field of media and communication studies as a "digitally saturated environment" (Couldry 2015) or as a "mediated construction of reality" (Couldry and Hepp 2016). In the technical sciences, architecture, human geography, and management system programming are called "hybrid space" (Saker and Frith 2019), "digiplace" (Zook and Graham 2007), and "code/space" (Kitchin and Dodge 2011). Eyal Weizman (2017) uses a helpful term—"media dense environment"—in his book *Forensic Architecture: Violence at the Threshold of Detectability*. There, he defines the situation in reference to contemporary cities, whose infrastructure and space during armed conflict become a record of crime:

> The urban environment is highly sentient in both material, analogue, and digital terms. It is a dense media environment saturated by optical and other sensors' photographs, noise, meteorology and pollution detectors, security cameras, fixed-orbit and image satellites, and smart phones. A conflict involves thousands, sometimes tens of thousands, of people entering into an unfamiliar environment that is also home to hundreds of thousands, sometimes millions of people. When this takes place, all elements of the city start recording, each in its own way. Buildings record vibrations and the force of impacts. Plants record—crushed fields around a city's agricultural outskirts register the movement of military vehicles on them when they stop photosynthesizing, a signal that is captured by remote sensors orbiting above and beamed back to earth. Air-quality sensors pick up increases in traffic as tanks roll in or refugees' escape. (Weizman 2017, 57–58)

All the sensors—technological and nontechnological—that Weizman indicates are abundant in contemporary cities register data that can later be used to reconstruct the situation in which violence occurred. Every element of the city's substance—its buildings, streets, and elements of infrastructure—can be evidence of a crime. Plants damaged by specific substances can provide traces of chemical weapons, while a photographed array of clouds can serve as evidence of the use of specific explosives. Modern cities are examples of extreme media saturation. They are becoming dense with media that capture sounds, images, motion, temperature levels, air composition, and any user-generated data online. Outside cities, media saturation is changing and is reduced. However, there is practically no place on the planet that is not recorded by satellites and therefore hybridized with digital technologies. It is increasingly difficult to find limits to the data-acquisition capabilities of remote sensing technologies. Everywhere that we use mobile devices, we leave data and traces. Sometimes we record videos, upload photos to social media platforms, and create further levels of complex mediatization of time and space. While this fact is evident from the perspective of any mobile technology user, its complex consequences for knowledge production are not always apparent.

Today the state of mediatization and mediation affects all animate and inanimate matter on earth (Cubitt 2014; Grusin 2015). This state of mediatization that creates planetary and supraplanetary infrastructures (Parikka 2015) triggers the need to explore and apply new ways and practices of tracking and exposing crimes and violence against humans and the environment. The ones we write about in this book employ very different strategies for both recording and mediating access to violence. Sometimes, as in the case of Forensic Architecture's investigations, these are complex chronospatial reconstructions that determine the precise location of ships, lifeboats, and people during rescue operations in the open waters of the Mediterranean. On other occasions, as in the case of Public Lab, it is the use of simple do-it-yourself activities, like releasing weather balloons with cameras attached to take pictures of the water surface, thus recording the state of contamination in the Gulf of Mexico after the environmental disaster caused by the BP refinery oil spill in 2010. Or in the case of Bellingcat, it is creating an open platform where socially harvested data and narratives about war crimes or evidence of war crimes committed by Russian troops against Ukrainian civilians are posted on the Timemap platform. Finally, there is the use of simple tools to detect radiation levels in given areas after the Fukushima contamination, as members of the Safecast group did. All these strategies that exploit the mechanisms of transversality of the physical and the digital are direct responses to the forms of violence they document and expose. The strategies of grassroots resistance have effected a change in their ontological and technical natures, and the media conditions in which violence is carried out also have changed. Defense mechanisms arise in response to specific threats, and therefore violence in media-dense environments demands digital and physical defense mechanisms. The transformations and systems of resilience enforced through the mechanisms of modern technological oppression are rife with broader implications for culture and society. The transformations addressed in this book, therefore, have the potential for effecting long-term social and cultural changes as they trigger a shift of public opinion and its attitude to unjust violence, the forms of production, and the organization of society.

AESTHETICS AS THE PERCEPTION BETWEEN POLITICS, NATURE, AND THE MATERIALITY OF VIOLENCE

Aesthetics are required to prove the truth, reveal it, and share it in society. Such an aesthetics becomes a process involving people, objects, facts, data, and images and thereby creates an ecosystem in which this process is carried out and shared. In this book, we envision aesthetics not as a static and finite research category but as a dynamic performance and cognitive paradigm. It determines how objects, facts, evidence, and testimonies are presented; how the course of an event is reconstructed; and what the process of obtaining materials, samples, and information about it looks like in aesthetic terms. Seen as ecosystem and relation, aesthetics is also closely linked to ethical and political ways of mediating things and objects (often as resistance, an alternative to top-down imposed information or ways of presenting evidence of violence). All these categories combine to form an open paradigm that we call the aesthetics of radical truth. We place AeRT among other definitions of aesthetics that perceive it as an environment—an ecosystem for the formation of communal, political, social, or ethical qualities within the framework of relations between people, things, situations, views, policies, economic, and communications systems.

Aesthetics is a discourse but also a way of establishing links and mediating between processes, objects, and recipients. For the practices discussed here, aesthetics is a sociocreative function that also introduces certain communicative and epistemic values for ways of revealing violence. This stems from the Greek etymology of the term *aisthetikos—aisthētikós* ("perceptive, sensitive, pertaining to sensory perception"), *aisthánomai* ("I perceive, sense, learn"), and *aísthēsis*, ("perception, sensation")—which means "recognized by the senses" as well as "sensing." Continuing along these lines, aesthetics can be seen as an environment that generates a new sensibility that is responsible for establishing relations between violence, facts, data, the process of collecting and analyzing them, the way they are made available to the public, and those who become cognizant and sensitized (through cognition) participants in this process. As we note in the introduction, the radicality of aesthetics refers primarily to the notion of *radix* ("root"). It therefore refers us "back to the roots"—to the grassroots, which are the shared practices that enable audiences to tap into the process of tracing, gathering evidence, and describing—but it also encourages us to learn about it in a practical way and to share in the creation of this cognition. Like radicalism, aesthetics in the twentieth century left behind its earlier domains of meaning as a study of beauty and expanded the field of its discursive and practical agency. It was also influenced by earlier recognitions, including the concepts of the eighteenth-century German philosopher Alexander Baumgarten, who said that aesthetics is the experience of a work of art and also produces understanding and cognition through these processes (Baumgarten 2013).

Most of the discourses and studies on the causality of aesthetics that have become important contexts for thinking about aesthetics as an environment and as a process of establishing relationships between objects, things, and audiences have been widely discussed since the late 1990s. The renaissance of this category begun at that time has led the term to be used and redefined in various research fields and disciplines. Aesthetics began to be strongly redefined in its etymology as affective and sensitive interfaces between objects, matter, and people and the ways in which these connections are experienced. The popularity of aesthetics as a realm of experimental practices and processual cognitive procedures was also influenced by concepts that arose within modernism and postmodernism in twentieth-century art. Aesthetics has become a space for interdisciplinary research linking pragmatists like John Dewey as well as widely represented feminist, posthumanist, and post- and decolonial discourses and practices. Finally, aesthetics has also become a tool for describing newly generated and technologically mediated entities and processes.

Below we would like to address four areas that are relevant from the perspective of our proposed aesthetics of radical truth and that involve the concept of aesthetics as a practice—an area linked to the expansion and entry of aesthetics into the field of politics and attempts to reclaim the causality of the actions of the participants in this process, a field linked to the acceleration of digital and communication technologies and the increasing integration of the digital and the physical, an area that concerns media aesthetics centered around environmental and ecological theories, and a field that describes the aesthetics of materiality as connecting human and nonhuman subjects. A separate section of this chapter is devoted to the agglomerative nature and structure of AeRT as a connective and collaborative aesthetics.

AESTHETICS AS SENSIBLE POLITICS

Around the year 2000, aesthetics began to strongly moderate the ways of capturing politics, resisting top-down social structures, and thus building new communities based on the notion of "sense." This aesthetics delineated two new epistemic areas for the practice of politics. *Sense-making* collectively establishes and negotiates the optics of cognition, and *sensemaking* affectively attunes participants to share and know this process.

In the late 1990s, French art critic and curator Nicolas Bourriaud described his concept of aesthetics as a mode of shaping social relations through artistic practices, including in the sense of political agency. His concept stems directly from his work as a curator, in which the practical interaction and design of exhibition space creates an aesthetic and simultaneously socially and politically causal space. For him, "the possibility of relational art (an art taking as its theoretical horizon the realm of human interactions and its social context, rather than the assertation of an independent and private symbolic space), points to a radical upheaval of the aesthetic, cultural and political goals introduced by modern art" (Bourriaud 1998, 14). In this perspective, artistic practice is a tool to generate social interactions through the production of a "space" for dialogue and relationship, which in a democratic society is political expression. In this sense, the art object has a primarily political function and produces form for social "co-existence" (Bourriaud 1998, 109).

The establishment of a community has a deeper meaning, as it is a strategy of both resistance and collective cognition. For Bourriaud, social qualities are produced in a real way in the situation of being together in the space of art. He calls this process "operational realism" and describes it as "presentation of the functional sphere in an aesthetic arrangement" (Bourriaud 1998, 112). This realm is not a model or a mock-up but is an actual space constructed through social and political relations. Of particular importance are the materiality of the object, the space in which the spectators are located, and the materialist approach to the sphere of social, economic, and political relations as embedded in Marx's critical texts.

Among other things, Bourriaud draws on the term "social interstice" that Marx uses to depict economic practices that elude the mechanisms of capitalism, based on the exchange of goods, autarkic types of production, and other means. In this case, through communal procedures, it is possible to create economic qualities based on nonexploitative and noncumulative social relations: "The interstice is a space in human relations which fits more or less harmoniously and openly into the overall system but suggests other trading possibilities than those in effect within this system" (Bourriaud 1998, 16). In the perspective of relational aesthetics, if social activity and communication always take place in the context of economics (corporations that produce living space and communication tools), then art becomes "the object and the subject of ethic. . . . Art is a state of encounter" (Bourriaud 1998, 18). Through its "form," art has tools for bringing people together and producing social relations. Form itself is an indefinite concept and is subject to constant transformation, unlike in classical aesthetics. Rather, it comes closer to social approaches, such as Émile Durkheim's sociological definitions where "social fact" is seen as a "thing." Thus, form in art becomes an amassment of "things" and "facts." Form is a "principle of dynamic agglutination" (Bourriaud 1998, 20). The relational nature in this concept is political, ensuring the linking of facts, things, and people in the process of form generation.

In 2000, Jacques Rancière published *The Politics of Aesthetics: The Distribution of the Sensible* (2004). The book presented a novel perception of aesthetics as politics and politics as aesthetics, doubly intertwined in the perspective of reason and sensibility. This concept was consistently developed by the philosopher and deeply connected to his antiauthoritarian and antielitist beliefs (Rancière 2004) as "the attempt to introduce the egalitarian effects of political and artistic action into the core of theory itself" (Rancière 2016, 2–3). Rancière draws on aesthetics to persuade his readers that politics should be a realm for the formation of concepts, practices, and ways of seeing things as collective action and negotiation that create "communities of sense" (Rancière 2009). Aesthetics introduces new experimental ways of aligning things. Being external to politics and its established powers, these "new regimes" (Rancière 2004) open political processes to broad understanding and the communal elaboration of cognitive modalities. Rancière analyzes selected works of art, especially experimental and avant-garde art, and shares insights into the political and social processes offered by works of art, both formally and semantically. Of prime importance for the author is the practice of "distribution of sensuality" that is produced by works of art that bring together audiences. Thus, Rancière deems aesthetics to be a way of producing new cognitive ecosystems for communities based on sense and sensibility. This function of art generates new practices among the socially political. Politics is a space of discussion, representation, and reproduction. Analyzing the French philosopher's concepts, Margus Vihalem writes that politics in Rancière's terms is experienced rather than invented, while sensibility "seems to be the very medium of politics: politics is what is sensed and what is felt" (Vihalem 2018, 2).

AESTHETICS AS A CRITIQUE OF DIGITAL AND DATA TECHNOCRACY

The accelerated development of technology—technologies that harvest data about people and tangible and intangible objects, advanced communication technologies, and the global accessibility of the internet—has led to attempts to define new digital aesthetics and the attendant challenges to sensitivity and experience. One of the seminal books on the subject is Séan Cubitt's 1998 *Digital Aesthetics*, where he looks critically at the new forms of digitization at the end of the millennium and highlights the need to rethink and rework a new ethic for a digitized world. The digital mode—an integral part of what Cubitt calls "digital aesthetics"—holds users responsible for how and why they use digital tools. The aesthetic is "the pursuit of an ethical mode of being in despite of the conditions in which we find ourselves" (Cubitt 1998, ix). The author notes the need for a critical approach to digital technologies due to their corporate and capitalist origin and their association with new technological forms of top-down violence, surveillance, colonialism, economic, and environmental exploitation. As he pointed out back then, the computerization of life began to be associated with the increased effects of technology and software producers on ever deeper layers of social, political, economic, and cultural life. Cubitt understood that digitalization is not just a process of technological change but an overall transformation of reality. Digitality is a new culture and a new ontology of the technology of everyday life that involves the integration of the physical and digital worlds. He therefore tried to define aesthetics as an essential force of resistance to technocapitalist tools of surveillance. He pointed out that, in such a reality, art and grassroots digital media practices have a vital critical function in diagnosing threats, abuse, violence, and systemic control.

Cubitt thus created a critical discourse and space for an "art that communicates, or that poses itself as communication, and questions whether any communication is possible that is not already aggression, command, power, submission" (Cubitt 1998, x). Cubitt's diagnosis, made at an early stage of global digitalization, was a precise critical prognosis of the aftermath of the growth of digital technologies. He described the hazards and processes of the grassroots "recovery" of communication and technology based on ethical imperatives. The practices we describe in this book are examples of just that. They create their own tools, setups, and strategies for using technology so that the process of finding the truth about violence is transparent, open, shareable, and mutually understandable. Cubitt seems to be proposing two approaches to the possible definition of digital aesthetics in relation to the environment. On the one hand, he points out that digital technologies plug into the environment as sensors—as remote sensing technologies that collect data to create digital representations of this environment. These sensors are subject to further forms of exploitation in the capitalist system. On the other hand, he refers to aesthetics as a sphere of possible practice of other forms and modalities of communication.

Cubitt addresses the technological and ontological natures of the digital image and digital data. Images and data acquired through remote sensing technologies can be capitalized on by "corporate cyborgs" (Cubitt 1998). GIS systems, like paper maps in earlier centuries, are not bottom-up practices of environmental knowledge production but rather visualized projects of colonization and exploitation. For Cubitt, the connections developing between digital technologies and new forms of natural resource exploitation are policies of economic pressure on local communities. The extraction of information about their territory by transnational corporations "not only infringes sovereignty, but more importantly enables massive investments in profit-oriented information gathering about mineral and hydrocarbon deposits, in any case far less likely to be exploited by a poor nation than a wealthy company, at the expense of vital local knowledge about inundation, drought, subsurface aquifers, overgrazing, poor irrigation and salt accumulation" (Cubitt 1998, 48).

These practices—working with remote sensing technologies, acquiring massive data, and feeding it into automated information systems—are violent and shortsighted. To prevent this outcome, greater emphasis should be placed on field research, which enables the verification of digital information through direct, on-the-ground observation. Data verification is becoming an ethical and socially significant activity. Cubitt thus marks a state of systemic suspension and continuous mediation between the material and the digital as a new cognitive mode that technological development generates.

The practice of detaching data from matter, environment, and terrain is also highlighted by Yanni Alexander Loukissas, the author of *All Data Are Local: Thinking Critically in a Data-Driven Society* (2019). Louikissas describes the consequences of the data automation processes, which aim at the aggregation of all data and its "simplification" according to specific methodologies. Thus, data is detached from local conditions and contexts and is subject to homogenization and algorithmic standardization. Qualitatively significant differences between individual datasets, which can be perceived only from a situated perspective, cease to be taken into account in the automation process. As a result, falsifications and internal conflicts arise within the dataset. Thus, subjected to automated visualization, datasets are associated with homogenizing aesthetics, whose goal is to subjugate the result achieved and conform it to a preconceived cognitive concept. Loukissas advocates a form of working with digital data based on the idea of "curation" (from the Latin *cura*, meaning "care"). Curation is not possible without extended ethnographic fieldwork; only in this way can digital data be situated in the local context: "More experimentally, reading locally can mean imagining how data might be seen in new ways, using speculative yet nevertheless locally imagined modes of visualization" (Loukissas 2019, 8). Situated data generates "friction" and calls for new non-normative and nonhomogenizing methods of analysis and visualization. Thus, questions about the aesthetics of data visualization are questions about the ethics of procedures, ways of acquiring data, methodologies for aggregating them, and methods of using them as forms of control and surveillance. Loukissas proposes a return of data to the terrain, the environment, matter, and people, thereby laying the groundwork for thinking and practicing a new environmental aesthetics of data that is meaningful not just as data taken from the environment but also as locally conditioned data and ways of acquiring, analyzing, visualizing, and sharing it.

AESTHETICS OF MEDIA AND COMMUNICATION ECOLOGY

An ever-greater fusion of the material and the digital is generating a new field for the formation of environmental and ecological aesthetics and models for analyzing and describing them. Within media studies, there is a long tradition of using environmental and ecological theory to describe media practices and to define the medium. This concept carries certain implications for viewing the aesthetics inherent in these practices by defining the structure, ontology, and relationship of various media to themselves and to social, political, and biological environments. Researchers taking the environmental perspective situate themselves in the optics of research proposed by Marshall McLuhan, Jacques Ellul, Walter Ong, James Carey, and Neil Postman are critical to technological determinism. Postman defined such a relation as the study of media as environments, meaning that "technological change is not additive, but ecological" (Postman 1998, 4). Emiliano Treré, in *Hybrid Media Activism:*

Ecologies, Imaginaries, Algorithms, suggests that we can think of media both as environments and as species within an ecosystem—entities that interact, compete, and form relationships with one another. Viewing media in this way allows us to adopt an evolutionary perspective, one that examines why certain media or technologies persist while others disappear and explores how various media forms evolve together over time (Treré 2019, 40). This perception of media introduces the new project of aesthetics into practices that use media as internally relational and evolutionary and is contingent on linkages and entanglements between the technological media themselves and more broadly between human and nonhuman entities and technology. Seen in this way, the aesthetics of media is a social practice that, as viewed by Bonnie Nardi and Vicky O'Day, is within "information ecology" and is "a system of people, practices, values, and technologies in a particular local environment" (Nardi and O'Day 1999, 49). Analyzing the development of this discourse, Treré indicates another major field that expands the definition of media as environments— "communicative ecology" (Foth and Hearn 2007). In digital technologies, it is a fusion of technological, social, and discursive contexts (Treré 2019).

A slightly different origin of the concept of media ecologies was introduced by Matthew Fuller, who drew on the philosophy of Gilles Deleuze and Félix Guattari (2004) and proposed a definition of the aesthetics of digital media as the aesthetics of multiplicity and layering—"of adding complication and filtering, and of joining processes to networks . . . alongside that of forces and powers" (Fuller 2005, 10). Fuller describes media as an open and dynamic composition of multiple relations: "these are dimensionalities operating as self-referencing structures that cooperate to produce something in excess of themselves and emerge in new structures of political, material, and aesthetic combination" (2005, x). He also applies to the definition of media ecologies the thinking in terms of metaphors that was proposed by Deleuze and Guattari and defined at length in *A Thousand Plateaus: Capitalism and Schizophrenia* (2004). Their term is the "machinic phylum," which simultaneously defines force and matter, allowing linkages between (living and nonliving) beings as forces of stretching, unfolding, shrinking, and folding (DeLanda 1997). Under such an approach, media enter structures of matter and contribute along with it to dynamic composition. As a metaphor, the machinic phylum allows for a sensual and technical aesthetics (Fuller 2005, 6). This results in an open virtuality of the "dynamic interrelation of processes and objects, beings and things, patterns and matter" (Fuller 2005, 2). Fuller stresses the material aspect of the media linked with the processes of subjectivation of matter itself. In his book *Media Ecologies: Materialist Energies in Art and Technoculture* (2005), in which he defines this concept, he refers to an analysis of the artistic and activist practices he describes using this aesthetic, which helps him navigate the political and social processes triggered and cocreated by the media.

In the optics of aesthetics as environment, the term "medianatures" was coined by Jussi Parikka to show that "natural ecology is entirely entangled with the technological one" (Parikka 2015, 63). It refers "to technology as an active agent in the ontological and epistemological sense. In other words, media structure how things are in the world and how things are known in the world. In fact, media analysis is an excellent way of 'giving material specificity to our descriptions of abstract concepts' of which materiality is oddly enough too easily one" (Parikka 2015, 1–2). Opting for such codeterminations and the coemergence of media and matter, Parikka places aesthetics in the ecology of mutual relations between technology and the environment and also in posthumanist and feminist metaphors and concepts (such as naturecultures) (Haraway 2003) or intra-actions between objects (Barad 2007).

Parikka points to a crucial aspect for a novel perception of the aesthetics of media as medianatures in his book *A Geology of Media* (2015). Here he indicates that media are merged with the matter of the planet as composites of various geological materials excavated in the processes of exploiting the earth, such as lithium, coltan, and other minerals indispensable for technological production. Technological media contribute to the degradation of the environment, effecting far-reaching climate change through the mass production of carbon dioxide, the consumption of huge amounts of energy, and the creation of physical data collection infrastructures that surround the entire planet. It is a concept "that crystallizes the 'double bind' of media and nature as co-constituting spheres, where the ties are intensively connected in material nonhuman realities as much as in relations of power, economy, and work. Indeed, it is a regime constituted as much by the work of micro-organisms, chemical components, minerals, and metals as by the work of underpaid laborers in mines or in high-tech entertainment device component production factories, or people in Pakistan and China sacrificing their health for scraps of leftover electronics" (Parikka 2015, 14). Through a materialist and infrastructural framing of media, Parikka points to the metaphor of medianatures as being instrumental for understanding and perceiving technology in relation to materiality and thus connects epistemics with ethics. As Cubitt did earlier, Parikka looks at the new forms of exploitation of the planet, and he includes mass-produced technological media (as corporate and industrial infrastructures) in the chain of responsibility for the climate crisis and exploitative policies. The ethics of environmental media is becoming so important today because it seeks to find a response to the need to break free from top-down mass modes of technological exploitation and adopt strategies that create new, purposeful, and committed projects that benefit nature and humans.

A major contribution to this debate is Cajethan Iheka's book *African Ecomedia: Networks Forms, Planetary Politics* (2021), which elaborates on the above concepts and invokes Séan Cubitt's media ecology. Situating his research on the ground and in the perspective of the African continent, Iheka shows yet another understanding of the media in ecological planetary politics. He points out that the media participate in the process of extraction and exploitation, especially of African states, and that this process has been going on since the fifteenth century. In this sense, the media are involved in infrastructures filled with violence, but they also produce waste—that is, a new technological layer covering vast territories of Africa. Iheka proposes a new understanding of media ecology that pays attention to the deliberate use and application of a specific media technology. It is impossible to turn off technology today, but it is possible to abandon many of its violent solutions in favor of ones that can bring justice through a deep understanding of the processes of planetary violence flowing from corporations, states, and technocrats. As we do in this book, Iheka argues for a broad definition of ecomedia, including infrastructures, technologies, software, and mass media. He goes back to the concept of media as systems of information, and civilizational systemic devices for social order and surveillance of individuals and groups.

For Iheka, media are also mineral resources such as oil, gold, diamonds, and uranium mined in Africa, which cause deep extraction of the land and economic, cultural, and ethnic degradation. In this sense, African media include, for example, bananas. The ways they are grown and imported are links in the violence policies of global economies. Iheka proposes the concept of supporting "imperfect media" that do not serve the consumption of production and distribution yet regain their agency as witnesses to the processes of this violence. For him "our responsibility as media producers and consumers therefore is to consider how to recalibrate their production, distribution, consumption, and recycling to mitigate those adverse ecological implications already outlined. How can we reorient media approaches toward 'low wattage culture' which attends to the practicality of 'ecological awareness'? Imperfect media, undergirded by finitude or the recognition of the dissipation of energy sources, is a major step in the direction of ecologically conscious media practices" (2021, 22).

Iheka believes that this approach to the media offers a chance for the deconstruction of African archives where mediatized black bodies are put side by side with objects and themselves objectified and stripped of the power of expression. A new perspective on both the media and the archives provides an opportunity to launch this discourse, which, through the new use of media, gives the excluded new possibilities for revealing the truth. In many places in this book, this approach to the media will prove relevant to individuals and groups that, for example, create media archives by giving voice to those who were previously deprived of it. Thus, through collaborative practices, the recovered and repurposed media provide an opportunity for suffering people to voice their own stories of violence. Aesthetics in this sense becomes a form of transmission and expression of what has been repressed, withheld, and abandoned. Furthermore, it is a strategy for sensitizing the structural violence of colonialism and racism.

AESTHETICS OF MATERIAL WITNESSES

Within this nexus of aesthetics generated by the interconnectedness of technology and the environment, there are also new perceptions and new practices of the aesthetics of materiality as a way of investigating and collecting traces of violence. The discussion of the material aesthetics of the trace, the evidence, and the object has been ongoing for several years as a description of investigative practices, in relation to the ways in which they are presented in public and artistic space (Jones 2022), through the creation of archives (Ernst 2013, 2021), and through the extension of the social functions of museums (Tybjerg 2017). Over the past decade, concepts have been developed that expand and intensify the perception of forensic aesthetics as a process combining media, matter, people, and objects within sensing and sense-making aesthetics (Fuller and Weizman 2021; Schuppli 2020). Such an aesthetics is based on new procedures for investigating and recording violence in organic and inorganic matter itself, on data acquired using sensory technologies, on facts contained in the stories of witnesses to events, and on ways of analyzing, processing, and making these stories sensitively available. New opportunities for this type of research and access to a variety of data have also created room for the development of experimental strategies for conducting investigations in a bottom-up manner within scientific disciplines (large research centers and laboratories) and in more situational and independent initiatives. This is also where new research and art practices have come to the fore, applying experimental techniques and tools to uncover violence in various spheres of social, political, and economic life (Jones 2022).

Rudolf Rugoff's 1997 book began a discussion of aesthetics as an environment for showing evidence, data, and images of violence and crime within artistic and curatorial practices. Rugoff uses the term "forensic aesthetics" to describe the phenomenon of the presence in these practices of media documents derived from or alluding to investigative and evidence-gathering strategies. As he points out, forensic aesthetics "engages the viewer in a process of mental reconstruction" (Rugoff 1997, 17). In such a case, a viewer's perception is more analytical as its essence lies in identification (reconstruction) of some event or situation based on dispersed bits and pieces of information, media documentaries, and discontinuous narratives. Mental reconstruction involves a form of development of a "forensic gaze" (Rugoff 1997, 61), which radically alters the receiving mode, setting in motion a new causal model of interaction between recipients, forensic objects and the history they tell: "Taken as a whole, this art puts us in a position akin to that of the forensic anthropologist or scientist, forcing us to speculatively piece together histories that remain largely invisible to the eye" (Rugoff 1997, 62). The dispersed bits and pieces open up to a new form of identifying an object and its significance. The presented object is only a fragment of a larger whole, and thus viewers become part of the entire process as they have to "complete" the link between it and other fragments and find out the inner relations and linkages between the various parts. For Rugoff, the nature of the forensic fragments is different from that of artefacts of traditional art, which seem to be "coherent, organized objects" (Rugoff 1997, 72). The author stresses that this process must pay attention to the role of the media, which offers complex forms of mediatization and complicates the relation of a media object (such as a photograph or film) toward physical reality and real time.

Forensic aesthetics was largely transformed in the 2010s. This transformation was due to the annexation of earlier theoretical concepts of social critique, the demand for political agency, the growth of exposure strategies using media as tools, and new tools and forms of work with persons and communities subject to violence. In this way, the definition of aesthetics has expanded toward a practical systemic methodology with elements of politics, critical theories, design, media, theory of objects (evidence, trace, waste), epistemics, and ethics.

In her 2020 book, *Material Witness: Media, Forensics, Evidence*, Susan Schuppli describes the aim of her own forensic practice as "ultimately to relink the material world and its affordances with the space of the aesthetic, the juridical, and the political. Consequently, my analysis often crosscuts between highly imagistic accounts and detailed technical descriptions. This is my mode of aesthetic assembly and narrative construction, which I borrow from my ongoing practice and sensibility as an artist-researcher" (2020, 4). Schuppli sees as an important point of reference the critical and philosophical theories of new materialism, so she defines the characteristics of forensic aesthetics from the perspective of matter—the material and the physical. Rather than a unified theory, she indicates forensic practice in art as "aesthetic assemblages" (Schuppli 2020, 39). As a researcher and an artist, she views the aesthetics setups of matter as indicating a specific political and social order. Pointing out these processes is important in approaching the evidence and the ways in which evidence is revealed, shown, and presented.

Referring to the relation between politics and aesthetics addressed by Rancière, Schuppli notes that "what is held in common between the spaces and discourses of public witnessing is revealed and the political, as that which exposes and disrupts this consensual order, is activated" (Schuppli 2020, 27). In forensic practice, aesthetics is functionalized and socialized. For Rancière, it possesses an agency that gathers communities of sense around the object. The word *sense* is doubly coded here as understanding and cognition but also as sensation and experience that can be had between recipients, object, and actual crime. It is therefore a practice of "exploring the evidential capacity of a particular aesthetic arrangement of matter in which properties and processes combine to express themselves as sensible events that render the political visible" (Schuppli 2020, 27). Forensic aesthetics extends from matter; through its analysis, data collection, and organization; and to its presentations in the media in the form of "various reports, videos, animations, and online platforms that make legible the multiple forces at play within the constitutive spaces of violence" (Schuppli 2020, 30). The goal of the whole process of using media, forms of laboratory cognition, and functional aesthetics is to bring the developed evidence into the space of art institutions and into forums of international law and human rights. Thus, Schuppli strongly connects politics, aesthetics, materiality, and mediality as core components for making public facts about violence.

Schuppli's aesthetic practice and theory are also reflected and elaborated on in the views of Eyal Weizman, founder of the Forensic Architecture research agency. He is a theorist and practitioner who designs systemic solutions for identifying violence and proving the truth publicly. As a new scientific discipline, forensic architecture is not simply another architectural discourse. It is a method of producing knowledge and proving the truth that is based on collected traces in a media-dense environment and that is later presented in the form of a temporal and spatial reconstruction. This reconstruction can be both analogue and digital. In this sense, aesthetics spans the entire process of finding the truth about violence. Weizman first used the term "forensic aesthetics" in the book he coauthored with Thomas Keenan, *Mengele's Skull: The Advent of a Forensic*

Architecture (Keenan and Weizman 2012), which discusses their research on proving the identity of the Nazi physician charged with crimes against humanity on the basis of his remains and bones.

In his numerous publications, Weizman elaborates on this aesthetics, which addresses three stages of the forensic process—the field, the laboratory or studio, and the forum (Weizman 2017, 94). These stages include the fact recorded in a matter, a medium, and sensors that collect data; its analysis in a laboratory along with technologies, media, and tools; and the presentation of evidence of its mode of appearance in the forum. This last stage calls for "different techniques and technologies of demonstration, rhetoric, and performance—gestures, narrative and dramatization, image enhancement and projection" (Weizman 2017, 96). Weizman refers to an architectural order with his forensic architecture, which he sees as an experimental and critical discipline that aims at forensic research and the preparation of "architectural evidence and to its presentation in juridical and political forums" (Weizman 2017, 9). In the book *Investigative Aesthetics: Conflicts and Commons in the Politics of Truth*, Fuller and Weizman propose a more ecological approach to aesthetics, combining the material and the digital. The aesthetization process is meant to foster conditions that allow observers to be "more attuned to sensing" (Fuller and Weizman 2021, 31). This focus on sensing and sense making as new and open aesthetic regimes, as Rancière would call them, introduces into forensic aesthetics nonhuman actors. The bodies of animals and plants record violence, and the data is harvested by technological devices, even the entire mediatized environment. As a way of sensing the world, "aesthetics does not exclusively refer to a property or capacity of humans. It equally refers to other sensing organisms, such as animals and plants, which themselves apprehend their environment. Further, we argue that sensing is also found in material surfaces and substances, on which traces of impact or slower processes of change are registered, including in digital and computational sensors, which themselves detect, register and predict in multiple novel ways" (Fuller and Weizman 2021, 33).

The different ways of capturing aesthetics as an environment provide new insights into interlocking political, social, and technological processes and into strategies for tracking and revealing violence in contemporary times. The relationships between phenomena, animate and inanimate matter, and humans and nonhumans introduced into media structures within the framework of the concepts discussed above have also become an important sphere for us. These relationships allow us to shape our research tools and perspectives on the analysis and perception of phenomena within the framework of the open paradigm of an aesthetic of radical truth proposed in this book.

AGGLOMERATIVE AESTHETICS AS A COLLABORATIVE FORCE

In this book, we analyze examples of practices that are diverse in genre, procedure, and research and aim to reveal latent structures of violence and socialize the truth about it. We discuss the activities of groups, laboratories, and teams that include artists, researchers, designers, journalists, architects, programmers, and activists. We could try to fix the resulting projects within disciplines and practices like digital media arts, independent journalism, digital forensics, network archives, interactive web documentaries, do-it-yourself physical computing, opensource software, digital watch dogs, human rights and environmental activism, open data activism, community-based science, and open laboratories. However, these practices are not homogeneous and do not have a concise set of characteristics. Assigning the projects to specific disciplines would contradict the idea that these groups function within their own internal heterogeneity. Their activity is a response to the emergence of new forms of violence, which in many situations is itself subject to processes of automation and digitization that produce new mechanisms of covert aggression and oppression and generate new indirect and direct forms of harm and traumatization. Since the perpetration of violence constantly changes its forms, transforming and masking itself, antiviolence efforts must reformulate and change strategies for collecting traces, presenting evidence, and socializing the truth about crimes.

As we thought about aesthetics in terms of relationality, ecology, environment, and digital media and politicization as possibilities for building communities based on sense and sense making, we were led to introduce yet another concept into the toolbox emerging from the concepts described above. This is the concept of agglomeration. We refer to its frequently overlooked Latin origin and meaning. The Latin term *agglomerare* means "to join forces, to gather into a body, to bring together." We therefore propose to see the aesthetics of radical truth in a perspective of dynamic agglomeration processes. In our study, the agglomerate we use remains genetically linked to discourses concerning naturocultures (Haraway), medianatures (Parikka), media ecologies (Cubitt, Fuller, Iheka), investigative aesthetics (Fuller, Weizman), and material aesthetics (Schuppli). It is also largely linked to concepts of new materialism and feminist science and technology studies (Barad, Bennett), the ethics of material work (Cubitt), new communities of sense (Rancière), and the decolonial need of finally being present (Iheka).

In geology, an agglomerate is a heterogeneous lump that is caused by a volcanic eruption and consists of aggregate elements—stones, sands, particles, splinters—fragments of biological and geological origin. The binder is hot lava, which absorbs and glues together the most diverse particles in a dynamic process. In chemistry, physics, and astrophysics, agglomeration is one of the basic processes that join particles under the influence of external and internal forces. Particles are agglomerated by a medium that surrounds each separate element and allows them to clump together into larger wholes. Agglomerates are not fixed formations. The process of their creation is reversible, so they are unstable. They are hybrid objects with internal and external dynamics. Agglomerates are created after significant external forces are experienced either in a violent manner or through long-term structural influence. Prone to disintegration, they are sensitive to various factors. When the physical conditions of the bond change, the elements that make up the agglomerate disintegrate and return to their original states. Because agglomerates are impermanent formations, time and environment are of crucial importance. Agglomerates have an interesting morphological structure. They can consist of very different elements, and their formation is a record of the situation in which they were born. Inside them are elements of various origins—biological and geological particles such as waste and dust.

A few factors are at the heart of the process. External forces act on the dispersed particles, which causes them to begin to compress; the properties of the binder depend on the characteristics of the medium; and internal dynamics occur between the compressed particles. Lava is the most common binder in geological formations. Binders can also include various liquids, which act as a transmitter medium that allows the processes of internal dynamics—the exchange of forces acting on the individual components of the agglomerate.

In industry and technical sciences, agglomeration is often a technological process that can be designed. The medium used to agglomerate particles and dust is enriched with various substances that affect the durability of the bond and the morphology of the agglomerate itself. The process is also sometimes used, for example, to purify air or water of harmful substances by binding them into larger wholes that can later be intercepted by filters. An agglomerate is a situated formation that contains information about a specific place and time. It is an integral part of the environment, without which it ceases to mean anything. Thus, anyone who wanted to create an agglomerative media theory would have to focus on the essence of the action of the medium or transmitter that surrounds and binds the compressed particles together, on the quality of the binder produced inside the agglomerate, on the particles that establish a relationship and interact with each other inside, and on the external forces and the genesis of the particular formation. Finally, any agglomerative media theory would have to consider the relations between the agglomerate and its surroundings and the possibility that new fragments might stick to the existing formation. All these elements and their interrelationships contain scattered information that can be identified and recovered only by collecting and analyzing particles in detail and studying the quality of the binder produced by the medium and the internal and external forces and relationships.

The agglomerate can be viewed as a traveling interdisciplinary concept (Bal 2002), as it appears across many disciplines and is also connected to other areas concepts. It refers to the synonymous term *gathering*, whose meaning relates primarily to the formation of human communities. Starting from the agglomerate as both a form and a process of forming matter and relations helps initiate analysis in environmental processes in which humans are involved. A concept semantically similar to agglomerate and agglomeration is accumulation. However, accumulation is more about "collecting something in one place." It often refers to the absorption and accumulation of energy or capital, and in geology it is also the process of building up sediment on the surfaces of land and the bottoms of water basins, leading to the formation of sedimentary rocks. In relation to agglomerate, the concept is based more on the processes of absorption than combination and the formation of stable forms at a specific location.

In our research, agglomerate extends dynamically between the situation of trace clumping and its social release. At each of these stages, it is a structure open to the attachment of further elements. Agglomerate is also a term closely related to the concept of assemblage, a term that is frequently used in the philosophy of new materialism, posthumanism, media studies and science and technology studies. Assemblage, however, does not produce objects as a specific form of matter, which is what we deal with in the case of agglomerates. Rather, it points to the causality of those already existing objects in the relations they establish. Agglomerate allows us to emphasize the simultaneity of process and form. It becomes a useful working concept. According to Mieke Bal, it is "a concept to work with and a concept that works—neither fixed and theorized nor slippery as a word" (Bal 2002, 99).

In the following chapters, we analyze specific case studies and discuss in detail the mechanisms of agglomerate formation. With each example, we are confronted with a different agglomerate morphology and different mechanisms of its production and impact. For us, it is vital that agglomeration processes involve two research perspectives—the formation processes and functioning strategies of individual cases and also their broad spectrum of social impact. These processes of sharing and absorbing more elements into the agglomerate generate the social meaning and sanctioning of truth. All the analyses reveal the important role played the media, which produce the binders and the morphological skeleton for the agglomerate. The media are responsible for gluing together tangible and intangible elements, physical evidence, and implicit policies of violence. The media are likewise responsible for the growth of agglomerates because they make more elements, issues, affects, and emotions, and people cluster around them. The ontology of the agglomerate is not fixed and homogeneous. It can change over time, so it is impossible to model it theoretically in isolation from the matter, from its location, and from the act of violence that initiated it.

The particles that make up the agglomerate in our study are biological, geological, and technological elements—everything that has a natural and cultural genesis, including rocks, sand, plants, clouds, elements of technical equipment, media infrastructure, fragments of politics, local economies, sensor data, readings from measuring stations, geo- and chronolocation data, photos from cell phones and satellites, witness testimonies, and living and dead human and nonhuman bodies. The particles are anything affected by the sudden energy of violence and compressed into its structure. The agglomerates that have a special morphology are those that either arose suddenly in a very short time or were formed over many years, grew over successive layers of sediment, and were revealed after a long time. Agglomerates that arise suddenly can be the result of an eruption or explosion, such as one-ton bombs dropped on civilian areas in Rafah in southern Gaza or chemical weapons used in Syria. Those that are formed over many years are most often the consequence of a buildup of violence. Violence forms sedimentary deposits that are perpetuated over the years and develop a hard shell. This happens with structural violence, such as racism (Rylko-Bauer and Farmer 2016), apartheid (Higginson 2015), all kinds of exploitation and slavery, colonialism (Mbembe 2001, 2021), exploitative natural resource policies, global warming, environmental disasters, and their broad spectrum of consequences degrading the living conditions of all species, including humans. Following Rob Nixon, we could call this type of latent violence "slow violence" (2011). Deep, sedimentary structures of violence are more complex as they incorporate the long-term effects of time, which must be considered in the analysis.

In each case, however, open ecosystem thinking cannot diffuse culpability and responsibility for violence. What must always be emphasized in such research methodologies is that violence is not an impersonal force that produces the conditions for an agglomeration of traces, people, and ways of recognizing them. Violence always has its perpetrators, whether direct perpetrators or those who created the specific conditions that allowed it to occur. Violence can also find justification in deep ideological, political, religious, national, ethnic, and institutional structures. In the case of such dispersed violence, the perpetrators are those who perpetrate it directly and those who create opportunities for its occurrence, benefit from it, and create mechanisms for its concealment. Violence inextricably and in a complex manner links and agglomerates the perpetrators, victims, places and tools of the crime, traces, motivation, and human and nonhuman witnesses.

Media are both the tools and the environment, and they have the capacity for agglomeration—that is, the production of relationships and bonds between their different elements, human and nonhuman. Media are the morphological skeleton of the agglomerate and its relations with the environment, introducing it into a broad ecological structure. Media are transmitters that enable the agglomeration processes—the tightening of relations between all these molecules, the exchange of energy and charge, the polarization, and their mediation. They are themselves dynamic technologies and active agents that generate the "media events" they store, process, and transmit (Ernst 2013; Kittler 1999). Media, as the binding agent of the agglomerate, create their own time ontology. We may refer to Wolfgang Ernst's observation that "media objects are radically present when they still function, even if their outside world has vanished. Their 'inner world' is still operative" (Ernst 2013, 57). Media as binding agents make up complex structures that do not follow the simple logic of relations between outside and inside or past and present. Thus, we no longer deal with a representation of violence but with a complex morphology of its mediation.

As impermanent formations, agglomerates can erode, be dismembered, or fully decompose. It is therefore essential to carefully collect their single elements, traces, and splinters. They can then be transferred to a new environment, where the morphological structure will be reconstructed and the relationships between the individual particles revealed. Each of these environments may demonstrate different characteristics. The production of media environments is always linked to individual methodologies as well as epistemological and aesthetic strategies. Agglomerates can also take the form of unstructured databases of heterogeneous data. Describing such formations, Ernst wrote that a change in internal morphology entails changes regarding epistemic strategies, which as of that moment are shared by human and nonhuman (technological and nontechnological). Ernst himself uses the term "media archaeography," which "describes modes of writing that are not human products but rather expressions of the machines themselves, functions of their very mediatic logic" (Ernst 2013, 58). This new situation requires a cautious approach that considers the technological and ontological aspects in the knowledge production process and in the identification of new forms of human and nonhuman memory. He states that "a radical metamorphosis of the aesthetics of storage is taking place in the media-technical field, which demands models for dealing with a new kind of dynamic memory" (Ernst 2013, 95).

These media environments also have the potential of the processes of following their fragments as accumulation, compression, and identification. Technological environments prepared in this way set in motion the potentialities of cosensing, identifying, and reconstructing (physically and mentally) the dynamics of internal and external forces affecting the agglomerate. The activity and instability of the accumulated elements also affect aesthetic and epistemic processes. Accumulation and agglomeration apply likewise to audiences, viewers, participants, and all who find, reconstruct, sense, and share. This process discloses the agglomerative nature of mediation. As Cubitt has it, "mediation is the ground of relationship, the relationship that precedes and constructs subjects and objects. Media matter, both in the sense of giving material specificity to our descriptions of such abstract concepts as society and environment, and in the sense of the active verb: mediation comes into being as matter, its mattering constitutes the knowable, experienceable world, making possible all sensing and being sensed, knowing and being known" (Cubitt 2014, 2).

This process cannot be closed. Even if it consists of sharing information or compiled data, it should also allow access to the raw elements—the process of morphological reconstruction—so that anyone can perform their own verification. This ethical imperative most often involves posting this information (and the methodology of its acquisition and development) on the websites of specific groups or dedicated network platforms. This process occurs simultaneously on two levels, as those clustered around issues of violence produce content and physical infrastructure through the sharing of resources and opportunities for collaborative work. In fact, it is impossible to separate the two levels. The infrastructure creates the conditions for the cognitive process, while the worldwide web provides opportunities to position the problem precisely. That is why the process of analyzing agglomerates must always combine technology with matter, locality, and location: "the technologies and platforms . . . are not just neutral vessels, but rather involve particular cultural techniques for mediating a body's phenomenal being-in the passage of time—that is, experience itself—by way of the aesthetic" (Ingraham 2020, 120).

Many of these projects find their forum through exhibitions. They also serve a social function of establishing communities that later sustain activities through networking tools, such as instant messaging, forums, discussion groups, joint subsequent projects, workshops, and other forms of sharing. Exhibitions in physical space become access points to digital platforms—coupled and extended places. Media structures seen in this way become, according to Parikka, "an epistemological framework, which enable one to perceive, simulate, design, and plan . . . ; media compose the framework that allows us to talk about . . . in the way in which we do nowadays" (Parikka 2015, 60). These *in situ* and yet open media structures and the practices clustered around them produce "materialist ethics" (Cubitt 1998, 57)—that is, assume the role of verifying truth and prevent the speculative and exploitative policies of capitalism. Thus, the very structure of exhibiting these projects means that they cannot be possessed in the gaze, at a glance. They cannot be easily inscribed into the system of capitalist circulation as objects of desire as they utilize a form of complicity that Bourriaud (1998), following Marx, called "social interstice." A materialist ethics is produced when the recipients begin to work with the individual fragments to unite, bind, stitch, and redefine them. It is through the agglomeration with the whole process of tracing, pinpointing, or investigating violence that they themselves become, so to speak, the media as the welders of successive agglomerative structures.

Participants in the process become enmeshed in these processes in a sensory and cognitive manner through the forces of the agglomerate. The work they must perform is far from easy. It requires a different sensory attunement, and often the experiences of the process stay with the participants for a long time, sedimenting themselves in their sensorium. The process of agglomeration has a broader meaning here. It also refers to the potential arising from grassroots dissent against injustice and harm, which calls for gathering around the work against violence identifiable in the morphology of the agglomerates. It has both the value of the physical work of the muscles of the body and the cognitive work of thinking bodies. In each case, this process opens up to the participation of those who begin the work and those who continue it by supplementing data, reconstructing, or even exerting political pressure. The process has no symbolic meaning. On the contrary, its agglomerative nature binds labor and matter. The participants who gather at each stage of the agglomeration process perform work and produce physical infrastructure, whether it is work performed *in situ*, in front of a computer screen, or in the process of engaging with the collected material in the physical space of the gallery. The same is true at the level of infrastructure. The agglomerative processes connect ever new media elements, further information, computers, and mobile devices and have a technical capacity to produce further connections. Through work whose meaning extends from the physical to the cognitive, the coupling of ground truth (collecting materials), materialist ethics (understanding the complexity of morphological mediations), and the ethics of care (sharing the process) takes place. In this cognitively difficult mode, the ethics of care is the approach to the whole process of unveiling and sharing as producing "practices of care, where relationships are cultivated, needs are responded to, and sensitivity is demonstrated" (Held 2006, 15–16). The ethics of care that reconnects recipients with the entire process and its materiality is a product of agglomeration, cultivation, and sharing.

Agglomerare as the gathering of a community around a specific problem with access to all elements and the sharing of tools (with their procedures and methodologies) leads to the proliferation of epistemic cultures and to a broad and communal process of knowledge production, social values, and political values. Defined in this way, media practices are an alternative to the laboratory that is based on counterinvestigation and countermapping, as their goal is to produce knowledge in close relation to the community and environment under conditions that cannot be predetermined or controlled. Through radical openness, coparticipation, and inclusion, the process produces socially sanctioned truth, which is shared knowledge that is supported by values and equitable and inclusive social and political relations.

An aesthetics of radical truth is an agglomerative process—an open and inclusive way of creating a bottom-up practice for tracking, pinpointing, and reconstructing violence at the nexus of the material and the digital and for communicating, sharing, and socializing the truth about it. Crimes and violence today are increasingly digital in nature. Their identification, cognition, comprehension, and sharing in society require the use of strategies, means, and tools that can integrally analyze material and technomedia phenomena. Only in this way can we today embrace issues of truth, especially those concerning violence as a vulnerable and radical process. As Seán Cubitt observes, "truth is a practice and therefore requires media through which it can be practiced: instruments for capturing evidence, means of storing and ordering arguments and beliefs, modes of transmission, persuasion, establishing. . . . Therefore, truth has a history. As a practice, truth therefore has a media history" (Cubitt 2018, n.p.). Each truth has its media history, which means also that it is recorded via various technologies; it is mediated and exposed. Media and technologies are not an addition to the process, and yet they are ontologically merged with the process as codetermining modes of cognition. Environmental categories help participants reexamine the nexuses and their potential for creating ever new linkages.

Digital media in the projects we write about make up a unique agglomerative morphology. They become structurally incorporated into the processes of mediation between fact, data, animate and inanimate matter, human and nonhuman subjects, policies, and economies. The radicalness of truth is inherent in the entire epistemic process, combining those who investigate, record, reconstruct, and publicly disseminate with those who familiarize themselves with these actions and violence. At the same time, we deal with a redefinition of the notion of radical and its liberation from primarily politicized practices for the sake of politics as an action aiming at an ethics of work with the matter of violence. In the introduction to the collective work *Aesthetics and Radical Politics*, Gavin Grindon mentions that radical aesthetics in relation to politics "often seeks to aestheticize politics or rather, to treat the aesthetic as a directly political terrain" (Grindon 2008, vii). In fact, the practices we examine show another possibility—a work *in situ* with tools, data, documents, and people in and with the environment. The *in situ* approach is a way to restore the radical truth about violence. Agglomerative work thus defines communities of sense as the "epistemic commons" (Fuller and Weizman

2021) or, more broadly, as "epistemic cultures" (Schatzki et al. 2001; Knorr-Cetina 1999).

Up to a point, these practices incorporate the Marxist ethics of the material work as labor (Wilde 1998), combining matter and work to reveal violence. Radical aesthetics is moreover linked to the ethics of radical transparency and openness by including human and nonhuman subjects as victims, witnesses, mediators, and recorders of violence. Each chapter of this book describes agglomerative processes from a different perspective, showing a plethora of agglomerative strategies of receptive and participatory processes. The processes can generate commiseration and compassion and, through transparent actions and labor, can immerse human and nonhuman subjects in the creation of epistemic cultures of radical truth.

2

RADICAL INVESTIGATORS OF MILITARY VIOLENCE

This chapter focuses on analysis of the social sharing of object-agglomerates as new mediatized witnesses to violence. We discuss experimental research and investigations done by Forensic Architecture, SITU Research, and Bellingcat. In these practices, the procedure for the creation of an agglomerative object of violence proceeds from the analysis and interpretation of all the collected data (both the mediatized data and the material traces present at the scene of violence). The agglomeration is the labor of gathering evidences of violence and therefore is subject to a constant process of intermediarity (Simondon 2017), oscillating between the physicality of violence; its mediatized images, sounds, and data; and the mediation procedure itself to create new binders that allow these violent events and situations to be narrated, shared, and made public.

The processes expose the sites of violence and its evidence, something Gilbert Simondon dubbed the *milieu* (Simondon 2017). In terms of the practices addressed here, the *milieu* is not merely a physical location but is a nexus that agglomerates a particular area with violent processes that are revealed in various forms of economic, social, racial exclusion, and policies of pressure operating in a particular place and time. The aesthetics of radical truth (AeRT), as a mode of producing knowledge about violence, reveals the entire process of the formation of media agglomerate bonds in the milieu. It focuses less on the objects themselves and more on the procedures of their formation and social circulation. AeRT is a method of analyzing the "relation between people and data, between a territory and money, citizenship status, and a racial category" (Fuller and Weizman 2021, 102). It exposes the appearance of intermediarity between physical violence and its mediatized recorded forms.

HOW TO AGGLOMERATE THINGS IN POLITICS?

Departing from the Latourian demand for the restoration of relational things and objects as causal and cocreative of new politics and democracies, we analyze in this vein agglomerative objects as witnesses to violence. At the same time, we seek to show some hope that practices and objects have the potential to produce new strategies of resistance to violence. Based on collaborative action, they center around real problems affecting people and the environment and have the potential to bring necessary changes to the procedures of legislation and the principles of open justice.

Before discussing specific examples, we revisit Bruno Latour's 2005 article "From Realpolitik to Dingpolitik, or How to Make Things Public," where the author discusses the crisis of the political at the beginning of the millennium. This crisis of politics has become a place of speculation via information, manipulation, and abuse of data and facts. The article is an introduction to the catalog accompanying the exhibition *Making Things Public: Atmospheres of Democracy.*[1] Latour asks here: "Can we trace again the frail conduits through which truths and proofs are allowed to enter the sphere of politics?" (Latour 2005, 19). He addresses a question relevant to our considerations, too—namely, how the practices of formation of evidence to truth can be politically and socially productive. He also wonders how the manipulation of things and their ideologization come about. What is the qualitative difference between the presentation of evidence and the honest process of its investigation and disclosure? In response to this question, he shows things and objects as relations in the process of representing facts and proving truth in public and political forums, and he points to the need to return to truth in its Foucauldian sense of straightforwardness and transparency (Foucault 2011).

Since the 1980s, Bruno Latour has consistently introduced thinking about "real things" into society and politics and has established truth within them via their representation as objects (Latour 1983). He invokes the notion of things that, transformed through research studies, return in the practices of their socialization (Latour 1993), transforming the very concept of society. He postulates abandoning the notion of society as attributed only to human subjects and opts for a new concept of a "parliament of things" (Latour 1993). He points to a need to reveal their functions and the patterns of producing relations, which we cannot identify and understand through traditional cognitive categories. He is interested not so much in the structure of the objects themselves but in the exploration of the "hidden geography of their relations" (Latour 2005, 15). This approach to objects as deeply mediated and intra-actional can also be found in feminist science and technology studies (STS). This is due primarily to the feminist tradition of introducing relational cognitive paradigms into modernist and positivist models of establishing fact and truth, including feminist empiricism (Longino 1990), the feminist standpoint theory (Crasnow and Intemann 2021; Harding 1991), and the subjectivity of the research process (Code 1993; Schnabel et al. 2016). The concept of the object is indebted to feminist STS's long history of rethinking objectivity (Keller 1995) in terms of the object and the subject of knowledge (Reardon et al. 2015). Redefining an object from the perspective of feminist studies brings a number of important questions into the perception of the researched object—a focus on relations and the relational aspect of generating knowledge about objects (Bennett 2010); a view of objects within an entanglement of multiple and heterogeneous agencies (Barad 2007); a shift from a closed positivist paradigm in the exact sciences toward an open, situated, multisubjective, and multisite mode of knowledge production (Haraway 1988, 2016; Reardon et al. 2015); the causality of objects and things included in intrarelationships with technological apparatus (Barad 2007); and the inclusion of nonhuman actants in the process of research and cognition (Bennett 2010; Puig de la Bellacasa 2017; Haraway 2016). This research process connected to the circulation of things, data, facts, and people is what Latour attempts to point to with the help of defined paradigms as a blueprint for a new politics of inclusion for things.

In "From Realpolitik to Dingpolitik"—where Latour traces things as real objects and refers to the notion of *res publica* as the union of things and people—he poses a slightly different question about what the "object-oriented democracy" might look like (Latour 2005). The relationships involving things, data, facts, and people became relevant to the researcher in the process of transforming and opening up the framework of the political agora. The reference point for the new social system in Latour's vision was also a reference to object-oriented programming (OOP). This programming paradigm defines programs by objects—elements that combine state (that is, data, usually called *attributes*) and behavior (that is, procedures and methods). An object-oriented computer program is expressed as a collection of such objects that communicate with each other to perform tasks. This method of programming allowed Latour to attempt to define an object with inner functionalities, methods, and procedures. However, part (content) of an object is also a functional relationship with the outside (reality). Latour makes object-oriented programming the metonymic framework on which he bases his concept of object-oriented democracy (OOD):

> What we call an "object-oriented democracy" tries to . . . bring together two different meanings of the word representation that have been kept separate in theory although they have remained always mixed in practice. The first one, so well-known in schools of law and political science, designates the ways to gather the legitimate people around some issue. In this case, a representation is said to be faithful if the right procedures have been followed. The second one, well known in science and in technology, presents or rather represents what is the object of concern to the eyes and ears of those who have been assembled around it. In this case, a representation is said to be good if the matters at hand have been accurately portrayed. (Latour 2005, 16)

Particularly relevant to both Latour's considerations and our research is his definition of representation, which involves setting before the researcher and the public things or objects that acquire a new meaning in these relations. Representation here means being seen and heard in a particular context, relation, or situation. In his other texts, Latour calls this form of representation aesthetics (Latour 2005) or positioning in relations. Object-oriented democracy can happen when things and people come together and form specific relationships around what relates to them (matters of concern) (Latour 2004). Thus, people establish frameworks for political actions and practices and also representations of objects that they present as evidence of their choices. To demonstrate his object-oriented democracy concept, Latour analyzes Colin Powell's address to the United Nations Security Council in February 2003 "about the unambiguous and undisputable fact of the presence of weapons of mass destructions in Iraq" (Latour 2005, 18). As we now know, no evidence was ever found to confirm Powell's allegations. Using this example, Latour is scathingly critical of the forms of representation that inform contemporary politics:

> No doubt, the first half of the representation—namely the assembly of legitimate speakers and listeners—was well taken care of. All of those sitting around the UN Security Council horseshoe table had a right to be there. But the same can't be said of the second half, namely the representation of the facts of the matter presented by the Secretary of State. Every one of the slides was a blatant lie—and the more that time has passed, the more blatant it has become. And yet their showing was prefaced by these words: "My colleagues, every statement I make today is backed up by sources, solid sources. These are not assertions. What we are giving you are facts and conclusions based on solid intelligence." (2005, 18)

Latour showed how, in order to manipulate, representation is separated from matter and remains solely a representation of political power: "To assemble is one thing; to represent to the eyes and ears of those assembled what is at stake is another. An object-oriented democracy should be concerned as much by the procedure to detect the relevant parties as to the methods to bring into the center of the debate the proof of what it is to be debated" (Latour 2005, 18). Thus, the object itself, becoming evidence in political practices and choices, cannot function without the honest exposure of the entire process and the method of its creation. The use of facts, figures, and data does not offer evidence but opens itself up to potential manipulation. "From Realpolitik to Dingpolitik" was created in a political context that was significant in transforming the concept of politics and the way it was practiced in international forums using objects as evidence. Europe and the United States were experiencing an onslaught of terrorism following the attacks on the World Trade Center in New York. Immediately after the September 11 attacks, in the fall of

2001, NATO invaded Afghanistan, where Osama bin Laden (then leader of al-Qaida, the terrorist group responsible for the New York attacks) was based. In 2003, under US leadership, coalition troops entered Iraq. Terrorism, however, was expanding its practices and scope of operations, including ISIS, which emerged in 2006. This was a time of tracking and tracing terrorists, which often exposed the chaotic decisions of politicians and individuals responsible for carrying out such activities. In the early twenty-first century, in the wake of the above developments, it became crucial in world politics to establish and show evidence in public forums of the presence of terrorists in a given place. These practices were vital for legitimizing eradication operations.

This is why Latour returned to the politics of things—so that objects could be shown as processes of reliable inquiry into their meanings and location. In the object-oriented democracy he advocated, this can be done by democratizing the things themselves. What does this mean? First, they acquire the right to be seen in their full epistemic dimension, along with the relationships that they enter, the situations that they originate in, and the evidence that gives them their meaning. They radically unveil the entire process of their establishment to lay it bare and make it transparent so that socially it can become a vehicle for truth. In many of his later texts and lectures, Latour stated that the idea of object-oriented democracy is to relocate the dispute with the things being heard and seen in the public space (Latour and Chakrabarty 2020). It therefore generates new rules for the place and location for conflicts—namely, a public debate based on dispute. This dispute is possible only with a transparent and open approach to creating objects as evidence and matters of concern that built the collective around relevant problems and issues.

This perception of the object as a process becomes crucial for the practices of exposing violence discussed in this chapter. The processual construction of objects uncovers the truth about violence and thus denounces this violence, producing a new location for the disputes. Discussions, dialogues, and political options and positions can be based on such strategies that make visible the entire structures and procedures that inform the objects: "What we need is to be able to bring inside the assemblies divisive issues with their long retinue of complicated proof-giving equipment" (Latour 2005, 21–22). Latour uses the notion of representation.

In our research, we are more inclined to use the notion of mediation or even more broadly the notion of inter- and intramediarity as we develop concepts of practices situated in media studies. This is because we are also interested in how media work as bonds in agglomerative AeRT processes and their epistemic procedures, which are established not only in relationships but also through hybrid (material-digital) infrastructures of data production, acquisition, and analysis.

WE DO NOT STEAL

"We do not steal, we do not hack" was one of the first sentences we heard during a online workshop conducted by Bellingcat members in the fall of 2020. Established in 2014 by Elliot Higgins, Bellingcat is an independent international collective of researchers, investigators, and citizen journalists. The multiday course introduced participants to the issues of open-source investigation (OSI), a technique that uses creative web search, methods of verification, digital maps and satellite images, geolocation and chronolocation, transport tracking, and searches of social media resources (popular platforms such as Facebook and Twitter but also less common ones such as Telegram, which is used for network communication in Russia and Eastern European countries, and 4chan/8kun, infamous due to its use in generating various forms of online violence and conspiracy theories). The statement "We do not steal" is a twist on the title of a 2013 documentary, *We Steal Secrets* (directed by Alex Gibney), which is about WikiLeaks and Julian Assange. In the film, the words are spoken by Michael V. Hayden, a retired US Air Force general and former director of the National Security Agency. The words are used in the context of the operational work of government agencies, which require discretion and confidentiality. This quote also refers to the practice of WikiLeaks and Julian Assange himself, who in the 1980s engaged in antiwar hacktivism while operating under the pseudonym Mendax. The hacking practices used later by WikiLeaks have changed public definitions of facts and truth by disconnecting the two in public opinion. Although the stolen and shared data may have pointed to the culprits of various crimes, little of it has been used as viable evidence against the abuses of the states and organizations that committed them. This is because the entire operation lacked an element of verification that would have exposed the process of establishing facts and radically embedded them in a network of sociopolitical contexts. As Eliot Higgins states, "WikiLeaks was about leaking classified information, while open-source investigators analyze what sits in public. The secrecy of WikiLeaks placed vast power into its hands, which became problematic when Julian Assange exhibited strong political preferences, timing drops to harm those he despised, . . . the problem with WikiLeaks is that it is hard to verify huge data dumps of shadowy origin" (Higgins 2021, 52). For both government agencies and hacking groups, the essence of their operations is the processing of classified information. The former want to acquire and conceal it, and the latter wish to "steal" and reveal it. The operating procedures of all participants in this game are secret, anonymous, and based on highly specialized and expert methods. In each case, hidden or disclosed information is used as a tool to gain control or power. Thus, this is an activity with antagonistic vectors—secret information (state, military, corporate) versus leaks and the game of power versus the game of subverting power. Still, at the core of these antagonistic relationships is the concept of information identified as a secret and used as a weapon against the other party.

In the case of groups such as Bellingcat that use open-source intelligence techniques (OSINT), information is treated as something transparent, and its acquisition is based on collecting fragments, traces, and data from publicly available sources. Because access to the extracted information is open and is not classified, many people can be involved in the process of finding and extracting it without incurring any legal consequences. The collaborative nature of the process makes an agglomerative object of evidence emerge from small fragments. This object is transparent, processual, and socialized and has the potential of revealing the truth about a particular incidence of violence. Higgins speaks of this process as follows: "We battle the counterfactual forces warping society. We insist on evidence. And we show ordinary citizens how to expose wrongdoing and demand accountability from the powerful" (Higgins 2021, 9). This method treats information as an open structure, and the strategies that arise for finding it and reconstructing it from fragments strengthen the grassroots practices of commons, for which access to information and knowledge can become shared values (Higgins 2021, 9). In this process, there is no direct attempt to influence and destabilize the entire information-sharing system or specific policies, but its basic imperative is the need to establish data and arrive at the truth. As Bellingcat members say of themselves: "This is not about Top Secret clearance, or restricting information to the initiated. Bellingcat is something that has never been before: an intelligence agency for the people" (Higgins 2021, 10). In this extended context, "we do not steal, we do not hack" becomes a vital credo, a *modus operandi*, and a work ethic that are based on treating information as a common good that all should have equal access to. This is critical at a time when data, facts, and figures concerning crimes, law infringement, and violence against people—the basic conditions necessary for justice and social security—are verified.

This new paradigm is transforming how contemporary communities produce the knowledge that they consider universally sanctioned. Many human rights theorists and practitioners note that this new paradigm of knowledge production is also linked to transformations of the roles and functions that formally trained experts, lawyers, and other professionals previously played in the process. Verification of data and information veracity has traditionally been entrusted to experts, representatives of various state institutions, or human rights advocates. They have confirmed the information *in situ* through interviews and the collection of traces, evidence, and witness testimonies.

As the entire internet becomes a space for collecting evidence and groups gather information, the role of verification of facts shifts to society as a whole. In a sense, we are witnessing a cultural and social transition where, through the development of digital media, the roles traditionally reserved for experts have eroded in favor of verification carried out not so much by individuals but by collectives supporting one another with practice and experience from many fields. A question arises about the reliability of the investigative process carried out in this way: How is it legitimized to the public? This is done primarily through a detailed disclosure of all investigative stages. The transparency of the investigative process is based on a clearly defined working method and ethics but also on extensive educational activities, such as holding open workshops where methods and tools in open-source intelligence techniques and the investigation and verification of information are discussed, shared, and taught. Equally significant is the inclusion of volunteers who are participants and also social observers and who design and share their own open-source software to support the conduct of research online. Agglomerated through these practices, people further hone their skills and work methodologies. This is how a new epistemic is produced, and it is integral to the process of designing and using tools. All the process participants (researchers, coders, designers, and volunteers) are involved in knowledge production. Thus, we are dealing with a new epistemic culture of the commons for which forms of cognition are linked to the process of open and transparent acquisition, verification, and sharing of information.

In this direct way, the transparency of tools is linked to the idea of open-source software. Again, this is the question of open access and the capacity to verify the source code, make changes, and develop functionalities collaboratively. Being able to review the source code of software is tantamount to the process of understanding how a particular digital tool works, what happens to the data at each stage of its processing, and whether the software and the processed data are safe. This is a significant part of the social legitimization of the veracity of the information obtained. In the case of Bellingcat, the process takes place in close collaboration within the community. As Johanna Wild, head of the Bellingcat tech team, observes, the aim of this collaboration is the "bridge-building" between open-source investigators and the open-source software community (Wild 2021, n.p.). Sharing the process of designing and using tools allows the development of methods and techniques previously unattainable for small research groups, and it is also a form of experimental agglomeration of competencies and practices.

Thanks to this approach, more people are participating in the movement, contributing their expertise and specializations, and collaboratively producing increasingly sophisticated and precise tools, solutions, and techniques that were initially dismissed. This type of collaboration is a sign of the cultural changes taking place in response to digital media and practices. The paradigm of collaborative research shifts the emphasis away from inter- and transdisciplinarity and toward collaborative processes that are contingent on multicompetence and on the sharing of research processes and skills, and it closely integrates the conduct of research with the design and production of experimental tools (software, hardware, and related procedures and practices). For Bellingcat practices, open-source intelligence techniques will become the primary method and toolbox. The analysis of open-source materials has also been used by human rights organizations such as Amnesty International and by dedicated units for this type of research set up in mainstream media such as the BBC and the *New York Times*. These techniques are becoming one of the most important methods of obtaining and analyzing data on violence in today's hybrid world.

MEDIA MORPHOLOGY OF MATERIAL AND DIGITAL TRACES

One of Bellingcat's investigations with international political relevance was a case of mass executions committed near Benghazi, Libya, by units reporting to Mahmoud Mustafa Al-Werfalli, an alleged commander of the Al-Saiqa Brigade of the Libyan National Army in 2016 and 2017. As part of their media propaganda, the terrorists published videos on social media of seven executions of captives. In 2017, the International Criminal Court (ICC) issued an arrest warrant of Al-Werfalli based solely on social media evidence. This was a first in judicial history. This also marked a turning point for the international, legal, and social relevance of open-source intelligence techniques, whose research tools were used in an internationally debated court case (Dubberley et al. 2020, 7). The videos the terrorists posted online, however, could not be regarded as bona fide forensic evidence because the time and place of the crimes could not be established on their basis. Stripped of their context, the materials circulating on the internet primarily fulfilled the terrorists' intentions to spread affective fear and anxiety online. That is why Bellingcat decided to investigate by means of open-source intelligence methods that aimed to situate the recordings in their proper political, social, chronolocation, and geolocation contexts. As Elliot Higgins explains in reference to the group's motivation: "we decided to dig into the seven videos cited in the Werfalli arrest warrant, to see exactly what the footage exposed, explain it to the public and lend our expertise to prosecutors so that they might understand better what they had" (Higgins 2021, 165). To gather as much information as possible about the locations of each of the seven executions, Bellingcat launched a crowdsourcing campaign that asked internet users to identify or point to distinctive elements in the landscape captured in the videos that could be used to narrow down the list of potential execution site locations. The investigation used a "wide variety of open-source information such as satellite imagery, geotagged photos, conflict context, geolocations from other sources and news articles" (Bellingcat 2017, n.p.). Finally, one video was identified and embedded in time and space. This was done on the basis of a multisite analysis and a precise reconstruction of media morphology (the relationship between different forms of media representation of the same place).

In the video recorded by the terrorists, the blood of the murdered victims formed dark puddles of a certain shape on the sandy soil, a visual (and digital) marker of the crime scene after the bodies of the slain had been removed. To identify the morphological relationship (sand, blood, media), it was therefore necessary to reconstruct the missing media coverage, which would establish an external point of view. This step applied satellite data. The satellite images of the potential execution site showed dark patches that formed unusual patterns that were absent at this location in images taken dozens of hours earlier (figures 2.1 and 2.2). As Aric Toler, who took part in this identification, explains, after "meticulously aligning the perspective of the camera showing the executions, along with the same approximate perspective overlooking the 17 July 2017 satellite image, the dark spots reveal themselves as blood—the bodies of the executed prisoners, as seen in the user-generated content cited by the ICC as evidence, aligns almost exactly with the dark spots on the satellite image" (Toler 2020, 216). A precise and complicated chrono- and geolocation gave rise to an agglomerate as a crime witness, a legitimate part of judicial proceedings. In this research—the collaborative collection of data and traces, their collation, and their analysis—Bellingcat demonstrates the potential of creating an agglomerative object that becomes evidence of a crime. This would not have been possible without the open-source intelligence techniques still being developed by the group or without the involvement of hundreds of volunteers who tracked the data and images circulating online. This is how an aesthetics of radical truth is produced

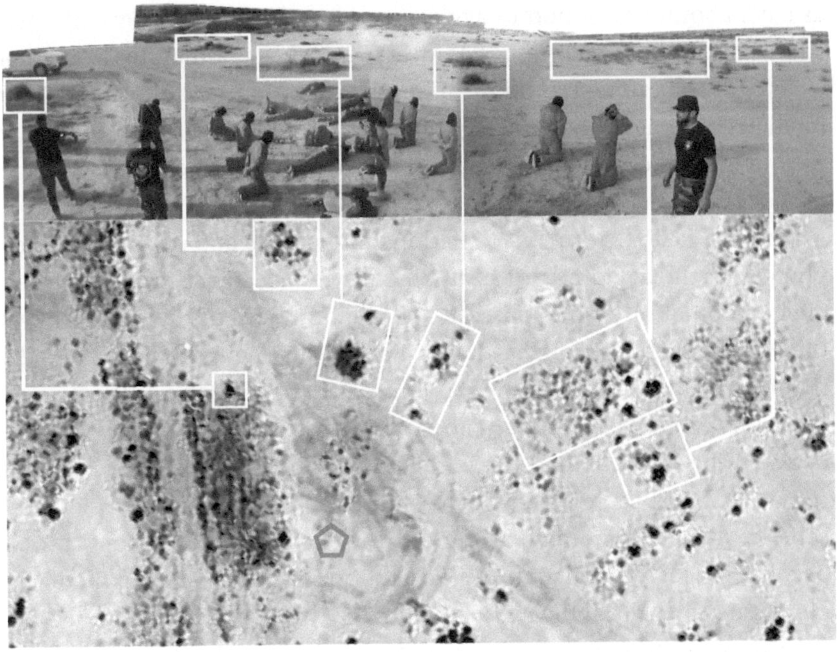

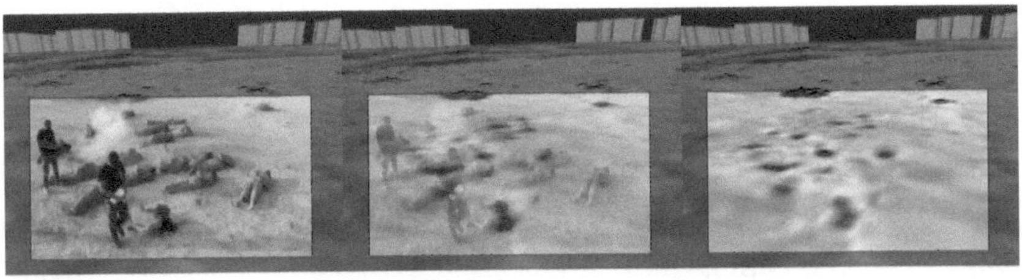

2.1

A stitched panorama of the Werfalli execution site made out of stills from the execution video. Bellingcat.

2.2

A comparison of the location of the Werfalli execution site bodies in the video and the spots in the satellite imagery. Bellingcat.

as a collaborative method of agglomeration, which, in the case of open-source intelligence techniques, is an activity that agglomerates the actual victims of the crime, the physical human blood in the desert, and their mediatized images. When conglomerated, these images turn out to be meaningful objects that make it possible to establish the place and time of the crime.

In this case, the intrinsic relationship became apparent in the morphology of the agglomerate as an object-evidence of the crime. The specific combination of the material and digital traces of the crime shows the complex intra-actions, as Karen Barad calls them. Applying Barad's theory to the agglomerate object as crime evidence in Bellingcat practices, these intra-actions and conglomerations are clearly visible. They emerge between the physical matter recording the crimes (as sand and blood in the desert) and their media representations (in the form of video and satellite images). The mediatized sand mixed with blood constitutes a peculiar object of medianatures (Parikka 2011) and results in a media agglomerate when combined with open-source intelligence techniques like procedures of searching for and combining data and facts.

SENSIBLE INVESTIGATION AND CURATED EVIDENCE

Participants in the democratic protests that swept across Ukraine in the fall of 2013 did not expect them to be the onset of a protracted war to regain full sovereignty from the Russian Federation. After the collapse of the Eastern Bloc in 1991, Ukraine declared independence and, in the early 2010s, began the process of preparing for association with the European Union, which was interrupted by Ukraine's pro-Russian president, Viktor Yanukovych. This sparked the pro-democracy protests called Euromaidan, Maidan Revolution, or the Revolution of Dignity. In the wake of these events, the Russian Federation was covertly involved in an internal war in eastern Ukraine via inspiring and funding separatist movements, covert military involvement, repression of citizens opposing the Russian regime, and the annexation of Ukrainian-owned Crimea in 2014. This seemingly internal and "crawling" conflict escalated into open warfare after Russian troops invaded sovereign Ukraine in February 2022.

The first victims of this brutal violence were the Euromaidan protesters demanding democratic change. Their peaceful protests were quickly suppressed by the brutal actions of the then pro-Russian Ukrainian authorities, which eventually led to a nationwide revolt in 2014. At that time, the main arena of the conflict, watched by the whole world, became the central square in Kiev, Maidan Nezalezhnosti (Independence Square). Officers of Berkut special units armed with live ammunition faced citizens organized as urban guerrillas, building makeshift shields for protection from telescopic batons and barricades made of tires, cars, buses, and garbage containers. The protective helmets worn by the demonstrators—construction hard hats, bicycle and motorcycle helmets, anything that could offer protection for demonstrators from gunfire—became symbols of the time. Before long, the protests (which became known as a revolution of helmets) were delegalized by the pro-Russian regime, and the wearing of helmets in public space was outlawed. Within a few days in February 2014, over a hundred demonstrators were killed. Some were shot by snipers from the rooftops of the buildings around Maidan Nezalezhnosti.

Documentation of February 20, 2014, one of the deadliest days of the protests, includes recordings from mobile phones of the protesters and observers and footage recorded by reporters. It was collected by Ukrainian activist Evelyn Nefertari, founder of the Jus Talionis Reconstruction Lab, a Ukrainian group involved in open-source intelligence techniques. After the initial identification work, consisting mainly of a temporal synchronization of the recordings, she handed them over to Pavel Dykan and Alexandra Iatsenko, attorneys who represented families of victims of Euromaidan protests in a Ukrainian court of law. These lawyers set out to prove that the authorities and Berkut officers used systematic violence against protesting citizens. The idea was to hold accountable the individual officers who fired live rounds and also to expose the political violence that inspired such a turn of events.

In 2015, they approached SITU Research with a proposal for cooperation to process all the available documentation as evidence to be submitted during court trials. SITU—a New York–based group of architects, researchers, and designers coordinated by Bradley Samuels, in collaboration with the Carnegie Mellon University Center for Human Rights Science (CHRS)—used 520 videos (totaling sixty-five hours) collected by

Nefertari for a synchronization of the footage in time and space. The investigation analyzed case studies of the deaths of three protesters. The video documents were synchronized with the sound rather than the image. Since most of the videos were made by the protesters, the recordings were chaotic, the shots were full of movement, and the images were often obscured by smoke from burning barricades and exploding smoke candles. Characteristic of the recordings was the crackling, roaring, and other sounds of ammunition being fired. These sounds made it possible to synchronize the various films and make a multisite study of the course of events. An algorithm was created to analyze the sound in the videos, which automated part of the identification process. The CHRS team created a unique sound print for each clip using an algorithm that recognized a standardized vocabulary of features (such as wind, screaming, gunshots, airplane noise, amplified speeches, music, and explosions). The algorithm then compared the sequence of these features in each clip to all others and looked for reasonable matches (Aronson et al. 2018, 169).

As the goal of the entire project was to present the analyzed material as evidence during the trial against Berkut officers in a Ukrainian court, and the material collected and analyzed was extensive, SITU Research decided to design an interactive platform called Euromaidan Event Reconstruction (figure 2.3). This platform allowed selective, multilinear viewing of various forms of evidence, analysis, comparisons, and expert evidence. It collected video footage from witnesses and participants, CCTV records, ballistic analyses of the trajectory determination of bullets fired at protesters (figure 2.4), medical reports on the injuries and causes of death of the victims, and photographic documentation of the clothes with the locations of gunshot wounds (figure 2.5). All this data was embedded in a virtual space of the city prepared on the basis of detailed cartographic data and Evelyn Nefertari's three-dimensional lidar (light detection and ranging) laser scans of the protest venues. In this way, a virtual urban

2.3

An audio latency analysis, from SITU Research's Euromaidan Event Reconstruction.

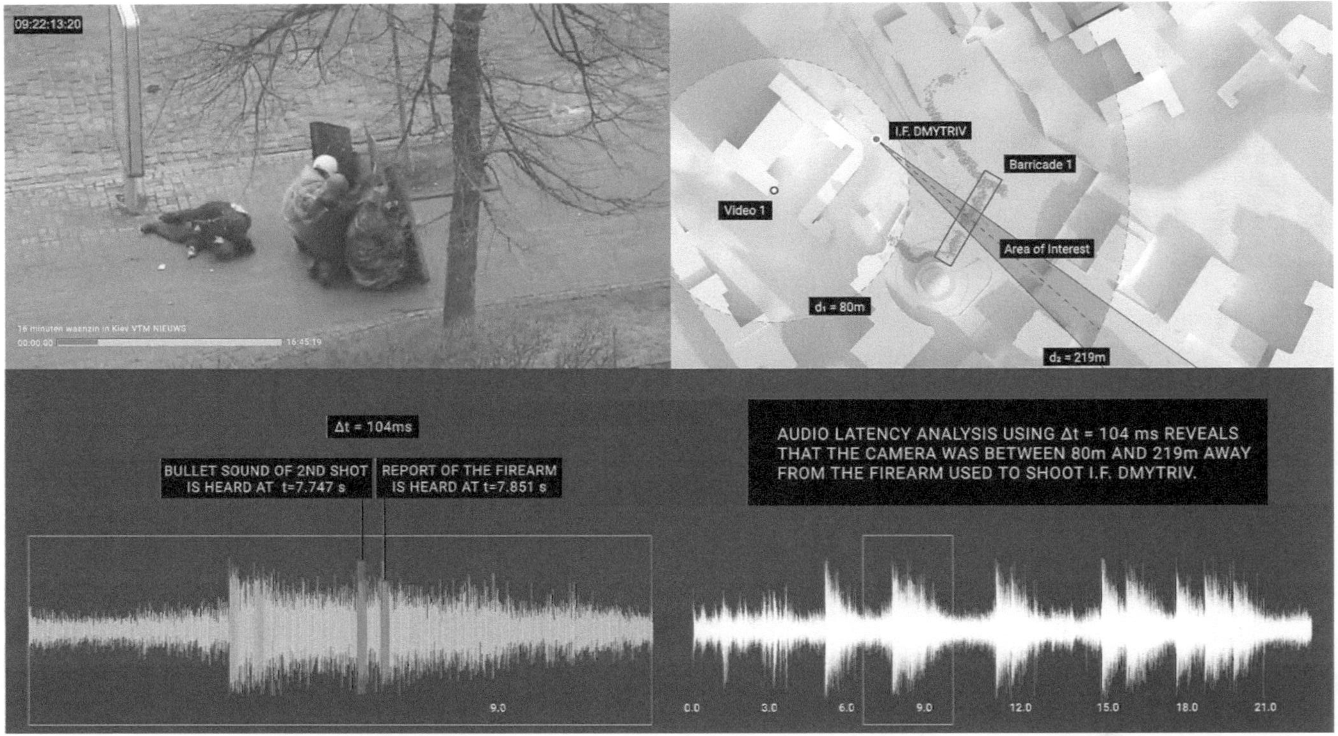
09:22:13:20
16 minuten waanzin in Kiev VTM NIEUWS
00:00:00
16:45:19
I.F. DMYTRIV
Barricade 1
Video 1
Area of Interest
d₁ = 80m
d₂ = 219m
Δt = 104ms
BULLET SOUND OF 2ND SHOT IS HEARD AT t=7.747 s
REPORT OF THE FIREARM IS HEARD AT t=7.851 s
AUDIO LATENCY ANALYSIS USING Δt = 104 ms REVEALS THAT THE CAMERA WAS BETWEEN 80m AND 219m AWAY FROM THE FIREARM USED TO SHOOT I.F. DMYTRIV.
9.0
0.0
3.0
6.0
9.0
12.0
15.0
18.0
21.0

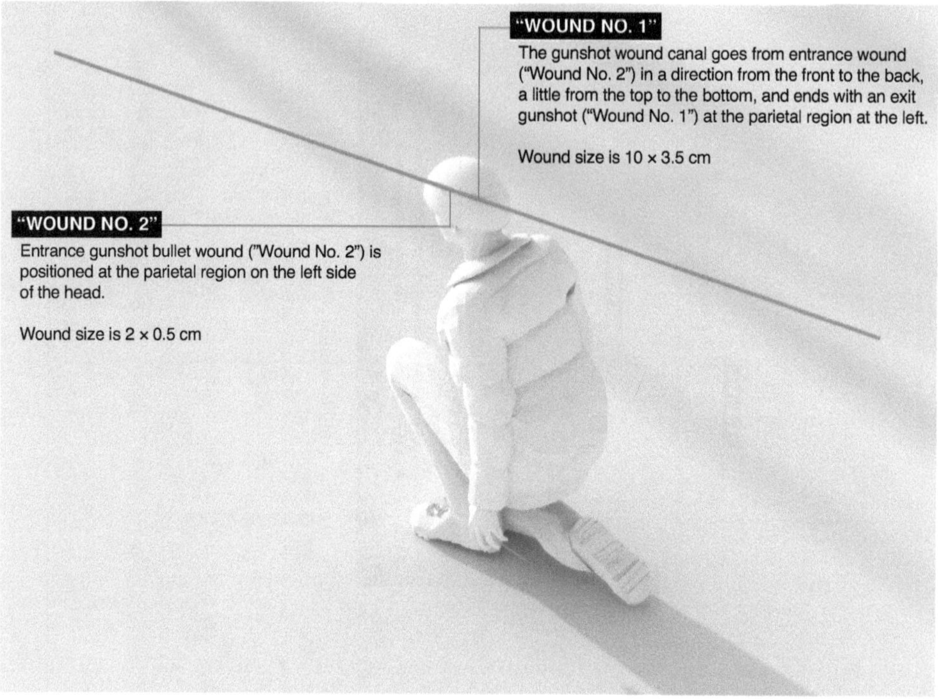

2.4

Ballistic analyses of the trajectory determination of bullets fired at protesters, from SITU Research's Euromaidan Event Reconstruction.

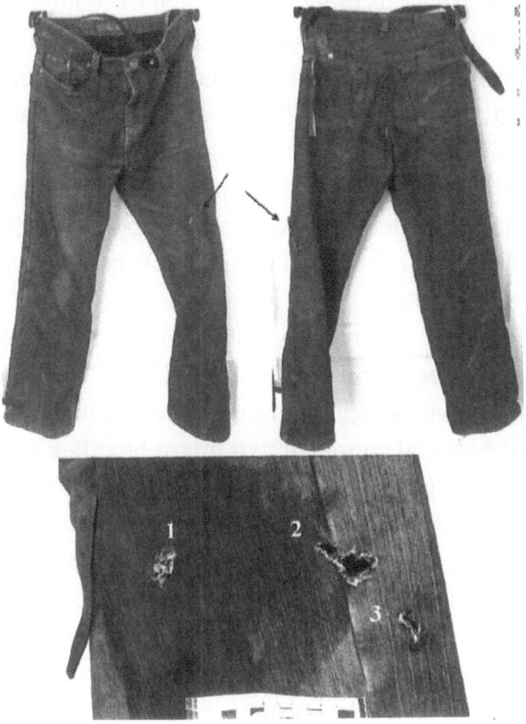

2.5

Photographic documentation of clothes with the locations of gunshot wounds, court evidence, and Kyiv Municipal Clinical Bureau of Forensic Medical Examination Report no. 278–2015/o, from SITU Research's Euromaidan Event Reconstruction.

model faithful to the physical space was prepared in which the course of the protest could be reconstructed with precision and with spatial and temporal synchronization, using the documentary material of February 20, 2014. Using such a strategy, the media morphology of the agglomerate was analyzed in detail and situated in space. The agglomerate's radical agency revealed the sensible relations between physical objects such as the victims' blood-soaked clothing, medical and forensic reports of injuries, and the mediatized sounds of gunshots and chaotic multiperspective video images recorded by the protesters.

Through the design of an interactive digital environment, SITU Research enabled an independent reception epistemic process. The Euromaidan Event Reconstruction—which agglomerates evidence, material, and analyses—is an effect of a special approach that might be called sensible investigation. It is meant to gather curated evidence. Care is a distinguishing mark of this type of work. As a result, the entire process, even though it uses design and laboratory methods and researcher-controlled procedures, helps us to get close to the process of violence identification and to participate in it by empathetic and epistemic involvement. The digital environment prepared for the court proceedings serves as a transversal presentation of materials, allows extensive familiarity with contexts, and provides access to temporal and spatial reconstruction. It simultaneously creates a public forum for presenting the voice of victims and the civic demand for justice. This new media milieu allows movement between situations and moments and becomes a new material fabric through which the agglomerative object as witness can be heard and seen in the public space. Spatial analysis, three-dimensional modeling, animation, interactive visualization expand the milieu in the same way, as it stretches into mediatized memory between there and here simultaneously. The crime took place on February 20, 2014, but its consequences have continued to this day. The war in Ukraine—which started in 2022 in a spectrum of historical, political conditions, and successive waves of violence and crime—is the tragic and tangible proof of this.

As part of many years of work in searching for evidence of crimes and violence, SITU Research also used open-source software called Codec, a collaborative tool for managing video evidence for use by legal and human rights organizations:

Codec originally emerged as a byproduct of attempting to solve recurring challenges in our investigative workflows—issues around collaboration, rapid visualization, and the management of video evidence. While the amount of user generated content has increased exponentially in recent years, managing the sheer volume of material can become inefficient at best and, often, simply prohibitive. Codec is designed to make this process collaborative, streamlined, efficient and intuitive. Research and development for this beta version of Codec unfolded across various cases of differing scales, and through collaborating with partners, including: Carnegie Mellon University's Center for Human Rights Science, Amnesty International, UC Berkeley's Human Rights Center, Columbia Law School's Human Rights Initiative, Human Rights Watch, UNITAD and many more. (SITU Research 2022)

CHRONOLOCATING HARM

In 2022, Bellingcat noted that "in the central Ukrainian city of Uman, a bloodied body lies lifeless in the street. It's February 24, and Russia's invasion of its neighbor has just begun. Debris is strewn across the road and the windows of nearby cars have been shattered. CCTV footage from a nearby shop shows a huge explosion took place here at just after 7 am local time. A crater, clearly visible in social media video, appears to confirm a rocket was the cause of the explosion, taking the life of the individual lying motionless nearby" (Bellingcat Investigative Team 2022, n.p.). As the Russian Federation's military aggression against Ukraine began in February 2022, Bellingcat researchers began collecting open-source evidence of war crimes committed against civilians by Russian troops as part of the Mapping Civilian Harm in Ukraine project. The database gathers media documents that provide evidence of the destruction of civilian infrastructure and that record violence against people (deaths and injuries due to the use of various types of weapons). After the materials are verified, their authenticity is confirmed (determining whether they have undergone additional digital processing, for example), and their geolocation and chronolocation are identified, they are placed on an interactive virtual map of Ukraine. Each media document includes a reference to the source (a link to the original place of publication on the web) and a brief

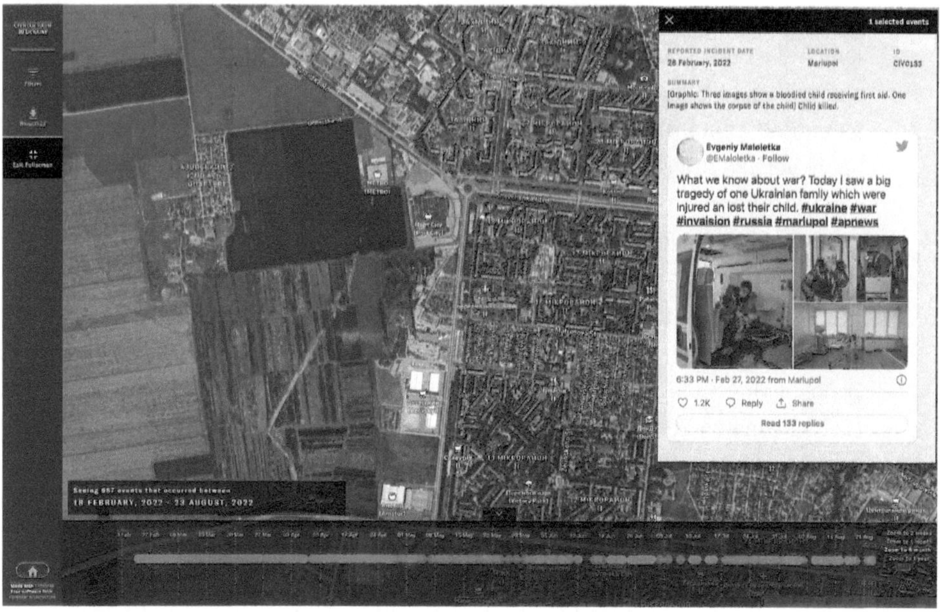

description of the event (figure 2.6). Photographs and video footage are anonymized to preserve the dignity of the casualties and to protect the identity and ensure the safety of those who were photographed. Besides visualizing all processed and verified materials on a digital platform, Bellingcat makes copies and archives all materials in case they are deleted in their original locations on the internet. This ensures that all collected material is available for legal proceedings.

The Timemap open-source software developed by Forensic Architecture is used to order and visualize the input obtained.[2] This software helps visualize geospatial events in an interactive platform and is used to gather evidence, conduct investigations, and thus shows course of events. The data, documents, and information uploaded to Timemap are temporally and spatially embedded in relation to the other materials collected. The

2.6

Database interface from Bellingcat's Mapping Civilian Harm in Ukraine project.

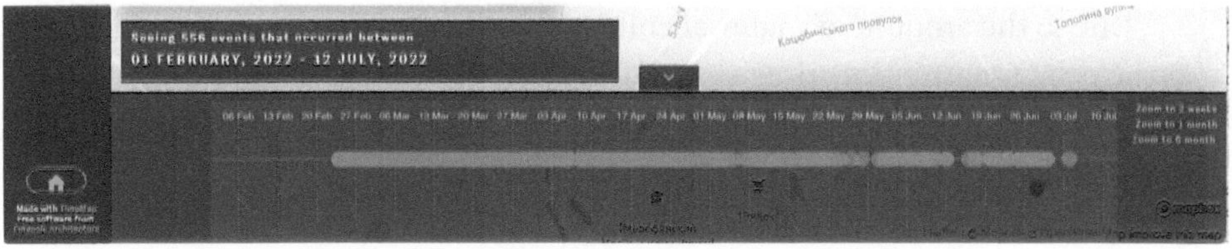

interface of the Mapping Civilian Harm in Ukraine database helps users review data from the level of a map, via zooming in on and opening documents directly in the site they were recorded in. Users can also access a scalable timeline that plays footage from a specific day, week, or month. The dataset can be filtered by using categories, which in this case are the types of public places attacked (residential, administrative, healthcare, school or childcare, or humanitarian) and the types of weapons used (cluster munition, thermobaric munition, rocket artillery, or vehicle-mounted weapon). Timemap helps users visualize the violence inflicted on innocent and defenseless people and reconstruct the dynamics of violence. The quantity, geographical spread, and temporal accumulation portray the real scale of violence committed against civilians in Ukraine. Zooming out the timeline to see the entire time axis of the war reveals that there are no time periods in which incidents of violence against civilians have not been documented. Therefore, the data collected reveals the scale and the systemic nature of violence. While the chart itself is neutral and abstract, consisting of overlapping points that are plotted on a timeline and make up a blurred line, in the situated context of war crimes it is a brutal image of the modern world. Every dot of this uneven line is connected to an image of actual violence and death (figure 2.7). Concealed under these dots are so many images that it is impossible to present them otherwise than through an agglomerative rendition revealing and embedding in time and space the enormity of violence.

2.7

Database timeline from Bellingcat's Mapping Civilian Harm in Ukraine project.

Due to the amount of material collected on an ongoing basis, as well as the need for attention, precision, and quality of verification, Bellingcat has formalized a mechanism of volunteers' participation in the core team. In its Global Authentication Project, volunteers from around the world are trained in open-source intelligence techniques (OSINT)—verification, geolocation, and data chronolocation techniques. Collaborative work has significantly increased the group's ability to process the large quantities of material pouring in every day from the war in Ukraine. Expanding collaborative methods and formalizing cooperation also requires common ethical standards. In working to identify crimes committed by Russian soldiers in Ukraine, Bellingcat refers to the *Berkeley Protocol on Digital Open Source Investigation: A Practical Guide on the Effective Use of Digital Open Source Information in Investigating Violations of International Criminal, Human Rights and Humanitarian Law* (United Nations Office of the High Commissioner for Human Rights and Human Rights Center, University of California, Berkeley 2022). The 2022 document was published jointly by the United Nations and the Human Rights Center at the University of California in Berkeley and represents a consensus on the ethics of OSINT practices. It is a major element in consolidating the community of open-source researchers. The protocol clarifies principles related to ethics and links ethics to work methods, legal issues, security, investigation preparation and procedure, data acquisition, processing, protection, and the sharing and disseminating of outcomes.

Radical truth in the data collection project on war crimes and violence in Ukraine emerges from the ethics of practices, methods, and methodologies of data acquisition and analysis and from open and inclusive structures of knowledge production. In the mediated-reality model, this appears to be one of the essential strategies for a sensible and sense-making way of sparking public debate regarding evidence of violence and crime.

LETHAL AIR AND WEAPONIZED CLOUDS

In 2020, the Forensic Architecture group (established by Eyal Weizman in 2010) premiered its Cloud Studies project. It appeared in the exhibition *Critical Zones: Observatories for Earthly Politics* curated by Peter Weibel

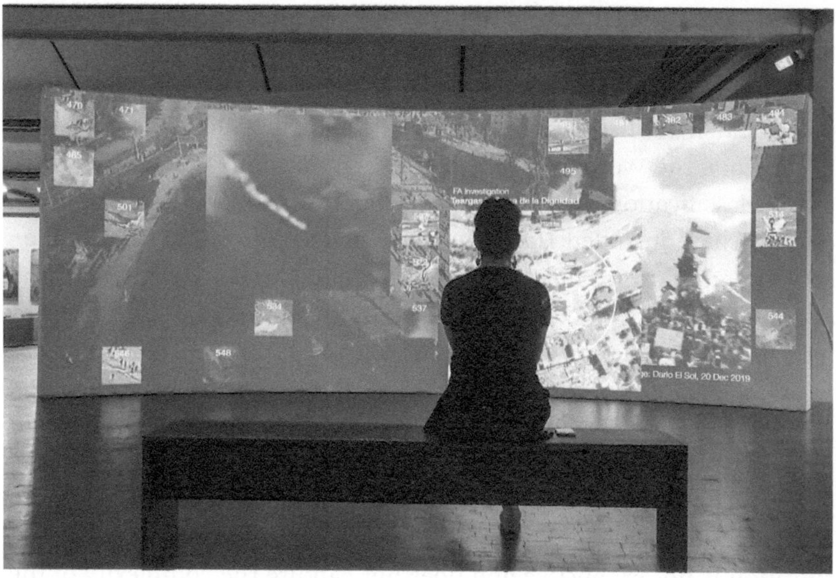

and Bruno Latour, along with Martin Guinard, and Bettina Korintenberg. Cloud Studies is based on previous investigations that produced a new epistemic perspective by revealing combined forms of violence against people and the environment. The epistemic framework adopted by Forensic Architecture presents forms of state, military, and corporate violence that produce or use agents like tear gas, white phosphorous, herbicides, airborne chemicals, and carcinogenic emissions. For the Forensic Architecture researchers, toxic chemicals create deadly artificial clouds of toxic pollutants (such as war gases) and harmful policies of repression, colonization, and exploitation. The Cloud Studies project reveals forms of violence that cannot be defended against (figure 2.8). The study expands between

2.8

Forensic Architecture, Cloud Studies, Berlin Biennale 2022. Photo by Michał Krawczak.

two extremes of violence resulting from the weaponization of clouds—the bomb cloud (the effect of an explosion that destroys everything within the range of its impact) and airborne chemicals (poisons that are difficult to detect and neutralize and that destroy the habitat of all species).

In 2017, the World Meteorological Organization (WMO) published a new classification of clouds that included some new types of special clouds. These included *Homogenitus* (a cloud that results from human activity and is formed due to the impact of industrial infrastructure) and *Flammagenitus* (a cloud that results from huge fires that are especially hard to control, such as forest fires or volcanic eruptions) (World Meteorological Organization 2017). From the perspective of the environmental crisis and critical discourse on the Anthropocene, both of these examples reveal the interdependence of the biosphere with the processes of global technologization and industrialization. From the perspective of contemporary media studies and postdigital violence studies, this classification is not exhaustive and does not capture the complexity of the processes involving human and nonhuman (also technological) actors. Forensic Architecture's Cloud Studies project therefore proposes a special cloud that, by virtue of its morphology, could expand the atlas developed by the WMO to include issues related to the atmospheric infrastructure of violence and dynamic social, political, biological, and meteorological processes: "Bomb clouds contain everything that a building once was: cement, plaster, plastic, glass, timber, fabric, paperwork, medicines, sometimes even human remains. Bomb clouds are architecture in gaseous form" (Forensic Architecture 2020, excerpt from a video). The definition coined by Forensic Architecture is a new unit in the taxonomy of meteorological phenomena and a new epistemic framework for a metadiscipline that would use aesthetic theory and practice to analyze the agglomerative morphology of clouds. Clouds can also represent metadata about the violence used. The classification created by the Forensic Architecture is a kind of atlas comparing the morphological characteristics of different toxic gas formations, enabling users to identify the types of weapons and violence used against people and the environment. The Cloud Studies project reveals technological patterns of violence and molecular policies of brutality that wreak havoc in a fraction of a second and persist in the form of deadly clouds, dust, fires, debris, and craters.

One of the investigations of the Cloud Studies series is The Use of White Phosphorus Munitions in Urban Environments, an investigation that was carried out jointly by Forensic Architecture and SITU Research. It examined the Israeli army's use of a controversial weapon against Palestinian civilians during the three-week armed conflict between Gazan paramilitary troops and the Israeli Defense Forces from late December 2008 to mid-January 2009. During Operation Cast Lead, known also as the First Gaza War or Gaza Massacre, the Israeli military carried out missile strikes of densely populated urban areas of Gaza in which a little-known weapon, white phosphorus munitions, was widely used. Witnesses recorded star-shaped explosions over Gaza City on video and smaller burning charges that later fell to the ground, triggering fires. White phosphorus is a substance that ignites on contact with air and burns at temperatures reaching 2,500 degrees Celsius. Falling to the ground, the burning phosphorus leads to widespread fires, fatal burns, and death. Phosphorus munitions fall in a hard-to-control manner in the form of a scattered rain of missiles, destroying large areas of land. Phosphorus munitions generate characteristic explosion clouds. When they drop, they are trailed by unnatural smudges and tentacles of thick smoke, and after they hit the ground, the smoke spreads across a wide area. The smoke formed by the combustion of phosphorus is very dense and poisonous to all living organisms. The Israeli troops' use of white phosphorus was documented in photographs and videos by multiple eyewitnesses and human rights organizations from both Gaza and Israel. Initially, the Israeli army denied using phosphorus and claimed that the only weapons used during Operation Cast Lead were "smoke curtains" and "smoke screens" generated by so-called quiet shells, with no explosives and no phosphorus (Amnesty International 2009, 35).

In its 2009 report, however, Amnesty International stated that military decision-makers were aware of the ramifications of deploying such weapons. The report quotes expert evidence from Israeli military documents from the time of Operation Cast Lead:

> When the phosphorus comes in contact with living tissue it causes its damage by "eating" away at it. Characteristics of a phosphorus wound are: chemical burns accompanied by extreme pain, damage to tissue . . . the phosphorus may seep

into the body and damage internal organs. In the long run, kidney failure and the spread of infection are characteristic. . . . In conclusion: a wound by an ordnance containing explosive phosphorus is inherently dangerous and has the potential to cause serious damage to tissue.

. . .

Most of the data on phosphorus wounds stems from animal testing and accidents. Exposure to white phosphorus is highly poisonous, according to many lab experiments. Burns covering a small area of the body, 12–15 percent in lab animals and less than 10 percent in humans, may be lethal as a result of its effects, mostly on the liver, heart and kidneys. (Amnesty International 2009, 36)

The use of weaponry so dangerous to civilians has been opposed by many international organizations and by activist groups on both sides of the conflict. Yesh Gvul, an Israeli human rights organization represented by attorneys Michael Sfard and Emily Schaeffer, lodged a petition to Israel's High Court of Justice demanding a ban on the use white phosphorus (Forensic Architecture 2014, 337–338). Working with Yesh Gvul, Forensic Architecture and SITU Research developed a report using novel methods to obtain data on postexplosion clouds. The aim of the report was to present the mechanisms of phosphorus bombs in detail. Based on an analysis of available photographic and video documentation showing phosphorus munitions falling to the ground in different parts of the city, researchers calculated the angle of charge propagation and the area of phosphorus burning fallout (figure 2.9). The analysis indicated that phosphorus bombs are weapons against civilians that cause uncontrollable losses, environmental damage, and deaths of innocent people. The lethality of phosphorus increases with the density of urban areas. In densely built-up areas, burns, toxic smoke, temperature, and induced fires are a deadly trap, making phosphorus munitions an extremely violent weapon. Forensic Architecture and SITU Research also developed a "parametric model to run iterative three-dimensional burst simulations" (Forensic Architecture and SITU Research 2012, 15). It enabled controlled virtual simulations in three-dimensional space on the impact of these types of weapons in urban spaces of varying densities. A cartographic grid of cities (including Gaza City, Tel Aviv, New York, and Paris) was used to conduct a simulation that shows the universal scale of destruction in relation to

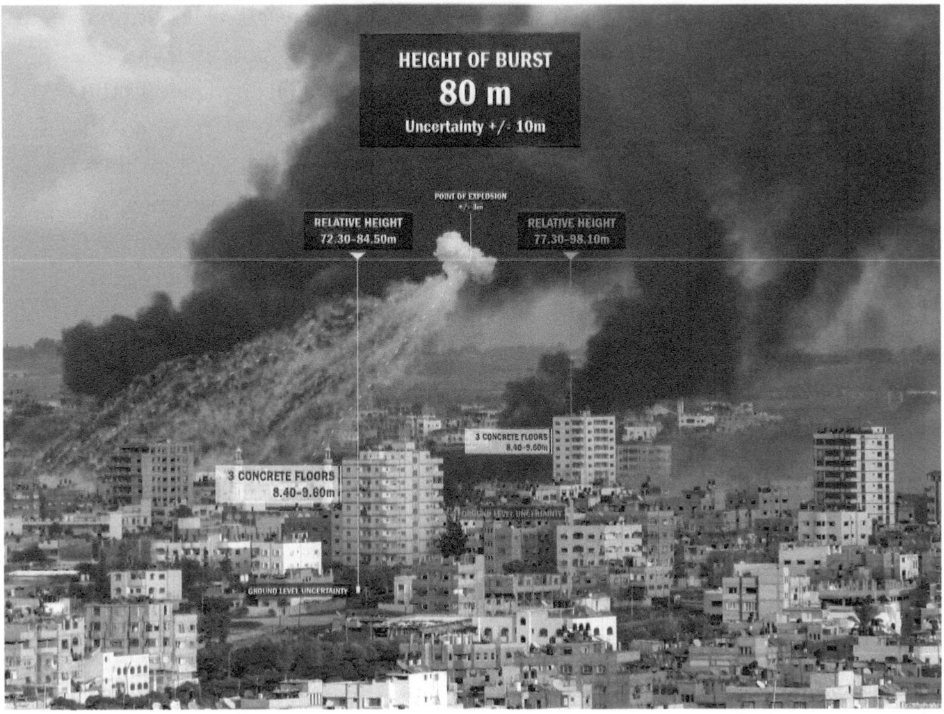

2.9

Height-of-burst calculations over an image of Rafah, Gaza. From Forensic Architecture's The Use of White Phosphorus Munitions in Urban Environments.

different types of buildings. In this way, violence reveals its relational nature. The strategy of transversal simulation involving potential victims from different continents and cultures is a tool for social engagement (on the basis of empathy and solidarity) and also helps to reveal the unconditional scale of violence, which in its physical, cartographic, and military principles would be the same for the residents of each of these cities.

The report *The Effects of White Phosphorus Munitions in Urban Environments* was presented at the 2012 Annual Meeting of States Parties to the Convention on Conventional Weapons in the UN Office for Disarmament Affairs in Geneva. It also was submitted with a petition developed by Yesh Gvul to Israel's High Court of Justice. These actions and strong public pressure led the Israeli military to declare in 2013 that it would stop using white phosphorus munitions in populated areas. According to a senior military commander: "As we learned during Cast Lead, [white phosphorus] doesn't photograph well, so we are reducing the supply and we will not purchase beyond what we already have" (Forensic Architecture 2014, 345).

The Cloud Studies project also includes The Bombing of Rafah, a study conducted by Amnesty International and Forensic Architecture (2014) that deals with bombings carried out by the Israeli Defense Forces in the Gaza Strip in July and August 2014. It focuses on the civilian consequences of the severe August 1, 2014, bombing of Rafah, and the results of the investigation were published as an interactive report. After Hamas captured an Israeli soldier despite a seventy-two-hour ceasefire announced earlier that day, Israel initiated the Hannibal Directive, a secret order for Israeli soldiers to use maximum firepower to rescue the soldier, regardless of the consequences for the lives of its own soldiers. The target of the bombing was the underground tunnels used by Hamas for the hijacking, but the shelling devastated civilian infrastructure and killed around two hundred people (Amnesty International and Forensic Architecture 2014).

Because Forensic Architecture members and Amnesty International activists were not allowed to enter the Gaza Strip, their investigation was based on open-source materials (including photographs, video footage, and witness statements) that were obtained from publicly available online sources and were sent to Forensic Architecture and Amnesty International

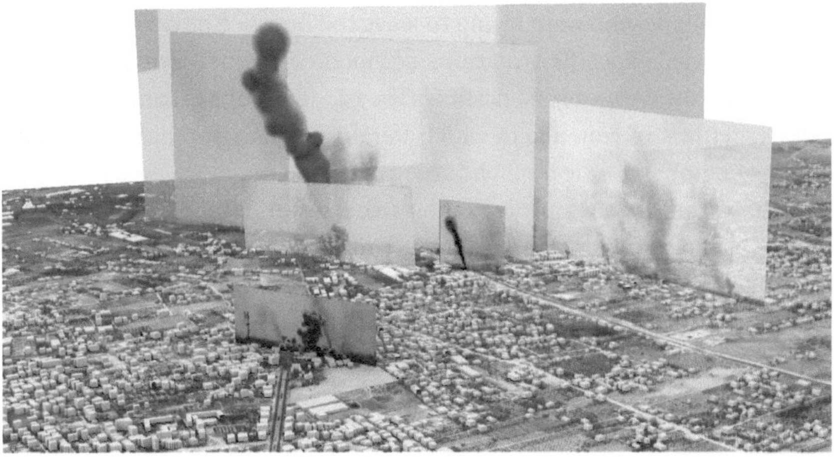

by journalists, witnesses, and activists. The materials helped reconstruct the bombings, create comparative morphological models of the postexplosion clouds, and create a synchronization of their development over time (figure 2.10). This enabled an accurate chronolocation of the explosions. The sizes of the craters produced by the bombing were also measured. By comparing pre- and postbombing satellite images, researchers located all the craters formed after the August 1, 2014, explosions previously identified on media footage. In this way, they created an accurate map of the urban areas affected by the bombing. Measurements of the size of the craters and the falling bombs (based on videos of the bombing) helped them identify the type of weapon used in the raids—the US-made Mark 84 bomb, which contained one ton of explosives. The report

2.10

Multiple images and reconstructed bomb clouds are arranged within a three-dimensional model of Rafah, Gaza. From Amnesty International and Forensic Architecture's *The Bombing of Rafah*.

describes the aftermath of the bombing and the shooting by Israeli soldiers of civilians who were trying to leave the bombed city. The Bombing of Rafah reveals specific situations of violence against civilians and, by identifying the weapons used, shows the broader political and economic infrastructures of violence in which Rafah's civilian population became victims of global political machinations.

The Cloud Studies project shows the systemic and regular use of chemicals and weapons and the recurring patterns and procedures concerning these forms of violence worldwide. "Atmospheric violence" (a term coined by Lawrence Abu Hamdan, a designer and artist who has collaborated with Forensic Architecture) is a form of violence that provides evidence for reevaluating earlier epistemic frameworks that linked to globalization processes in the context of economics and politics. Regardless of whether there is fast violence (an explosion that brings immediate destruction and casualties) or slow violence (the long-term consequences of environmental contamination on human and nonhuman health), this is systemic violence, and the infrastructures of this system are the regime's policies of colonization, exploitation, and the intertwined forms of state and corporate capital linked to the military and extractive industries.

PUBLIC OBJECTS OF TRUTH

The aesthetics of radical truth is of particular importance in all the projects described in this chapter. The analysis of what has been recorded—albeit chaotically and incompletely, lacking temporal and spatial context, through ordering and resituating in space, time, and in political, military, social context—exposes the actual course of the event and lays bare the aggressors' intentions. In his book *Forensic Architecture: Violence at the Threshold of Detectability*, Eyal Weizman writes that "forensics is an aesthetic practice because it depends on both the modes and the means by which reality is sensed and presented publicly. Investigative aesthetics slows down time and intensifies sensibility to space, matter, and image. It also seeks to devise new modes of narration and the articulation of truth claims" (Weizman 2017, 96). An aesthetics of radical truth as forensics is about new tools and strategies to identify violence, collaborative and solidarity-based resistance to it, and gradual and painstaking exposure of the politics that objectify the victims of this violence, taking away their voice and agency. The projects discussed in this chapter can empower all those who suffer military violence, but above all those who died, who can speak only through the reconstructed events, the digital and material traces that witness their deaths, and the narrative that these projects publicly present. These groups conduct investigations and prepare evidence that is later used in international and local courts. The new forms of evidence and the techniques and methodologies for producing it expand the definitions of open justice. Under this legal principle, court proceedings must be conducted transparently and under public scrutiny to safeguard the rights of those who are subject to the court's authority and allow the public to monitor the proceedings. SITU Research, Forensic Architecture, and Bellingcat have extended this definition to include the openness and transparency of the evidence itself as agglomerative objects that are made available on websites and online platforms designed for this purpose, through strategies for discussing and showing them at international art exhibitions, and through dissemination in the press and scholarly publications. The social circulation of the witness-object provides a new field for rethinking legal procedures for analyzing crime and violence in the mediatized culture, where the digital fuses with the material and both digital and material must be present. These agglomerative objects become witnesses to contemporary forms of violence and crime. This is also how the new parliament of things that Latour advocated is to be formed. It is vital not only to give things a voice but, as the philosopher would have it, to relocate the debate about specific acts of violence by allowing them to be seen, heard, and commonly understood in the public space (Latour and Chakrabarty 2020).

In this chapter, we use the notion of the agglomerative object of truth, although social, and media discourse sometimes uses substitute and near-substitute terms, such as *thing* (Latour uses this term more than once), *matter*, *trace*, or, in the discourse of the legal sciences, *fact*, *evidence*, *witness*, and *testimony*. The agglomerative object concept combines the different semantic scopes of those mentioned above and, at the same time, has an open, connective structure. It expands by transversally linking physical violence and its forms of mediatization and allows a new affective experience of violence through a multimediated cognition of its strategies of action. Using this concept, we return to the relational object of learning. We embed the agglomerate in the definitions of scientific objects, because all the examples cited above elaborate the agglomerative object within specific, situated, established parameters, using technological apparatus and employing ethical and transparent methodological standards. Thus, it can be said that new experimental systems are created for the study of violence. As new epistemic modalities, they are transparent, open, socially shared, and inclusive for more people who want to engage in this research. At the same time, they offer new experimental research strategies in fields such as the humanities or social sciences, where practice, collective knowledge production, and the shaping of social circulations of knowledge are increasingly essential.

One of the first to study the essence of "experimental systems" in science was Ludwik Fleck (2011), a Pole with Jewish roots, a physician, a microbiologist, and a philosopher of medicine. Fleck is seen as a precursor of the sociology of science and studies on science and technology. He inspired the research of Bruno Latour and Thomas Kuhn. He scrutinized this notion among others in the book *Genesis and Development of a Scientific Fact*, first published in German in 1935 (Fleck 2008). Here Fleck focuses primarily on the fact that in many disciplines scientists use systems of experiments that are not defined top-down and fail to offer clear answers from the start, producing the right result only in a complex nexus. As the German philosopher of experimental science Hans-Jörg Reinberger wrote about Fleck's work, "in permanently changing and varying patterns, experimental systems mix up elements that historians and philosophers of science usually wish to have properly separated: research objects, theories, technical arrangements, and instruments as well as disciplinary, institutional, social, and cultural dispositifs. An analysis of the ways in which different experimental systems interact—how they overlap, delimit, exclude, or supplement each other—provided insights into the developmental dynamics of broader fields of science" (Reinberger 2014, n.p.).

Through their laboratory and experimental workshops and methodologies, the groups and methods of work we write about spark a debate on the "broader fields of science," pointing to the need to change and redefine stagnant university disciplines and ways of doing research, especially in the humanities and social sciences (Dersley 2025). Analyzing the turn to experimentation in science, Fleck launched a debate on the relationship between reality and the ways in which it is represented scientifically and the need to understand its modes of socialization. This debate created opportunities for a new relational approach to the research object, the experiment, and the position of the researcher in science, which was later continued, among other things, in the study of science and laboratories in science and technology studies (STS) and feminist STS. Karen Barad sees this debate as falling within the relationship between nature and culture: As "the discursive practices by which we seek to describe phenomena do not refer to properties of abstract objects or observation-independent beings but rather actively reconfigure the world in its becoming, then what is being described by our epistemic practices is not nature itself but our intra-activity as part of nature. That is, realism is reformulated in terms of the goal of providing accurate descriptions of that reality of which we are a part and with which we intra-act, rather than some imagined and idealized human-independent reality" (Barad 2007, 207).

In the projects we write about, intra-actions allow for the analysis of agglomerative objects that enter public circulation as witnesses to violence. They regain agency and have the potential to produce new practices against violence. In the case of the agglomerative objects created by SITU Research, Forensic Architecture, and Bellingcat, intra-acts expand in the transversal movement between physical violence and its mediatization—between the sand and blood in the desert and the conglomerated propaganda images of executions circulating inertly on the internet, between the human and nonhuman bodies burned using white phosphorus and the politically concealed consequences of that action, between the bullets killing demonstrators and the imperialist policies of territorial aggression. Intramediarity is being generated everywhere. We deal here with a situation of creating an agglomerative object "between" (as intermediarity) but also "within," as the meaning of the prefix *intra-* should be read in this case (as a mutual constitution of agglomerative entities). This is because, with the use of media as joints, there is a process of rematerialization. It takes place through intra-actions and the ability to act that emerges from within the relationship and not outside of it. This process simultaneously incorporates human and nonhuman subjects into the framework of the agglomerative object. They become a form of new collectives that produce agency against violence, as the agency does not preexist separately but emerges from relationships in the intra-actions (Barad 2007).

One of Ludwik Fleck's major metatheoretical accomplishments was noting that scientific objects have collective authorship. Fleck had not yet considered the category of relationality between human and nonhuman. He focused on the researchers, apparatus, and social systems that determine scientific objects. As he pointed out, "collective cognition" and "collective knowledge" are required for research and experimental practices to happen, as the scholarly and cognitive practice is a "collective activity." Its knowledge product "is a certain picture, which is visible only to anybody who takes part in this social activity, or a thought which is also clear to the members of the collective only. What we do think and how we do see depends on the thought-collective to which we belong" (Fleck 2011, 77). The collaborative nature of the practices we discuss consists also in groups often working together, exchanging tools and methodologies by adapting and updating them to specific problems, investigations, and processes. Within the teams described, there are also often internal units set up to continuously work on tool development, such as Bellingcat's tech team, which is led by Johanna Wild. The tech team develops new open-source tools and research strategies that it shares with the community at large, collects and analyzes the changing technical needs of the open-source intelligence techniques community, and actively seeks designers and coders to collaborate on these new tools. Forensic Architecture and SITU Research are also creating much larger systems, such as the collaborative platforms described in this chapter (Forensic Architecture's Timemap and SITU Research's Codec) but also more precise and sophisticated tools using machine learning classifiers (developed by Forensic Architecture) to automatically recognize different types of munitions and weapons in photos and videos. Such tools significantly speed up investigations and the process of evidence collection. These nonstandard and innovative methods of conducting research through collaboration on specific projects and the training obtained in workshops also expand the toolbox, competence, and proficiency of various nongovernmental organizations, activist groups, independent open-source researchers, and journalists. Examples of this include the Citizen Evidence Lab founded by

Amnesty International and the incorporation of open-source investigative methods into the journalistic practices of large media outlets, such as the *New York Times*, the BBC, and *Der Spiegel*.

The collective nature of the research is crucial since it involves academics, researchers, and practitioners outside the academy (designers, architects, artists, journalists, activists, volunteers, and anyone else who wants to commit time and energy to a project). They meet the criteria of transdisciplinary research and practice, but they transcend the frameworks and cognitive modalities sanctioned in research institutions, pointing to the need for universities and research units to devise new strategies, practices, and collective studies. Rather than individuals, radical investigators are whole groups that are producing new experimental systems for combating violence. New collective knowledge-shaping practices are based on engaging humans and nonhumans as causal witnesses to violence (Jelewska et al. 2024). Through the elaborate, multisite structure of presenting agglomerative objects—including art shows, online platforms, publicly available reports, workshops, and forums for sharing tools and methods—agglomerative objects are not merely a one-time viewing experience. They have unfolding ontologies and ask viewers to piece them together, learn about and understand them, and have a say in the public debate. The matters of concern attract people who want to dispute and understand (Latour and Chakrabarty 2020).

3

SLOW VIOLENCE AND DATA RESISTANCE

In his 2011 widely discussed book *Slow Violence and the Environmentalism of the Poor*, Rob Nixon observes that "climate change, the thawing cryosphere, toxic drift, biomagnification, deforestation, the radioactive aftermaths of wars, acidifying oceans, and a host of other slowly unfolding environmental catastrophes present formidable representational obstacles that can hinder our efforts to mobilize and act decisively. The long dyings—the staggered and staggeringly discounted casualties, both human and ecological that result from war's toxic aftermaths or climate change—are underrepresented in strategic planning as well as in human memory" (Nixon 2011, 2–3). Noting the various forms of environmental violence that have gained momentum over the past century, Nixon introduces the concept of slow violence in the above contexts. He points to the anthropogenic origins of most modern environmental disasters (all of which are the outcomes of actions of specific people at a specific time) and their lasting consequences, which are often difficult to predict. He focuses on "the representational challenges and imaginative dilemmas posed not just by imperceptible violence but by imperceptible change whereby violence is decoupled from its original causes by the workings of time" (Nixon 2011, 11).

Protracted violence and its harmful effects may, according to Nixon, be more difficult to combat than we currently imagine. "The long dyings" of humans and nonhumans assume different forms of slow temporal and spatial destruction at local and planetary levels. Environmental slow violence is marked by unfolding structures and processes, and its consequences are often scientifically unpredictable. For example, it is hard to obtain unequivocal data on the direct effects of radioactive contamination of the environment (Jelewska and Krawczak 2018, 2025). Diseases caused when the human body is exposed to radiation or environmental pollution are difficult to study. In fact, long-time radioactive elements are present in the earth's matter. Once contaminated, soil or water can remain in this state for hundreds of years. Only from a long-term perspective can hypotheses be made about how radioactivity transforms the natural environment and human health. The situation is similar in the case of contamination by chemicals or oil spills. Often, the consequences of disasters are impossible to predict due to the complexity of the ecosystem of the affected areas. Diagnosing their immediate impact on people and the environment may be fairly precise, but the effects of ecosystem transformation over time are not obvious and have their own internal unfolding ontology.

The concept of time is critical to Nixon's definition of slow violence. Expanding on Johan Galtung's (1969) concept of structural violence, Nixon recognizes time as a key factor in defining violence with far-reaching consequences (Kaufman 2014). In his 1969 text, Galtung writes that "we shall refer to the type of violence where there is an actor that commits the violence as *personal* or *direct*, and to violence where there is not such actor as *structural* or *indirect*. There may not be any person who directly harms another person in the structure. The violence is built into the structure and shows up as unequal power and consequently as unequal life chances" (Galtung 1969, 170–171). According to Galtung, it is often hard to pinpoint a single culprit in cases of structural violence. Rather, economic, social, or ideological systems are responsible for these forms of violence because they are the result of racial injustice, unequal access to education and health care, and the inequitable distribution of resources, which are due to place of origin or socioeconomic status. Galtung links its emergence primarily to "the power to decide over the distribution of resources, which is unevenly distributed" (Galtung 1969, 171).

In addition to his structural and deeply embedded view of violence in societies, Nixon augments the understanding of its causes in environmental actions when he includes time as a necessary element for describing the process. Galtung was referring largely to racial violence and economic violence as the foundations of modern societies in the global north. The time of slow violence, as produced mainly by the global north's anthropogenic catastrophes and abuses, extends into the future, which is impossible to delineate and define, and embeds an ever-recurring trauma in the past. Nixon thus adopts a topological figure of time and links the past with an indefinable future on a grid of references. This is especially true of the violence that began with the first European colonization practices in the fifteenth century in the Americas, Africa, and Asia and continues as the extraction of land resources exploits and destroys the environment, causes climatic migrations, creates forced displacement, and leads to the deaths of community members.

Slow violence is present in capitalism as a state of mind of the global north, which invariably inserts the present into the technofuture model as the potential and only legitimate course of development. This type of development, however—especially its endless open horizon of events—seems to be slowly fading. Under the impact of slow violence, the earth as a planet is increasingly demonstrating its potential temporal limitations:

> Ours is an age of onrushing turbo-capitalism, wherein the present feels more abbreviated than it used to—at least for the world's privileged classes who live surrounded by technological time-savers that often compound the sensation of not having enough time. Consequently, one of the most pressing challenges of our age is how to adjust our rapidly eroding attention spans to the slow erosions of environmental justice. If, under neoliberalism, the gulf between enclaved rich and outcast poor has become ever more pronounced, ours is also an era of enclaved time wherein for many speed has become a self-justifying, propulsive ethic that "renders uneventful" violence (to those who live remote from its attritional lethality) a weak claimant on our time. (Nixon 2011, 8)

In this age of "turbo-capitalism," time is scarce and postpones environmental justice to the future. As researchers point out, however, this may prove precarious for the existence of humanity. During the 2016 seminar he led at the University of Aarhus, Bruno Latour (2017) noted that a significant shift in the design of the earth occurred in the twentieth and twenty-first centuries. Until modern times, the human race oscillated between the concept of the earth as a place to cultivate and a place to modernize and colonize—that is, between cultivated land and the globe. In recent decades, climate change data from researchers in many disciplines have indicated that the model of an endless horizon of possibilities no longer holds true. Latour asserts that we need to return to the earth, Gaia, which is the system of interaction of which we humans are components. Such thinking will allow us to look at certain processes with an awareness of how slow violence affects topological and temporal contortions (Latour 2017).

Nixon points out similar aspects of the slow attrition of the horizon of the future as an arrow of time. In his book, he gives space to "stories, images, and symbols adequate to the pervasive but elusive violence of delayed effects" (Nixon 2011, 3) as signs or witnesses to violence. He cites many narratives on slow violence—stories, testimonies, novels, film documentaries, and journalistic and scientific articles—as a form of writing activism. Many of the authors cited in the pages of this book are from outside the global north and can identify specific problems of anthropogenic destruction of the planet in their local human and nonhuman communities. Nixon positions his book as an activist voice in the debate on environmental violence and the need for justice.

A decade after Nixon's book was published, political geographer Shannon O'Lear (2021) commented on Nixon's assertions from the perspective of the planet's ever-deteriorating situation. O'Lear adds the need to "decode" political and economic claims about the environment. In her introduction to *A Research Agenda for Geographies of Slow Violence: Making Social and Environmental Injustice Visible*, she writes that before we design meaningful alternative stories, images, and scenarios for a planetary rescue, "it is necessary to examine dominant narratives, practices, and geopolitical agendas that enable harmful structures to exist" (O'Lear 2021, 3).

In this chapter, we are following Nixon's directives to seek activist practices that confront locally situated violence against people and the environment in its topological temporal structures, and we concur with researchers such as O'Lear who see a need to point to the causes and the individuals, corporations, and states that bring about this violence. We address grassroots, community-based, and engaged practices for uncovering slow violence and various types of contemporary environmental harm (Kahn 1999, 2011). We examine collaborative practices carried out in tandem with local communities, applying media tools designed for specific conditions to collect and secure data on violence. We discuss examples of practices that use new do-it-yourself ways to construct devices and sensors for community members to download data. A process is taking place in which local communities create tools and methods for analyzing environmental disaster data and discover the first steps to take toward the reinvention of environmental rights (Gabrys 2019), the return of data to the local communities that collect it (Loukissas 2019; Murillo and Dosemagen 2022), and a turn toward data-decentralizing practices.

SITUATED DATA

Most economic, political, and cognitive processes depend on the collection, administration, and use of data for specific purposes. Data has thus become a corporate, state, ideological, and economic force in the modern postdigital world (Thatcher and Dalton 2022). However, in this system, data can also be a tool of resistance and struggle for and by those who suffer forms of structural violence. In a sense, data becomes a double-edged weapon that, depending on who wields it, can be a major driver of change (Thatcher et al. 2018, xvi). Grassroots collaborative data-collection initiatives can be used to resist or legitimize a position, and they are particularly relevant to slow violence. Because the effects of slow violence are long-term, monitoring and data often are multisite, time-consuming, and experimental. Just as tools need to be designed for a specific need, location, and question so that they can be epistemic tools in the process, the collected data needs to be properly processed so that it does not lose its original quality and can be accurately read and interpreted. Important aspects include how environmental data is collected and organized, how and to whom it is made available, and what technological devices and media practices are necessary to obtain such data in relation to the place and local communities affected by violence. The data must be situated, transparent, and open to forms of sharing and joint use.

Yanni Alexander Loukissas wrote about the need for deeply situated data in his book *All Data Are Local: Thinking Critically in a Data-Driven Society* (2019). In this work, he proposed a broad definition of data that includes all elements of locating or situating data in political, social, economic, and scholarly contexts. A transdisciplinary, transversal, and open understanding of data also allows Loukissas to showcase contemporary grassroots practices that, using experimental techniques and methods of data collection, offer counterstrategies to global, corporate, and political models of data aggregation to achieve a specific goal.

This is the definition of data that we use in this chapter. It helps explain why data must belong to the local communities that collect it, why its analyses must be situated and open-ended, why grassroots monitoring of the environment and the effects of violence mean more than global aid projects, and why data today is a new form of resistance to top-down policies, the capital of large corporations, and the often ethically questionable projects of the technofuture.

The first example we discuss concerns Safecast's organization of a social way to collect radiation data. The second concerns Public Lab's use of grassroots mapping for the monitoring on the ground of petrochemical contamination in the Gulf of Mexico. In this section, we also address the manufacture of do-it-yourself tools and ways to create relationships with environmental monitoring volunteers. In the second part of the chapter, we scrutinize resistance strategies, new media, and mapping practices of indigenous communities in Indonesia, Peru, Guyana, and Panama. These include monitoring the environment, countering deforestation, creating detailed digital maps of protected areas, and collecting and archiving data on environmental harm and violence. The projects examined here are unique in that local communities are applying modern technologies (such as do-it-yourself drones and open-source software) to compile data and create digital maps for their information gathering and monitoring processes. In this way, through their practices, they are deconstructing both the colonial basis of cartography and the military origins of drone-related technologies.

In all these activities, data is situated in local contexts, collected through DIY tools, and analyzed through open and transparent methodologies, and it thereby becomes a potential power of resistance. This resistance is primarily against the violent, unethical, and exploitative environmental and human policies of corporations and top-down designed data analyses that often obscure the scale of environmental violence. The events we write about are linked to both immediate, direct violence and to long-term violence affecting people and the environment. But all environmental violence affects specific people and communities. As Donna Haraway (2016) writes, as humans we are connected to the environment in both planetary and local perspectives. When environmental disasters occur, there is heavy periodic pollution in an area and exposure to radiation, and this violence directly affects human and nonhuman bodies by penetrating their structures and doing damage. However, all these forms of environmental exploitation have a long-term aspect, too. These events—the BP oil spill into the Gulf of Mexico in 2010, the radioactive contamination of the areas around the Fukushima nuclear power plant accident in 2011, ongoing pollution of the air with harmful substances, the unwarranted clearing of forests—have a slow violence dimension. They cause successive waves of disease, degrade local and global ecosystems, and bring about new forms of arousing and managing fear and insecurity about the living conditions in local communities.

The second part of the chapter reveals another brutal fact—the intertwining of violence against the environment with violence against people. Individuals from indigenous communities who express their opposition to harmful environmental activities and who engage in efforts to monitor and protect natural areas often die in unclear circumstances. They sometimes are killed on the orders of companies that are violating the law or carrying out illegal activities in protected areas. This kind of entanglement of violence against the environment and people defines environmental violence today as "slowly unfolding" (Nixon 2011) and triggering immediate losses and violent consequences for human and nonhuman entanglements.

CROWD SCIENCE AND DECENTRALIZING RADIATION DATA

In her research on disasters, environmental anthropologists Kim Fortun and Alli Morgan point out that although environmental disasters are unique and have differing consequences in space and time, they share some "recurrent patterns" that can be read as they unfold (Fortun and Morgan 2015). This methodological approach makes it possible to study and describe them in combinations rather than as separate and disconnected phenomena. This is also the principle behind the operation of slow violence disasters. Their effects locally destroy the environment but globally attach themselves to one another, thereby destroying the planetary system. The context of individual disasters produces health, social, and economic damage locally, but more broadly it is attached to many other smaller and larger environmental forms of violence. This agglomerative addition of successive disasters necessitates increasingly involved ways of monitoring and studying their effects. In "Thinking across Disaster," Kim Fortun and Alli Morgan note that "disasters are always unique, resulting from multiple failures (organizational, technological, educational, etc.), producing cascades of effects (ecological, biological, emotive, conceptual, etc.)—all forcefully shaped by context. Yet there are also patterns across disaster that when recognized can orient disaster mitigation, preparedness, immediate response, and long-term recovery. The Fukushima nuclear plant disaster is no exception. Its tragic unfolding has been both unique and illustrative of patterns that recur across disaster" (Fortun and Morgan 2015, 1).

Fortun and Morgan place the environmental disaster that occurred in Fukushima side by side with other industrial disasters that cause catastrophic consequences—such as the Chernobyl nuclear power plant explosion in Ukraine in 1986 and the Union Carbide pesticide plant disaster in Bhopal, India, in 1984 that released chemicals into the environment. The recurrent patterns of disasters also reveal their causes, which the authors define collectively. The disasters have an anthropogenic provenance and originate in the acceleration of industrial development, which the authors see as the prime cause of such phenomena in the modernized world. Because accelerated time is a compulsion of technocapitalist development, scant attention is paid to creating safeguards in the design of complex systems such as nuclear power plants or factories producing high-risk materials and substance. Disaster scenarios are not part of such systems, which has implications for the aftermath of such events. The rapid development of infrastructures does not inevitably include the design of appropriate safeguards. The lack of these designs in corporations and states reveals recurrent patterns of industrial disaster.

A similar situation occurred at Fukushima, where it was clear "that the promise of nuclear power as an energy source undercut recognition of associated risks. Hospitals and medical staff in Fukushima prefecture report being almost completely unprepared for disaster, for example. It was assumed that there would never be problems with the nuclear power plants in the region. Deeply institutionalized overconfidence in the safety of nuclear power in Japan was carried and exacerbated by Japan's media ecology" (Fortun and Morgan 2015, 56).

In March 2011, a huge earthquake struck the island of Honshu, Japan, and caused a tsunami that affected twenty different countries in the Pacific region, with most of the damage occurring in Japan (Coletti et al. 2017, 2). The devastation caused by the earthquake and tsunami caused the Fukushima Daiichi nuclear power plant to suffer a catastrophic level 7 nuclear accident, the highest rating on the International Nuclear and Radiological Event Scale (INES). The partial meltdown of the reactor cores resulted in substantial radiation being emitted into the atmosphere and the ocean (Coletti et al. 2017; Funabashi and Kitazawa 2012; Nakamura and Kikuchi 2011). As tsunamis and earthquakes in this part of the world are commonplace, numerous organizations recommended that power plant safeguards be constructed to meet high standards. As Patricia Swann writes, Tokyo Electric Power Co. (TEPCO), the corporation that constructed the nuclear power plant in 1971, was aware of potential disasters and yet disregarded the warnings:

> an internal report by Tokyo Electric Power Co. (TEPCO) in 2008 . . . suggested that a tsunami 10.2 meters high could damage the Fukushima plant. It was ignored. TEPCO had predicted Fukushima's reactors could withstand a tsunami height of 3.1 meters (10.2 feet) when the nuclear power station was built in 1971. This was later upgraded to a new maximum height of 5.7 meters (18.7 feet) in 2002. TEPCO ignored other simulations showing waves between 13.6 and 15.7 meters (44.6–51.5 feet) based on previous Japanese tsunamis because there had been no recorded tsunamis in the Fukushima location. In 2009, the Nuclear and Industrial Safety Agency (NISA) asked TEPCO to consider the Jogan earthquake of 869 AD, but because it had not occurred in the Fukushima area it was ignored. (Swann 2014, 612)

The tsunami that struck Fukushima was fourteen meters in height, and the plant's protective sea wall was designed to withstand a three-meter wave (Swann 2014, 611). Fortun and Morgan consider this type of negligence, which disregarded various negative scenarios at the design stage, to be critical for defining responsibility for the occurrence of industrial-based disasters. Most significant in terms of how the Fukushima disaster situation was handled, however, were the lack of preparation of medical infrastructure; the lack of clear evacuation procedures for the people living in the area; and the actions taken by TEPCO, the Japanese government, and the national media that created confusion about radiation levels in specific locations and generated fear and trauma. Fukushima reminded the Japanese of their ongoing fears that their nation would be attacked by a nuclear bomb. On the fifth day after the explosion, the journalist Keiji Takeuchi, in an article titled "Unprecedented Disaster Tests Resilience of Society," said that "Japan should have developed nuclear energy not only with pride in its advanced technology, but also with cautiousness as a nation hit by atomic bombs" (Swann 2014, 627).

For the first tens of hours after the tsunami hit, the Japanese government and TEPCO claimed that the disaster was causing little harm, which later proved untrue: "During the initial weeks of the disaster in particular, citizens were given little actionable information concerning actual radiation levels, and what was presented both by official spokespersons and in the media was often incomplete and/or contradictory" (Brown et al. 2016, 82). The absence of trustworthy information regarding the contamination and the ways that information was communicated to the public triggered another crisis as people grew anxious about potential radiation exposure. Their frustration and disillusionment with how the situation was being handled gave rise to a Japanese movement called "post-Fukushima DIY networks" (Abe 2014, 1). This was the largest nuclear disaster to occur in the internet era, and people quickly organized and began collecting data and information about radiation. They used their own Geiger counters for this purpose but did not always read them properly, and few were available in the weeks after the disaster. Another initiative was the creation of a website called Radio Monitor 311, where scientists summarized radiation monitoring (Abe 2014, 2). It was insufficient as a source of reliable data, however, because Japanese scientists were generating a different narrative about nuclear risks. One notorious example involved Yamashita Shunichi, a professor at Nagasaki University, who claimed in the media that nuclear radiation at Fukushima would not affect people who smiled (Abe 2014, 3). In this context, Yasuhito Abe writes that "contradictory information has thus been widely circulated via media and social media. As a result, Japanese citizens have been struggling to determine the most reliable information on nuclear radiation and what decisions they should take to protect their health and safety" (Abe 2014, 2). Out of this information chaos, a strong need for real data on radiation was born.

The Safecast group was founded on March 12, 2011, as a digital citizen science project to collect radiation measurement data at the grassroots level and share it online. At first, it was simply a website for uploading data, but it soon became clear that measurement equipment was needed to make the data reliable, confirmable, and socially shareable according to certain rules:

> At a group meeting in Tokyo on 17 April 2011, attended by experts in hardware and software design, radiation detection, communication, and development, a decision was made to rapidly develop and test a new type of mobile detector which could be attached to a vehicle and linked to GPS and a data logging system. The necessary features of a publicly available online database and map system for communicating the measurements openly to the public were also discussed. The need for an independent identity for this newly focused activity was recognized by all, and the group name "Safecast" was chosen at this time. (Brown et al. 2016, 83)

The group quickly developed an open-source device for collecting radiation data. The mobile radiation detector was in the shape of a bento lunch box and was called the Bento Geiger counter (or bGeigie, for short) (figure 3.1). The current version was based on the Arduino platform and fitted out with special modules and detectors. As this is an open technology, the users may buy complete sets or build the device following shared specifications. The software is also available in open access. The bGeigie device measures radiation levels in regular intervals of a few dozen seconds. Each readout is supplemented with metadata such as time stamp and GPS coordinates. All the data is recorded locally on a memory drive in

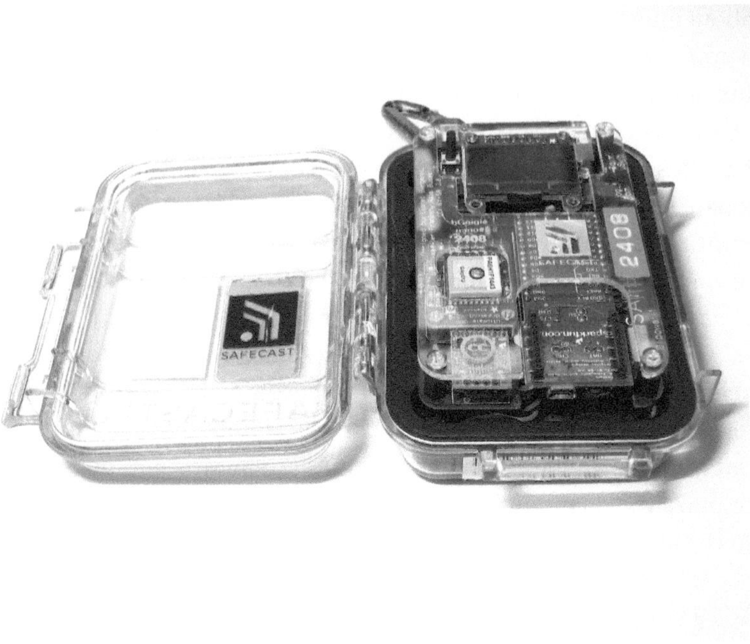

the device and may be automatically sent in real time to a central register. The data is uploaded to the Safecast database, and each user can verify the readouts, check errors, and add other metadata (such as explanations for mistakes).

The data collected by the bGeigie takes the form of a text or is presented directly on a digital map (readouts are localized on the basis of GPS metadata). Before the data is entered into the global database, it is subject to evaluation by the system administrator, who controls its correctness and verifies that no falsified readings are uploaded to the central register. The administrator can contact all users and clarify doubts. The data is collected by one type of device and by means of the same

3.1

bGeigie Nano. Photo by Jan Helebrant, CC BY-SA 2.0.

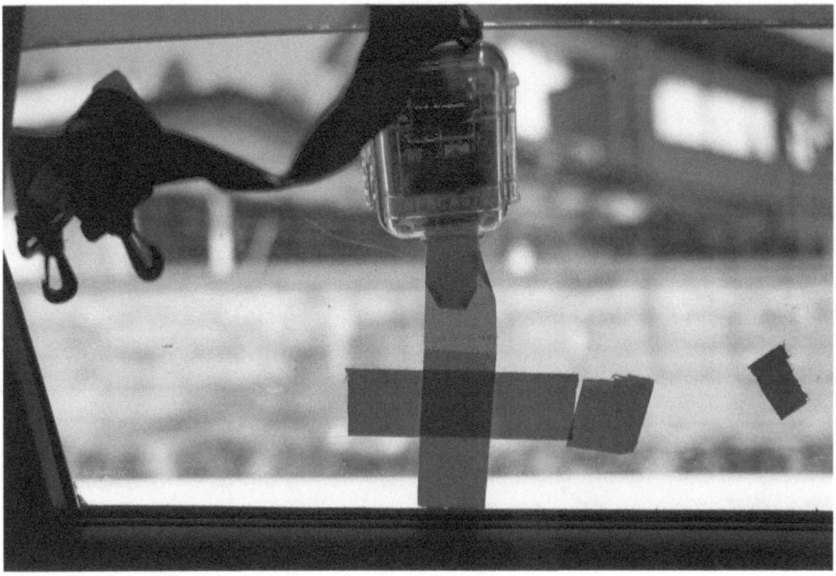

measurement sensors (the construction instructions are very detailed, and the same certified sensor is used for the measurement), so it can be aggregated and compared within a single database, which is later used to create a map showing the recorded changes in radiation levels in individual areas. These devices are portable. They are not stationary measuring instruments but small mobile sensors that help collect data from large areas (figure 3.2). By using this instrument, the crowdsource repository that was created as part of Safecast's media practices can provide high-quality scientific measurements. All data is subject to visualization and placement on a publicly accessible map. The map shows all the currently operational measurement sensors as well as the newest and past readouts (figure 3.3).

3.2

A bGeigie Nano attached to a car window.
Photo by Guido van Nispen, CC BY-SA 2.0.

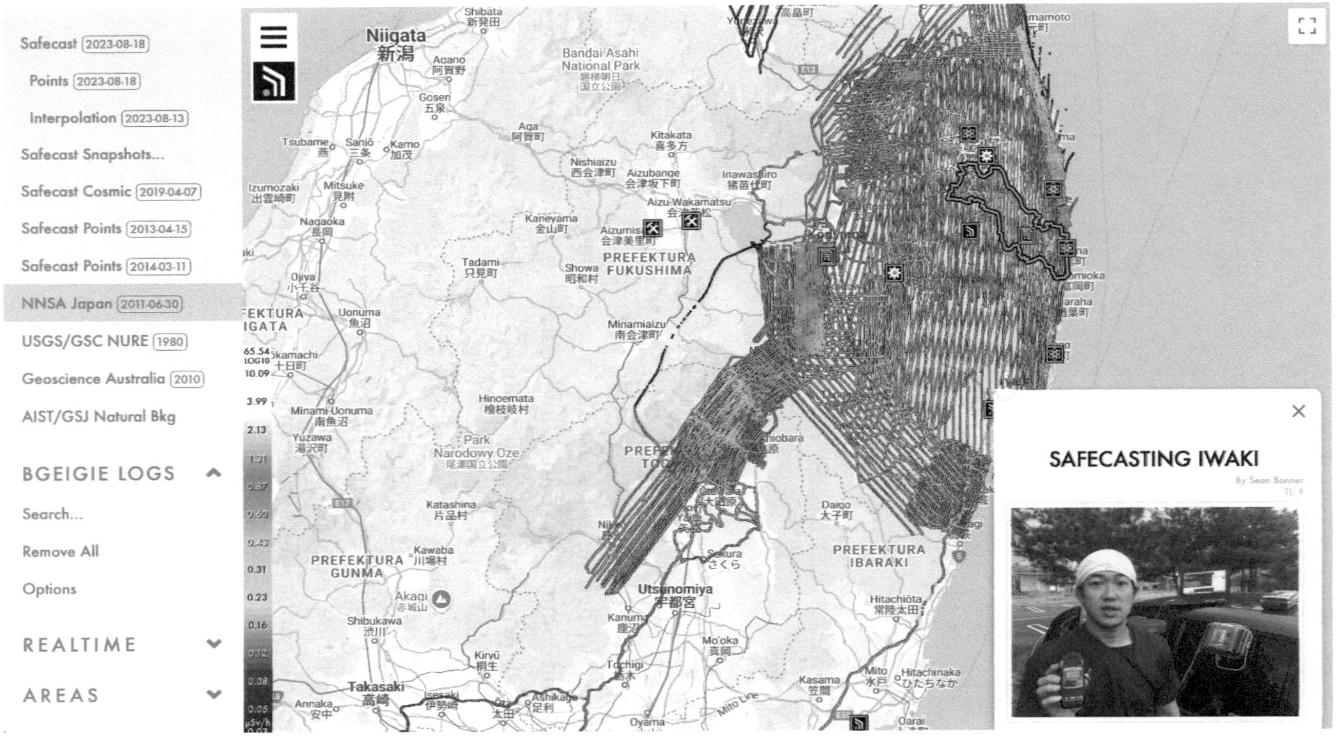
Safecast 2023-08-18
Points 2023-08-18
Interpolation 2023-08-13
Safecast Snapshots...
Safecast Cosmic 2019-04-07
Safecast Points 2013-04-15
Safecast Points 2014-03-11
NNSA Japan 2011-06-30
USGS/GSC NURE 1980
Geoscience Australia 2010
AIST/GSJ Natural Bkg
BGEIGIE LOGS
Search...
Remove All
Options
REALTIME
AREAS
Niigata 新潟
PREFEKTURA FUKUSHIMA
PREFEKTURA GUNMA
PREFEKTURA IBARAKI
Utsunomiya 宇都宮
Takasaki 高崎
Bandai Asahi National Park
SAFECASTING IWAKI
By Sean Bonner

Characteristic of Safecast is the creation of open structures of cooperation among volunteers. In addition, all data is published free of charge in the public domain, and the group designs devices as open technology that anyone can build at home. Safecast also holds numerous conferences, lectures, and workshops (including some for schoolchildren) to raise public awareness about radiation and teach people how to build sensors under their license. This transparency and the grassroots efforts of civilians who monitored their own environment after Fukushima were why, by February 2023, the radiation measurements collected through the Safecast project surpassed 200 million data points worldwide (Safecast 2023). In the same year, a team of social psychologists published the results of a study on the values and motivations of people who participated in digital citizen science projects. Some of the subjects were long-term Safecast volunteers. The study results indicated that "self-direction, stimulation, and achievement were important values to participants when joining Safecast. These were enhanced by a strong need for security and sense of benevolence, whilst conformity/tradition, universalism, and power were the least influential values to drive participation. . . . the value of hedonism (doing something because it is enjoyable) was not important at all at the time of joining Safecast" (Palacin et al. 2020, 10). This means that the unifying values behind such a broadly effective project were the open and transparent form of data collection and visualization and the participants' sense of social responsibility. The study reveals another crucial issue. Disasters such as the one that took place in Fukushima demonstrate a social need to build knowledge based on information-flow infrastructures other than those offered by governments, corporations, or national media. In this key moment, the expanding outreach of online communication platforms and social media is helping digital communities create spaces for data speculation. That is the significance of building counterinfrastructures

3.3

A Safecast radiation map showing a 2011 data visualization.

based on reliable data, creating open technologies used for downloading this data, and developing strategies used for administering data, visualizing data as situated, and following and commenting on it (Jelewska and Krawczak 2025, 100–110).

The reliability of the data collected by volunteers is yet another major question in the process of producing knowledge about radiation in different places on the planet. In 2017, an interdisciplinary team of researchers published an article titled "Validating Safecast Data by Comparisons to a U.S. Department of Energy Fukushima Prefecture Aerial Survey" in the *Journal of Environmental Radioactivity* (Coletti et al. 2017). The researchers compared Safecast-collected data with authoritative data collected by the United States Department of Energy (DOE) and the United States National Nuclear Security Administration (NNSA) in the Fukushima prefecture shortly after the Daiichi nuclear power plant catastrophe. Detailed analyses of the data show "that the two sets of observations were highly correlated, but that the DOE/NNSA measurements were somewhat higher. Nonetheless, despite the differences, we feel that the Safecast data is useful for public safety given that it identified similar regions of high radiation as did the DOE/NNSA" (Coletti et al. 2017, 7). This is one of few texts that analyze the validation of Safecast data in the context of highly technologically developed and equipped scientific and governmental organizations. The text points to the social and scientific value of the Safecast data and the reliability and appropriateness of the technological devices the group's volunteers used. Safecast data should be considered within the whole system of their positioning (Loukissas 2019). What matters is not only the data itself but also the formats of the measuring devices, the forms of administration and archiving, and the involvement of the participants. This comparison is an example of how a well-organized social initiative creates new models for knowledge acquisition.

These reliable and transparent counterinfrastructures have proved helpful to the affected communities and even to Japanese authorities. According to the research report of the social psychologists cited above, "Safecast is largely trusted by the population in Japan, which in turn has led to its use by the Japanese government as an official source for radiation measures. This level of trust was achieved by opening the entire process of radiation monitoring to everyone, from the recording of measures and data verification, to knowledge-sharing and the release of open data" (Palacin et al. 2020, 15).

Safecast has developed a model of digital citizen science that is much closer to the practices defined as "crowd science" (Franzoni and Sauermann 2014), "networked science," and "massively collaborative science" (Nielsen 2014; Wiggins and Crowston 2011) than to a classically defined citizen science that is seen as complementary to that produced by scholars. "Citizen science"—a term coined in the 1990s (Bonney 1996; Irwin 1995) even if rooted in earlier projects (Strasser et al. 2018)—"conveys both senses of the relationship between science and citizens" (Irwin 1995, xi). However, the relationship often remains hierarchical. The volunteers are included in the research mainly as those who acquire data that is later analyzed by researchers. In most cases where this practice is applied, the data is ultimately owned by scientists who publish research results, earn degrees, and share data at closed scientific conferences. The open science model developed by Safecast is different. It is based on collective intelligence in a hyperconnected world (Brown et al. 2016). In a September 2021 lecture for TEDxOgikubo, "The Future of Trust = Decentralized Data," Pieter Franken, one of Safecast's founders, emphasized the relevance, in today's post-truth world, of the activities of the group and the community as a whole for the recovery of data and, by extension, the creation and development of community knowledge about radiation. In doing so, they are decentralized (the "DeDa process," as Safecast's creators sometimes refer to it) and become a recovered force for building a knowledge-based community (Franken 2021).

The aim of such activities can be also observed in Jenifer Gabrys's Citizen Sense project, which creates open technologies for measuring environmental contamination, socializing research practices, and bridging the boundaries between traditional institutions of science, art, and culture (Gabrys 2019). Recalling the bygone directives of pragmatists such as William James, John Dewey, and Cornel West, Gabrys points to the need to link research practices to social and cultural processes by developing do-it-yourself sensors to measure various indicators of environmental violence. In this model, the design of research tools (essentially, experimental media) is a process of social sharing of research procedures and practices. Individuals, groups, and communities learn to construct the devices themselves, thus establishing a relationship and producing what John Dewey calls "communities of inquiry" (Gabrys 2019, 76–77). The processes of producing tools and procedures are linked to the processes of socioconstruction, by which technology begins to coexist and evolve with communities according to principles of internal coherence (Simondon 2017). Socializing research practices and instruments on a wider scale may help to change the cultural system that identifies separate areas for science, culture, and artistic practices: "Instruments are invariably involved with social relations. Any change to them . . . will also shift social conditions" (Gabrys 2019, 56). Therefore, a change in instruments is a transformation of the entire social theory that begins to produce new models of cultural human, technology, and environment interactions.

GRASSROOT MAPPING AS A SHARED WAY OF DEALING WITH CATASTROPHE

A similar shared and nonhierarchical approach to the creation of knowledge during a crisis is practiced by the Public Laboratory for Open Technology and Science (Public Lab). The group emerged out of the need to organize local communities to garner data on an ecological disaster that occurred from mid-April to mid-September 2010 in the Gulf of Mexico. It was the largest environmental and industrial disaster in history. An explosion on British Petroleum's Deepwater Horizon platform caused oil to leak into the waters of the Gulf of Mexico for eighty-seven days. The scale of the disaster was unprecedented and its environmental ramifications were irreversible (McNutt et al. 2012). According to official estimates, between 1,000 and 62,000 barrels of oil spilled into the ocean every day (McNutt et al. 2012). BP made the data public, and although some thought that BP attempted to conceal the massive scale of the catastrophe, it later was revealed that the company, even in internal classified correspondence, used estimates that were similar to those presented by the Flow Rate Technical Group, a team of scientists and engineers appointed by the US government to assess the disaster's consequences.

As Rob Nixon (2011) has written, the long-term effects of a disaster can be understood only if we consider its complex nature, the multifaceted harm is caused, and its environmental, social, economic, and cultural dimensions. Peter Kahn (2011), an American psychologist who works on issues of environmental harm, analyzes the factors that cause multigenerational trauma and harm in this regard. He considers the situation of "direct and indirect harm" and makes clear the differences between these states and also the possible combination of them in the case of borderline situations, such as environmental disasters or pandemic diseases (Kahn 2011, 198). Some situations—such as oil spills in the ocean, pollution of the seas with toxins and waste, and chemical contamination of rivers—have no definite time of impact. Due to the penetration of contaminants into the soil and organisms, their effects can last for many generations, changing the bio- and hydrospheres of the places where the contamination occurred as well as entire areas of the globe. When a disaster occurs, we are aware of the contamination, but we do not know how far-reaching its environmental consequences might be. In the scientific systems created for the analysis of such disasters, bodies of water—oceans, seas, rivers, and lakes—become mainly algorithmically modulated constructs based on big data analysis systems. The idea is to quickly monitor and prevent a possible recurrence. For human and nonhuman communities, the initial disaster triggers a long-term crisis and profound consequences that cannot be fully recognized with such tools.

After the Deepwater Horizon disaster, political and corporate actors manipulated the data to reassure and blunt the vigilance of the global public (Bradshaw 2012, 2015). Some of their behaviors—a lack of clear consequences for the BP corporation, the destruction of the environment and economy in the Gulf of Mexico, and the concealment of the scale and true measurement data of the disaster—also revealed the principles of the scientific system in the face of the mechanisms of the global corporate economy and national interests. The oil spill was extensive, disaggregated, and difficult to track as the oil spill moved in different directions. When BP and the media suggested that a quick return to normal conditions would be possible, environmental activists questioned this limited and constrained response to the disaster. They argued that this response neglected to consider how the oil residue would disrupt the seasonal and spatial movements of migrating marine mammals and fish, their reproductive cycles, and the stability of the ecosystem (Davies 2022).

The activists were rightly concerned. Ten years after the BP oil spill, the ecologist and environmental data researcher Joan Meiners (2020) wrote an article for the National Geographic website in which she quoted researchers who were involved in information gathering on the ground and who claimed that it was impossible to make an unequivocal determination of the devastation due to the complexity of the ecosystem:

> Eleven rig workers lost their lives. So did untold millions of marine mammals, sea turtles, birds, and fish. While the world watched, helpless, oil gushed into one of the planet's most biodiverse marine habitats for 87 long days. . . . A decade later, many species, such as deep-sea coral, common loons, and spotted sea trout, are still struggling, their populations lower than before. By contrast, a few Gulf inhabitants have shown a robust recovery—among them, menhaden fish and the brown pelican, Louisiana's state bird. Scientists say it's still too early to tell definitively what the impact has been for longer-lived species such as dolphins, whales, and sea turtles. (Meiners 2020)

All these elements sparked the emergence of new bottom-up information-gathering strategies. Local communities—not the big international players and governmental experts—began to carry out wide-ranging control and monitoring research to develop reliable knowledge concerning actual problems present in a specific place. Collective initiatives played an important role. Among them, Public Lab began to develop new methods and methodologies for community science. Members of Public Lab began to organize grassroots ways of acquiring oil-spill data at specific ocean sites. These researchers came primarily from the grassroot mapping movement, and they decided to share these experiences with local communities: "Grassroots Mapping, an early project of the Public Laboratory for Open Technology and Science, began in 2010 in Lima, Peru. Using balloons and kites to launch cameras as 'community satellites,' grassroots mappers around the world have engaged in local-level, activist remote sensing—building upon the critical cartography and participatory mapping movements to investigate local environmental and social issues with inexpensive 'Do-It-Yourself' technologies" (Breen et al. 2015, 850).

In the case of the 2010 Gulf of Mexico oil spill that sparked the creation of Public Lab, the research began with a collaboration between designers and researchers Stewart Long, Jeffrey Yoo Warren, and Oliver Yeh and community activist Shannon Dosemagen, from the Louisiana Bucket Brigade (LABB). LABB is an organization dedicated to monitoring the impact of the petrochemical industry on the local environment.[1] Since its inception, the Bucket Brigade has used distributed leadership and developed an individual research approach based on scientific foundations and the collective production of new methods and tools to handle the problem at hand with community involvement.

Community-based participatory research (CBPR) has been used for a few decades, but Public Lab relies heavily on the active participation of local communities in research and in the cocreation of tools and measurement instruments through simple prototyping and do-it-yourself methods. Another important element that has been developed via researching the effects of the Gulf of Mexico disaster is the self-determination of communities to own their research data and thus to participate in the system of knowledge circulation and production. The BP disaster revealed deep inequalities in access to data and the capacity of affected communities to analyze it. By becoming culturally authoritative and reliable, data can inspire trust among people in the local community. To become a social practice, knowledge requires a system of trust. The mechanisms for spreading knowledge are more effective in smaller fields of manipulation and in groups where the people themselves pass information among themselves—in small groups, during debates, in discussions, in conversations with family members and groups of friends—rather than in top-down science and education management systems (Breen et al. 2015).

After the BP disaster in the Gulf of Mexico, low-cost and locally producible methods and techniques were used to monitor and document the state of pollution as well as water and shoreline contamination. All photographic documentation capturing the state of the water and shoreline was done with the aid of weather balloons and kites, which carried cameras mounted in stabilizing structures made from used plastic cans (figure 3.4). These simple devices helped take terrain photographs that bridged the important gap between ground-based observations and satellite imagery.

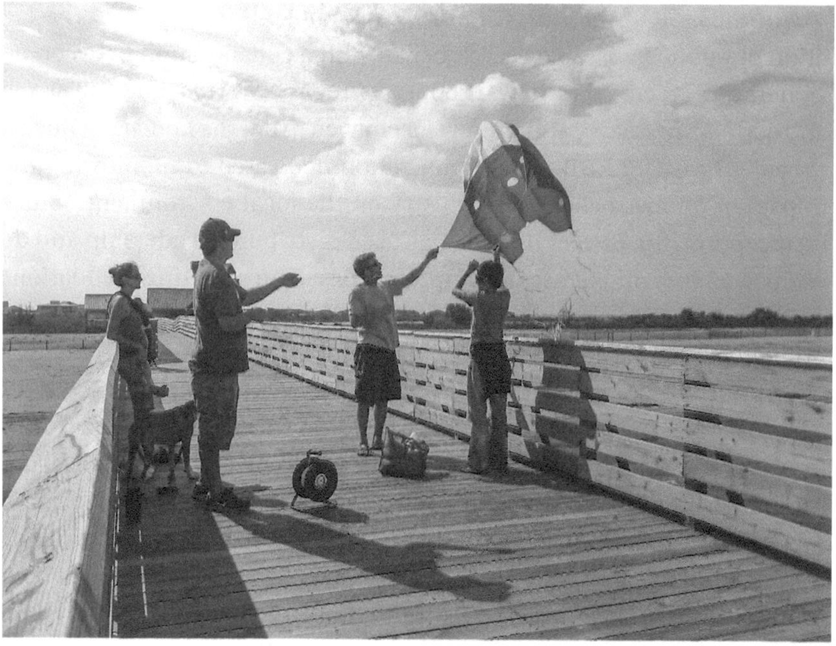

The resolution of photographs taken from a height of between 60 and 450 meters above water level, for example, helped to identify vegetation, schools of fish, and individual bird specimens. After many months of monitoring, the data showed evidence of the scale of the oil pollution in the bay and its effects on the environmental degradation taking place over specific time periods.

To acquire sufficient visual material of adequate quality, Public Lab organized workshops and training for volunteers who learned to use grassroot mapping techniques, to control balloons and kites, and to adapt equipment to meteorological conditions. The quality of the photographs

3.4

Kite mapping the oil spill at Grand Isle State Park, Louisiana. Photo by Jeff Warren, CC BY-SA 2.0.

that could be obtained using balloons was far greater than the quality of satellite images, due to resolution. The smaller the element, the more difficult it is to record it via a satellite (Kurgan 2013):

> While the rise of free online satellite imagery services like Google Maps has made access to imagery commonplace, the relatively low resolution and lack of control over *when* images are collected has limited the degree to which such maps may be used to capture specific time-situated narratives. While it is impressive that one can view 1 meter imagery (where each pixel represents 1 square meter of the earth's surface) of many urban areas, many parts of the world are represented only in out-of-date imagery at poorer resolutions, where individual roads and buildings are hard to see, let alone people. Balloon and kite mapping have allowed practitioners to choose not only a place to describe through photographs, but a moment in time to capture events unfolding, such as a protest or a chemical spill. (Breen et al. 2015, 852–853)

One method of data sharing was the creation of open maps that included all the information collected during the study. Public Lab's mapping practice has a laboratory and collaborative dimension, with maps being created from prepared documentary photographs of the area. In the case of the Gulf of Mexico disaster, individual photographs were stitched "manually" by means of graphic processing software. The stitched photographs were combined into a single large image, which helped observers detect significant elements and changes in entire coastlines or larger areas of land. The maps were supplemented with additional information and comments and were made available to members of the community, who could make further use of them.

In the years that followed the 2010 BP oil spill, Public Lab developed the "stitching" technique, and it is now possible for people to create maps without having specialized skills in using graphics software. The maps are created in the Map Knitter software environment, which is available as a free web-based platform allowing for collective work, map creation, information sharing, and peer commenting (figure 3.5). These practices, launched to examine the consequences of the Deepwater Horizon spill, "represented a break from the primarily Cartesian, or vector-based representations of space, in favor of raster photographic imagery, as in remote

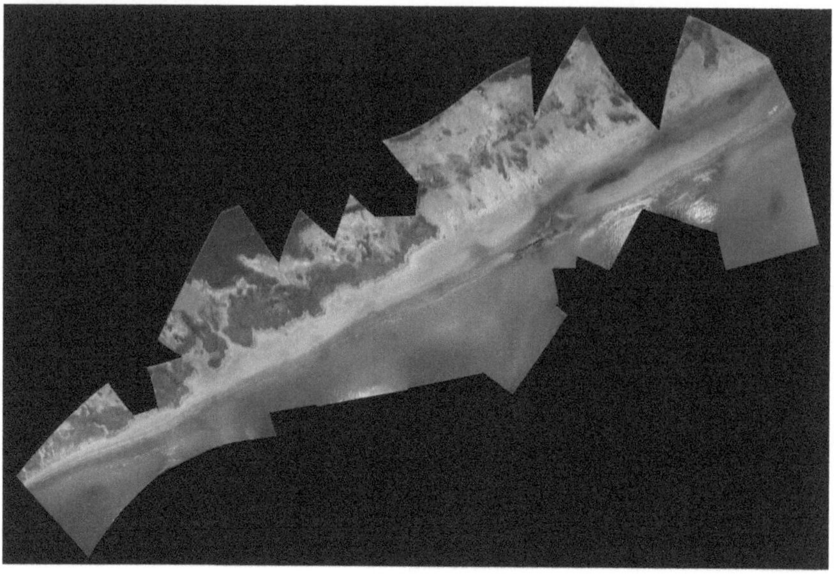

sensing. . . . Grassroots Mapping has sought to challenge the idea that raster mapping is a more objective way to describe a geography" (Breen et al. 2015, 852). Because this type of map tries to situate mapping with aerial photography as a narrative or journalistic tool, it was also important to find ways of "narrating" these maps, analyzing their data, and developing them within a transparent methodology. At the same time, meetings and discussions were held with the local community. In the long term, these activities helped gather people who wished to be involved in grassroot mapping and organize an independent infrastructure for the research process (logistics, technical facilities, and information exchange). Thanks to sustained commitment and continuous work with local volunteers who

3.5

A "stitched" pollution map with photos of oil patches at the coast of Grand Isle, Louisiana. Photo by Stewart Long, CC BY 2.0.

had a vested interest in the issue at hand, it was possible to continue the research in the long term.

As members of Public Lab point out, the initial enthusiasm in the group wears off over time during the first stage of the work. Overcoming this lapse is essential for sustainable long-term research (Warren 2010). Furthermore, embedding the research process in the local community enables an in-depth analysis of the situation of cultural trauma and ecosystem damage. In this case, the damage had long-term effects and harmed a specific social group, the members of a South Asian minority of Vietnamese origin who made a living from fisheries and shrimp businesses.[2]

In addition to the collection of data on pollution and the extent of the environmental disaster, social data collection began. The digital reporting system was based on the Usahahidi platform,[3] which allowed participants to send information (including audio recordings and mobile text messages). The system greatly extended crowdsourcing research, which continued with interviews that provided detailed information from those directly affected by the disaster. As Shannon Dosemagen and Jeffrey Yoo Warren wrote in the entry "Leftovers" on the Public Lab website in 2011:

> In contrast to the typical model of harvesting data from communities, our approach . . . is to commoditize the expertise, and the experts, rather than the public. Instead of a scientist culling data from a sea of participants, we hope to create tools and a platform that will allow independent groups to gather, interpret and discuss the results of their work based not only on the use of scientific data. We are also intent on building a community and a culture of critical inquiry, and to emphasize the intimate awareness of one's environment brought by local community inhabitants. The desire to bridge the divide between the "experts" and local communities is one that came to the forefront in the above example of the BP Oil Spill, by residents that sought (then and now) to conduct their own discussion of spill impacts. (Dosemagen and Warren 2011, n.p.)

As the contamination spread, the authorities began to restrict access to the contaminated areas, fencing them off and placing guards, and the result was a media blackout. The intent was to nullify the presence of images documenting the disaster in the public media space and limit discussion of the issue. Attempts to ban access to the disaster sites and the possibilities for documenting it were perceived by the local community as efforts to discriminate, exclude, ration access to information, and manipulate the economic future of the community. A group of local fishermen became involved in the activities organized by Public Lab, which allowed those mapping the contamination to have access to closed areas. The fishermen began to lend their boats and organize documentation cruises. These interactions helped researchers collect and secure visual footage that the mainstream media did not possess. Mainstream media outlets therefore began to ask the community to provide material on pollution levels. This later became a major argument for the idea that the local community should always be a co-owner of the research material acquired, regardless of what kind of data it is. Over time, it becomes an important element of the media and communitywide debate in which local people must have a say.

Public Lab's approach to radical openness realizes that data belong to communities and requires it to pursue a form of working with digital data that Loukissas (2019) calls "data curation" (from the Latin *cura*, meaning "care"). Curation is impossible without extensive ethnographic fieldwork, which situates digital data in a local context of workshops, meetings, and open debates. This helps to develop a data curation project that involves "imagining how data might be seen in new ways, using speculative yet nevertheless locally imagined modes of visualization" (Loukissas 2019, 8). However, such an approach may "create communities around data, as one should approach keepers and subjects first, by engaging them in a process of participation, not after the project is complete, at which time all we can do is conduct an anodyne evaluation" (Loukissas 2019, 186).

In its projects, Public Lab develops and redefines methods of community science. Its research into the effects of the environmental catastrophe in the Gulf of Mexico also laid the foundations of its interspecies research methodology, which included both the ocean (which was perceived not as an abstract entity but as a set of selected contaminated areas that needed to be reidentified and monitored) and local communities (not as recipients of expert data or objects of research but as coresearchers who were contributing their experience and knowledge). Involving people in the entire data lifecycle means "that individuals don't just enter a project at the stage of collecting data for a preconceived research project. Beyond those initial activities, they are empowered to become active and involved collaborators at every step of the process from problem identification and engaging with hardware and software tool creation (as collaborators) to further data collection, analysis and localized instances of advocacy" (Breen et al. 2015, 851).

WHO CONTROLS THE POSTCOLONIAL MAPS?

Defending the environment in various places around the world and collecting data on its devastation can involve loss of health and life. As research shows, this process has intensified over the past dozen or so years. According to the Global Witness report, "the process of climate breakdown is violent, and it manifests not just in violence against the natural world, but against people as well" (Global Witness 2021, 15). Between 2012 and 2020, 1,540 land and environmental defenders were killed. Data gathered by Global Witness on the basis of monitoring and open-source investigations show that in 2012, 139 people died; in 2020, the death toll was as high as 228. Most lost their lives in Central and South America; 70 percent of the victims were working to defend the world's forests from deforestation and industrial development. In 2020, all but one of the 228 recorded killings of defenders took place in the countries of the global south. More than a third of deaths are of indigenous people, even though indigenous communities make up only 5 percent of the world's population (Global Witness 2021).

These deaths can also be seen as an effect of a global ecological disaster that brings together corporate capital and covert colonialism. The direct result of this entanglement is the degradation and devastation of the environment and the deaths of the human beings who cocreated these environments. The Anthropocene—as an era of human impact on the environment and a political and economic coupling—was founded on an extractive model that pairs those who colonize and those who have been colonized (Yusoff 2018). These processes have been ongoing since the first European conquests in the fifteenth century. They now contribute to the progressive destruction of the planetary ecosystem, the depletion of green spaces, and the intimidation of those who protest against environmental exploitation, displacement, and degradation. The actions of these processes reveal what is still insufficiently present in public discourse—the coupling of industrialization and exploitative use of natural resources with direct violence against people. In the introduction to the 2021 Global Witness report, on the basis of which we cited above the figures for the killings of environmental defenders, Bill McKibben writes:

> Strong local people, attached to place and community, seeing their role in defending terrain or ancestral territory. Every person like this around the world is at risk. And they are at risk, in the end, not just because of another local person who pulls the trigger or plunges the blade; they're at risk because they find themselves living on or near something that some corporation is demanding. That demand—the demand for the highest possible profit, the quickest possible timeline, the cheapest possible operation. . . . colonialism is still running strong, even if it's dressed up with corporate logos or hidden with offshore bank accounts. (Global Witness 2021, 7)

As we try to show in this chapter, indigenous communities, by using the collective practices of data resistance, are an obstacle to the exploitative directives of many modern corporations. They are also the embryo of a new social force that has the potential to deconstruct the foundations on which these industries have built their power and global position. These practices, which are centered on data collection and analysis, are gaining relevance in the fight against corporate violence against groups, communities, and the environment.

To legitimize their extractive actions, global corporations use arguments of power (embedded in politics and capital) and top-down data collection (such as strategically crafted development forecasts, geological data, and satellite imagery). Corporations aggregate these methods within a common geographic information system (GIS) and often build their "expression of power" by subordinating and using the data for their own benefit. It is a very old technique. It is worth recalling that until the sixteenth century, the meaning of the word *discover* (from the medieval French *descovrir*, based on the medieval Latin *discooperire*) was "to remove the veil from an object or subject" rather than "to learn something new and unforeseen." When Renaissance Europeans began to speak of a discovery (*une découverte* or *un descumbrimiento*), they linked it to uncovering something or to finding something to emphasize their possession of the earth. This was done primarily by constantly redrawing maps. Through their expanded maps, colonizers annexed new territories and people. Maps announced the seizure and possession of new territories and the establishment of new legal rules for human life over nonhuman life. They were treated as universal tools for securing what had been revealed and what was already in the possession of the people who worked with the territory, object, or species that was shown on the map. Maps were treated as political land ledgers. They legitimized the use of other means to subjugate, maintain, terrorize, exterminate, enslave, and resettle people, biological resources, and mineral deposits of given areas.

Present-day forms of violence against humans and the environment are changing, and their strategies may not be easy to prove to the general public, especially if violence was earlier recorded on maps in consultation and agreement with multiple agencies and central authorities. Such kinds of violence have triggered resistance based on grassroot practices and participatory mapping in Central America, South America, and Indonesia at least since the 1990s (Paneque-Gálvez et al. 2017). Over the last decade, these practices acquired new technological tools and computer software that, from the perspective of media and environmental studies, ushered in major cultural transformations. Media practices of the local communities in the Amazon and in Indonesia are collectively known as *indigenous digital mapping*.

Bottom-up mapping practices carried out by volunteer environmental defenders are important for marking places that are remote from central authorities and difficult to access and where little data is collected *in situ*. They counter the planning models of capitalism and have the potential to produce decolonized maps that invert the hierarchies of cartographic representation. Instead of classifying, identifying, valuing, and containing an implicit plan of expansion and exploitation, they can express local cultural practices linked to relationships with the environment. But "if mapping by the state is enthused with categorizing power connected to the representation and production of space, then so too must the counter-mapping movement ask who controls the production of these counter-maps, who fills them with meaning, and how mapping technology and activities change relations of power, gender and knowledge production within the participating community" (Radjawali and Pye 2017, 25). Collaborative, community-based practices of indigenous digital mapping have more in common with critical cartographic projects (such as those proposed by scholars Rob Kitchin and Martin Dodge in their 2007 article "Rethinking Maps") than with maps as terrain representations. In this case, mapping is a set of "spatial practices enacted to solve relational problems," and the map itself is an unstable form that "emerges through practices and has no secure ontological status" (Kitchin and Dodge 2007, 331). Here we invoke agglomerative processes of countermapping and countercartography that link a local community (in its social, cultural, political, and economic relations) with its environment and ecosystem. More broadly, the phenomenon is also a form of knowledge production. It takes place from the bottom up as part of the redefinition of a fixed knowledge system.

By pursuing a meta-approach, indigenous digital mapping simultaneously does not negate the existing standards of map construction. Cartography is not attacked here from the position of critical theories, but it is exposed and decolonized from within by the creation of its own scientifically correct digital maps based on transparent data-acquisition practices. Indigenous mapping thus situates itself in a field of action in which "the mapping process itself becomes a site of politics" (Herb et al. 2009, 339). The collaborative *in situ* practices that were conducted in the Amazon and in the forests of Indonesia are examples of the practical decolonization of white cartography and the creation of activist and militant cartographies (Herb et al. 2009) that targeted contemporary forms of slavery and colonization. Militant cartography is a concept coined by social geographer Sebastian Cobarrubias and anthropologist Maribel Casas-Cortes and originates in activist cartography (Herb et al. 2009). They call for new tools, infrastructures, and media practices of data resistance. In the 2010s, solutions arose that defied exploitative corporate policies in unprecedented ways. Community collaborative practices, data collection, and the production of digital maps became forms of local resistance and began to be seen as a kind of last-frontier defense that could delay the effects of a planetary disaster.

DRONE SCHOOLS AND "WEAPON OF THE WEAKS"

The Indonesian province of West Kalimantan in the island of Borneo continues to be one of the few heavily forested places on the planet. Historically, the area was of agricultural importance to local communities. Timber was the staple of the economy, followed by land cultivation and fishing. It has a complex history and currently is inhabited by several ethnic groups, including Dayaks, Madurese, and Chinese. Rural sociologist Nancy Lee Peluso highlights the profound racialization and political transformations that occurred in the eighteenth and nineteenth centuries under Dutch colonial rule, which began in the early seventeenth century. The Dutch introduced top-down divisive ethnic categories for local communities that served as a policy of control and surveillance (Peluso 2008). One executive tool of this control was to incite and initiate communal violence between different ethnic groups. Peluso observes that recurrent episodes of ethnic violence

> helped naturalize and harden categories of ethnic difference. . . . Ethnic difference was constructed—and lived—through government policies, colonial and contemporary law, through integration into a post-colonial national state, as well as through . . . explicit efforts to revitalise and reconfigure "culture." Because ethnicity or "race" was the basis by which territory, authority, and land rights were allocated under Dutch colonial legal pluralism, territory and ethnicity had become conjoined in new and unprecedented ways, most importantly in the ways individuals were allowed access to land or governed. (Peluso 2008, 56)

Forms of ethnic violence embedded in the colonial model of exploitation and politics survived Indonesia's twentieth-century independence processes and continue to be a problem in Kalimantan today. The activist geographers Oliver Pye and Irendra Radjawali note that contemporary Indonesian government institutions continue to persist in the colonial model of land governance. Government agencies "that exert territorial control, in particular the Ministry of Forestry and the administrations of the national parks, have inherited state-colonial mindsets and ways of working" (Pye and Radjawali 2017, 387). In recent years, these agencies have allocated licenses to multinational corporations to use land for operating mines or industrial oil palm plantations. The central government granted licenses for resource exploitation and industrial plantations on the basis of the companies' land-use plans, which failed to acknowledge the forms of ownership and use of these lands by indigenous communities. The territorial scope of such activities was established top-down on the basis of a geographic map, with no checks and balances on the ground to determine that the map realistically represented the territorial reality and what the consequences of these activities would be for the local ecosphere. The issue of modern land grabbing must be embedded within the intertwining of these contexts (Radjawali and Pye 2017)—the historical context (the colonial powers' taking of lands occupied by indigenous people and inciting of ethnic violence) and the postcolonial context (the contemporary ecological degradation executed by powerful global corporations).

In the 1980s and 1990s, a rapid expansion of the extraction and plantation industry brought about irreversible transformations in the region's economic, geographic, ethnic, and cultural landscapes. These changes are occurring through industrial cultivation of oil palms, expansion of gold mine sites and particularly damaging bauxite mines, and deforestation. Affecting both ecology and economics, they are an undercurrent force responsible for fueling new ethnic tensions. These industries are extremely hazardous to the environment. In addition to devasting green spaces, they contaminate river waters, which sustain the region's socioeconomic development. Their toxicity disrupts traditional methods of land cultivation and fishing and prevents the development of ecological tourism that was planned by the region's residents. Working at the nexus of all these issues, Irendra Radjawali, a scientist-activist from Indonesia, uses drones as tools of data resistance and as a way to construct digital indigenous maps ("militant maps"). Radjawali has been using drones in his research and practice since 2012 and first turned to drone images while collecting data on the pollution of the Kapuas River in West Kalimantan. His goal was to study the impacts and ecological transformations occurring due to "fossil fuel-based capitalism . . . , a growth model based on extractivism" (Pye and Radjawali 2017, 379). Understanding the transformation of the river's ecosystem involved recognizing the infrastructural, economic, and cultural relationships that existed between the Kapuas River and the people living around it. In his original research methodology, Radjawali proposed integrating scientific and activist activities that collected, compiled, and shared data for environmental justice and the rights of indigenous people. At stake in this process are the rights to community property, territorial unity, ecological development and annexation, and technological solutions relevant to the protection of these rights. Radjawali's approach challenges the long-established western type of researchers who distance themselves from the research problem by making a broad analysis "from the outside." Considering the rapid pace of ecological transformation under the shortsighted extractive economics, Radjawali is more concerned with "arming" local communities with scientific and political "weapons" so that, with the help of independently collected data, they can make analyses and assess the risks and consequences of actions by embedding them in a broader ecological context. In this way, the illegal actions of corporations that carry out deforestation or unjustified exploitation of natural resources begin to be seen as interfering with the rights of local communities, as threatening the larger community, and as fueling the global environmental crisis.

The Dayak people are one of the ethnic groups subjected to institutional and exploitative violence by corporate industry in the Kapuas River region of West Kalimantan. The land traditionally cultivated by Dayaks is subject to corporate land grabbing because some of the villages and lands cultivated and exploited by Dayak communities do not appear on official government maps, on the basis of which land-use plans are made. At the scale the official maps are made, Radjawali points out, only forests are visible on the state map. The goal of the defense may therefore be to create precise alternative maps that can be used legally to claim indigenous rights (figure 3.6). If the maps produced by local communities are to become part of scientific and legal arguments, they must be prepared at a much higher resolution and in a way that allows them to be incorporated into official maps of Indonesian lands. Drones have proven to be handy tools for acquiring terrain images and creating maps from them.

Mapmaking always begins with the reconstruction of important historical and cultural contexts. Radjawali and Pye call this "place biography narratives" (Radjawali and Pye 2017, 20). Group debates, field trips, and "spatial problem analysis" help reconstruct key problems, the history of ecological transformations, and forms of the inhabitants' relations with

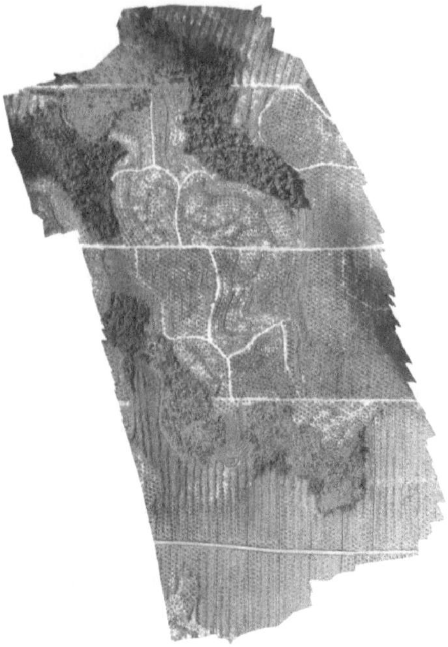

the environment. This method helps to situate the digital map and the digital data close to material objects. Maps are "developed from the biographies and perspectives of the local activists themselves" (Radjawali and Pye 2017, 22). According to this perspective, the perception of space itself changes, too. It is not just an area described via specific geographic qualifiers but is a multidimensional place with social, political, economic, cultural, and ecological contexts.

The next step is to establish "drone communities" that collect data, produce maps, and later carry out monitoring, service the devices, update

3.6

A drone-produced orthophoto shows palm oil planted on local farmland, rubber gardens, and customary forest in West Kalimantan. Irendra Radjawali and Oliver Pye, CC BY SA 3.0.

the data, and transfer their skills to others through educational activities. If local communities are to benefit from such a drone solution in the long term, costs must be reduced, and service facilities must be provided to repair drones on site. For this reason, Radjawali designed the drones. The do-it-yourself approach significantly reduced the cost of building and servicing the equipment, influenced the skills development of local communities, and ensured that local people could control and shape the development of the project. Open-source software is used to manage and plan drone flights and stitch maps from digital photographs. To disseminate the collaborative media practices, Radjawali's team created a "drone school in order to train locals how to fly the drone and how to use the software to stitch the orthophotographs together" (Radjawali and Pye 2017, 23). In referring to the function of drones in creating digital indigenous maps, Radjawali and Pye say that "in a world where corporate land grabbing is leading to land conflicts and environmental destruction in the Global South, we expect that drones will increasingly become a 'weapon of the weaks' to fight for a more just and inclusive spatial planning" (Radjawali and Pye 2017, 25).

The importance of the projects initiated by Radjawali and carried out using reweaponized drones as scientific instruments is best illustrated by the fact that in 2014, for the first time, digital maps that were prepared by indigenous communities were used in an Indonesian court in a case against the aggressive activities of extraction corporations. The Constitutional Court of Indonesia accepted the maps prepared by local activists and admitted them as evidence in court proceedings. Since then, the activities of corporations involved in oil palm plantations and bauxite mines have been legally reviewed. Some of them, due to proven license violations, have had their contracts terminated and been banned from operating in the country (Radjawali and Pye 2017, 24).

THE AMAZONIZATION OF TECHNOLOGY

For millennia, the indigenous people of the Amazon have independently dealt with forest conservation, sustainable forms of cultivation, and the management of logging. These processes have been shaped over hundreds of years in relation to locally changing ecological conditions (Paneque-Gálvez et al. 2018; Posey 1985) and helped develop multiple unique systems of local agriculture, hydroculture, and biodiversity conservation. In traditional communities, coexistence with a surrounding biological system reflects intertwined material culture (forest culture) and nontangible culture (traditional forms of knowledge and cosmology) (Paneque-Gálvez et al. 2018). These inseparable elements—material culture, intangible culture, cultivation, management, protection, forms of local beliefs, and a value system—make up traditional ecological knowledge (TEK) (Posey and Balick 2006). A set of radically situated diverse practices and forms of knowledge production codetermines the ecological quality of a particular place.

Western perceptions of traditional ecological knowledge are often marked by xenophobic stereotypes. As ethnobiologist Darrel A. Posey writes in the introduction to the edited book *Human Impacts on Amazonia: The Role of Traditional Ecological Knowledge in Conservation and Development* (Posey and Balick 2006), the cultural visions ingrained in the colonial European imagination neutralize traditional forms of ecological knowledge and practices. The objective is supported by cultural falsifications carried out by colonization and modern extractive capitalism: "indigenous and traditional peoples have been treated as 'backward and primitive,' and as such are viewed as barriers to development and modernization. Those attitudes fuel and justify policies that strip native Amazonians of their lands, territories, and resources—all in the name of development, progress, and conservation. Scientists, too, continue to believe that traditional knowledge is mere folklore; this in turn leads to the replacement of local-knowledge specialists and leaders with alien scientific and technical 'experts'" (Posey and Balick 2006, xii).

The founding myth that justified subjecting indigenous peoples to cultural practices of subjugation and control required manufacturing a fictional identity that corresponded to the visions of European explorers and their narratives legitimizing colonial violence. The identity of the "noble savage" imposed by them resulted from romanticizing projections and implementation of European fantasies fueled by the art and literature of the time (Hemming 2006). As ethnobiologist John Hemming notes, "Such visions of indigenous peoples may have been exaggerated and inaccurate, but they contained a powerful political message" (2008, 9). This kind of political agenda underlay the land grabbing, slavery, and violence practiced during colonial expansion.

The identity of indigenous communities was not the only element subject to deliberate cultural annihilation. A category of "tropical nature" was imposed within which "tropical has been positioned as an area of pure nature, as opposed to one of culture and history" (Stepan 2006, 17). It allowed settlers' discourses to strip Amazonia of its cultural, ethnic, biological, and historical continuity. In fact, Amazonia was not recognized but discovered by those who had long assumed its existence. Its possession was merely the execution of a vision of development written in plans and on maps. The tropics with their material objects, therefore, were invented as a landscape. They were not something to be known but something to be fitted into the projected image.

Analyzing the visual forms of colonial representations of material objects of the tropics, anthropologist Nancy Leys Stepan (2001) writes that there are no pure forms of visual representation. Even scientific forms of graphic representations are unconsciously embedded in cultural projections. Stepan argues that "history shows us that there is no single map or picture of the natural world that increasing knowledge progressively fills in, but rather many different maps and representations, articulated and shaped by numerous factors of politics, culture and aesthetics, by beliefs about reality, codes of seeing and representational conventions. Even the most scientific of our pictures of natural objects are not a matter of a simple transfer of perceptions into representations" (Stepan 2001, 14).

In recent decades, recovering these representations and local identities has been part of a strategy to decolonize maps of Amazonian territories. In the 2010s, attempts were made to deconstruct stereotypical cultural visions of the Amazon and to restore many aspects of traditional ecological knowledge. Media practices have used drones to create digital maps developed *in situ* by indigenous Amazonian communities and to amalgamate grassroots data (scientific, cultural, and cosmological) that contribute to traditional ecological knowledge with visual representations of the land and natural objects. The practices described in the following section of this chapter—which environmental geographer and ethnoecologist Jaime Paneque-Gálvez calls the "Amazonization of technology" (Paneque-Gálvez et al. 2018)—are forms of practice-based decolonization and functional counterinfrastructure within which traditional knowledge systems are integrated into a broader system of scientific information exchange. They become an important strategy of data resistance and a political argument against land grabbing and top-down ways of protecting nature and using land and its resources in new forms of "green grabbing" (Fairhead et al. 2012).

Between 2014 and 2016, pilot projects were carried out in South America using simple technologies—such as unmanned aerial devices (UADs) with video cameras, satellite imagery, and GPS locators—to monitor Amazon forest areas for illegal deforestation and ecological degradation in areas inhabited by indigenous people. Pilot programs conducted by various groups—Rainforest Foundation US, Digital Democracy in collaboration with indigenous organizations such as the Interethnic Association for the Development of the Peruvian Rainforest (Asociación Interétnica de Desarrollo de la Selva Peruana) (AIDESEP), and Coordinator of Indigenous Organizations of the Amazon River Basin (Coordinadora de las Organizaciones Indígenas de la Cuenca Amazónica) (COICA)—were carried out in the Peruvian Amazon in areas inhabited by the Kukama Kukamiria (2014) and Harakmbut (2015), in the Rupununi region of Guyana inhabited by the Wapichana and Makushi (2014 and 2016), and in the Emberá-Wounaan region of Panama inhabited by the Emberá-Wounaan (2015).

These activities were initiated by local communities and included workshops on the use, maintenance, and repair of small drones; techniques for constructing simple drones using do-it-yourself methods, for mapping the area using video cameras installed on drones, and for using simple geographic information systems to create and supplement digital maps with acquired data and photographs; and the organization of an information and communications technology (ICT) system for alerting people to deforestation, illegal plantations, cattle ranching, oil and gas extraction, and environmental pollution. Some deforestation has been carried out by drug cartels that seek space in remote corners of the Amazon forest to establish illegal coca plantations. Because it can be dangerous to monitor the forest and communities face threats and direct kinds of violence, forms of systemic support are indispensable. This is what indigenous Amazonians are seeking by acquiring data together, designing collaborative media practices, and networking to share experiences.

Drones are much more effective than kites or balloons in surveilling large areas of land in the Amazon forest. Balloons and kites are not suitable for this type of task, and controlling them in a terrain with a dense forest cover is difficult. It is also necessary to adjust the technology to local contexts and conditions. Every time, in every community, and in every area, researchers need to "Amazonize drone technology so that it can become truly useful in such a socially and environmentally challenging context" (Paneque-Gálvez et al. 2017, 16). The process of Amazonization cannot be designed remotely. Only *in situ* experiments and practice can help researchers generate conclusions about constraints and adaptations of technical solutions to local conditions.

Amazonization also means taking into account the lack of infrastructure (such as electricity, cellular coverage, and the internet) in many heavily forested areas. It is necessary to adapt technology to the prevailing conditions and to create counterinfrastructures (in cooperation with organizations, universities, independent researchers, and other communities) to ensure that projects are sustainable and feasible. In this case, collaborative media practices are the essence of functionality. So a major part of the media practices of resilience is to develop technology prototypes in a local context without standardizing and universalizing practices. Through "the acquisition of new data, knowledge and skills from the utilization of drones in indigenous communities, together with the collaboration of cross-scalar allies . . . have the potential to play a key role in empowering disempowered indigenous communities toward achieving greater levels of territorial protection and justice" (Paneque-Gálvez et al. 2017, 15–16).

Creating grassroots media infrastructures also means sharing digital tools with even the smallest indigenous communities. Jaime Paneque-Gálvez, a workshop moderator in the Amazon communities, observes that many participants in the workshops "had smartphones and laptops, and were active users of social networks such as Facebook, a situation that is increasingly common even in isolated communities in the Amazon basin. Moreover, digital tools have progressively been adopted for conservation tasks, including community-based monitoring. Therefore, communities that are becoming involved in conservation activities in partnership with the State, NGOs and/or academic research projects . . . are gradually becoming more familiar with contemporary technology" (Paneque-Gálvez et al. 2017, 16).

The projects that Amazonize technology agglomerate an increasing number of communities and generate permanent cooperation networks. For example, projects conducted in Peru by the Rainforest Foundation increasingly rely on an organized, coherent system for monitoring, collecting data, and countering environmental crimes. The monitoring system now makes up a network of local communities that watch sections of the forest entrusted to their care. At the Global Land Analysis and Discovery (GLAD) laboratory in the Department of Geographical Sciences at the University of Maryland, alerts are created when satellite pictures indicate changes in the forest cover. The information is automatically sent to smartphones with applications like Global Forest Watcher. With precisely pinpointed locations, local observers can verify the information captured by drones via the satellite system. After unlawful behaviors—logging, pollution, or other encroachments on forest land—are confirmed, this information is sent (along with geotag photos as evidence) to the relevant departments and authorities, which can take legal action (Capello et al. 2022). As indicated earlier, indigenous forest defenders sometimes are subjected to violence and become victims of killings, which indicates how dangerous it is to act in defense of the environment and a community's rights. Therefore, it is vital to implement any strategy or technology that reduces the risk of direct contact between defenders and criminals.

Indigenous media practices against environmental violence are becoming a radical agglomerative tool that can change the perceptions of situated data and global ecological disasters. Sometimes remote sensing technologies and simple technical systems enable monitoring from the air. Drones have become a symbol of revolution and a new weapon against extractive capitalism. Drones are intriguing from the perspective of earlier Western concepts of grassroots mapping, media activism, and digital decolonization. They are also interesting from the perspective of critical media studies as originally military devices that are deconstructed and reconstructed via DIY and reweaponized for the sake of local communities. The examples of agglomerative digital indigenous mapping provided in this chapter make up a critical discourse within militant cartographies. Collaborative media practices generate community knowledge and establish relations with other research groups and with people from outside who engage in the work as collaborators or in the name of environmental or political solidarity. The relationship established through Amazonized technologies is symmetrical. The goal of indigenous media practices is both to defend local communities and to act in the ecological interests of a much broader group that fights for environmental justice. The decolonization process relates to media, technologies, and data and information exchange.

To a certain extent, the practices are a grassroots response to the Belém Declaration, which was adopted in 1988 under the auspices of Darrell A. Posey at the First International Congress of Ethnobiology in Belém, Brazil. The declaration defined research ethics in relations with indigenous people, especially their intellectual property rights and their status as authorities in their fields. It also required disseminating local-language versions of the outcomes of studies conducted in collaboration with traditional communities (Posey 1990). The Belém Declaration was the first formal acknowledgment of the "responsibilities of researchers and practitioners to address the needs of Indigenous Peoples and local communities, and to recognize the critical role of these cultural groups in biodiversity conservation and global planning" (Golan et al. 2019, 90). These militant indigenous cartographies are a critical practice that builds communities and helps generate knowledge, and they should be taken into account in global planning so that local communities maintain rights to the data gathered.

WE MUST MAKE DATA OURS

In the conclusions of their 2022 book *Data Power: Radical Geographies of Control and Resistance*, Jim E. Thatcher and Craig M. Dalton state that "data crafting projects, data hacking projects, data dérives, and other opportunities to explore and take control of the data produced through our digital devices hold promise for improving our lives and making society more equitable. Spatial data technologies are impoverished by a one-dimensional pursuit of profit. They have much to offer, for they allow us to reach beyond the limits of our senses to experience and come into contact with new knowledges, places, peoples, and ways of living. The data we produce are us, and the future demands that we make them ours" (Thatcher and Dalton 2022, 130). The authors note that a significant shift has occurred in critical data studies as denialism and apocalyptic visions of the end of humanity in big data systems have been overtaken by new practical projects that socially reclaim data: "Our data are us, so make them ours" (Thatcher and Dalton 2022, 128), say the authors, demonstrating that this is an important way to resist the exploitation of data in the hypercapitalist systems of global corporations. Initiatives to reclaim data and resituate it in local social, cultural, and economic contexts and to point out the forms of violence and exploitation carried out in its use represent a new kind of grassroots social resistance to this violence.

The practices described in this chapter also implement these demands in original and individual ways. They are embedded in communitarian methods of mapping based on data collected independently by community members using simple do-it-yourself technologies. Safecast and Public Lab's data-acquisition principles and digital indigenous mapping practices are based on transparent procedures that legitimize their veracity and accuracy within scientific comparative processes. Collaborative media practices offer counterinfrastructures against closed systems of science and top-down systems of data collection. These counterinfrastructures agglomerate people within specific communities, making technological tools tailored to specific needs, places, and situations and providing an opportunity to incorporate the experiences of historical communities, stories, and traditional practices of situated knowledge acquisition. This is the case with many indigenous communities that have always collected data about their neighborhood. In her article "Building a Data Revolution in Indian Country," Desi Rodriguez-Lonebear, a sociologist and member of the Northern Cheyenne Nation community, observes that "despite centuries of indigenous knowledge production steeped in histories of data collection and analysis . . . , progress is defined largely in Western terms and measured by Western-identified and controlled indices. . . . For indigenous peoples, data were everywhere, and survival was often tied to one's ability to gather, analyze and share this knowledge" (2016, 254).

In the projects we write about, technological tools and software can be seen in Gilbert Simondon's concept of "technical object as event" (Simondon 2017). Media can create morphological bonds that help agglomerate new relationships and opportunities to create grassroots practices of resistance. One lesson we can take from these practices (especially those in Indonesia and the Amazon) is that we need to redefine the technology itself. This extends Simondon's concept (which identified the human and technology relationship in relation to the global north) to include practices in which the technical object—properly tailored and refined and sometimes hacked and adapted to specific needs and conditions—exerts new political and social ontological relations. Situated media tools can help us decolonize stagnant structures, plug indigenous projects into global data-gathering processes, and allow local communities to retain the right to their own data. Broadly defined, data can function as "'skilled data workforce,' or 'data warriors'" (Rodriguez-Lonebear 2016, 268).

Viewed from a broader perspective, depending on the cultural context, these processes create new communities of inquiry (Gabrys 2019) by assuming different forms in different locations. These forms include crowd science in the case of Safecast, participatory grassroots mapping in Public Lab projects, and community-based digital indigenous mapping in the case of practices from Indonesia and South America. All are based on data, a new form of resistance to neocolonial violence and to top-down systems of knowledge creation and information management about the effects of disasters and forms of environmental degradation.

Our study of the media practices that have emerged in response to environmental disasters extends Nixon's concept of slow violence to include agglomerative processes. This is because a disaster has both a local impact and a global impact. The local effects involve directly generated environmental harm, and the global consequences involve environmental crises that feed the destruction of the entire planetary ecosystem. Local traumas, diseases, health issues, and social and economic problems are subject to agglomeration, creating a force seen on a macro scale as environmental violence. These disasters generate the need for increasingly engaged, grassroots, and situated ways of monitoring and studying their effects. In this chapter, we focus on examples of violence generated primarily by corporate-based processes because it is often overlooked and its perpetrators are often hard to hold accountable. In corporations, the people responsible for making decisions hide behind a complex management system. In such cases, creating counterinfrastructures to assert community rights based on collected data and mapping practices is all the more pressing and can be a powerful weapon of resistance against global corporate tycoons or mafia systems, as in the Amazon.

An aesthetics of radical truth—as a practice of community data collection, grassroots mapping, and the situating of data in local contexts, traditional knowledge, and narratives—becomes a tool for revealing hidden violence and proving truth. The kinds of maps discussed in this chapter represent previously unrepresented and invisible data about people and the environment and have become curated arguments that help empower marginalized communities. Deconstructed by grassroots collaborative practices, these maps become tools for political and economic emancipation, for decolonization, and for repairing and even ending the slow violence perpetrated against the environment and humans. This always-situated, peaceful form of militant mapping defends the rights of those who have been deprived of them by top-down management projects and develops data that can be used for the benefit of these communities. As Donna Haraway says, "staying with the trouble does not require such a relationship to times called the future. In fact, staying with the trouble requires learning to be truly present, not as a vanishing pivot between awful or Edenic pasts and apocalyptic or salvific futures, but as mortal critters entwined in myriad unfinished configurations of places, times, matters, meanings" (2016, 1).

4

THE LIQUID VIOLENCE OF BORDERIZATION REGIMES

> We live in the age of the migrant. . . . Today, there are over 1 billion migrants. Each decade, the percentage of migrants as a share of the total population continues to rise. In the next 25 years, the rate of migration is predicted to be higher than over the last 25 years. More than ever, it has become a necessity for people to migrate due to environmental, economic, and political instability. Climate change, in particular, may even double international migration over the next 40 years. Even more, the percentage of total migrants who are non-status or un-documented is further increasing, which poses a serious challenge to democracy and political representation. (Nail 2020, 148)

This chapter is about the collaborative practices of combating and reconstructing the violence against migrants, refugees, and asylum seekers across European borders. The increasing migration rate is caused by complex cofactors and is considered to be an important challenge to current conceptual and social constructs of state, border, nation, and citizenship. This ongoing and infinite process has been growing in intensity recently in many aspects and in numerous geographical locations. It affects the futures of nations, states, and the planet. The above quote from Thomas Nail's article "Migrant Images" shows the enormous scale of migration, which is an urgent political, economic, social, and human problem (Nail 2020). The very notion of migrants is objectified in political discourse, loses its significance and power, and changes its nature.

Political, journalistic, and scholarly discourses describe the refugee phenomenon primarily by means of three terms—*migrant*, *refugee*, and *asylum seeker*. According to Daniel Trilling in his book *Lights in the Distance: Exile and Refuge at the Borders of Europe*, "the word 'migrant' describes a person on the move for an unspecified reason. 'Refugee' has both a legal meaning, in that it describes a person who is eligible for asylum under international refugee law, and a colloquial meaning, in that it describes a person who has fled their home. 'Asylum seeker' describes a person who has come to a country in order to claim asylum, but whose claim has not yet been either accepted or rejected" (Trilling 2018, 20). In many cases, however, differentiating among the three words is far from easy because the overlapping reasons for migrating in the modern world. As Trilling notes, the personal details that emerge in migration stories do not always match established concepts and definitions. Therefore, the instability, bifurcations, and transversalities of these definitions should be kept in mind when we talk about refugees and migration (Atoui 2020).

In the European Union, borders and border zones have become sites of new forms of violence, cyber regimes, and practices of radical solidarity opposed to those regimes. This direct and systemic violence is fed by complex historical, political, and cultural prejudices and regulations. When combined with the digitization of national borders, they generate procedures of exclusion and segregation. As Nicholas De Genova writes, discussing and analyzing the migration crisis is impossible without understanding Europe's borders because the migration crisis, as a crisis of borders, is primarily a political spectacle (De Genova 2013). It has simultaneously become necropolitical (Mbembe 2003), as it has converted many European borderline spaces, especially the Mediterranean Sea, into mass graves (Heller and Pezzani 2020a, 2020b). The borderline spaces of Europe are irreducible to "anything resembling immutable, integral, internally consistent, or objective boundaries corresponding to any self-evident 'natural' fact of physical geography . . . nor can [they] be apprehensible as simply the outward projections of a stable and coherent centre, whereby the sociopolitical, cultural, or civilizational identity and spatial integrity of Europe may be presupposed in contradistinction with a variety of alterities beyond or outside the ostensible limits demarcated by those boundaries" (De Genova 2017, 20).

Europe's borders materialize the sociopolitical regimes of both individual states and the broader borders adopted by the European Union to separate its territory from the rest of the world. The mediation of what borders mean externally and internally in terms of geopolitics and economics often begins far beyond the geographical framework of present-day Europe. For De Genova, "the borders of Europe are simultaneously entangled with a global (postcolonial) politics of race that redraws the proverbial color line and refortifies European-ness as a racial formation of whiteness and a comparably global (neoliberal) politics of transnational labor mobility and capitalist labor subordination that produces such spatialized (and racialized) differences, above all, to capitalize upon them" (De Genova 2017, 21). The almost spectral nature of borders (Lymes et al. 2020) and the simultaneous political pressure for their physical stability is most evident in the digital systems used to collect data on migration and migrants. Borders are a political construct (Novak 2017) that is governed by technologies and algorithms that record all data about the persons crossing these borders. Europe's borders become a game of political forces that implement state directives that determine who can be accepted and who must be rejected and of cyber regimes that management the refugee crisis via data surveillance and monitoring systems (Paul 2020).

This spectacle has irreversible consequences in the violence it perpetrates. The borders of Europe and its border strips and zones (also known as cross-border facilities or green natural barriers) become sites of violence. In these areas—the Mediterranean Sea; the Evros River (Maritsa in Bulgarian, Meric in Turkish) separating Greece from Turkey; the forests between Belarus, Poland, Lithuania, and Latvia—violence is inflicted on migrants and refugees. Each natural border becomes an archive recording *in situ* devastation and death.

These new forms of borderization regimes (systems through which borders are actively produced, maintained, and enforced) link various processes and beings—policies, technologies, operations, legal and social systems, human life, and nature (nonhuman actants)—within so-called natural zone borders. In the first part of this chapter, we analyze the principles of dividuating migrants by collecting data about them and positioning them within a social, economic, and cultural system. In the second part, we focus on natural zone borders and direct forms of violence. We look broadly at the pan-European perspective on migration processes, the technologization and mediatization of borders, and a "cybernetic regime" paradigm. Using the example of borders in the Mediterranean, we also point to the phenomena of resistance and the construction of a bottom-up countersurveillance based on collaborative media practices. In the last part, we present a study of the border between Poland and Belarus. We show the processes of border expression in practical and critical terms—including the post-Soviet historical and social traumas that feed national and cultural chauvinisms, the development of cybernetic regimes that include remote sensing technologies and an electronic firewall, and the various forms of direct violence that is perpetrated against migrants and refugees.

DIGITAL FORTRESS EUROPE AND ITS CYBERNETIC SOVEREIGNTY

Since the 1990s, the term *Fortress Europe* has been repurposed to define issues related to migration policies and European Union (EU) borders. The EU has accompanied its internal integration process with an intensified sealing of its external borders. This process has expanded, militarized, and digitalized the EU's architectural infrastructure by adding walls, fences, and guards who use sophisticated technological methods of reconnaissance, communications, and data exchange during their surveillance activities. It also has established institutions that coordinate the operation of borders and the work being done at the borders. The EU members states and the pan-European institutions operate in a network of interdependencies, exchange data and information, and use autonomous crisis management systems. The border is administered not by a single coherent organization but by complex entities guided by different legal and political regulations. Frontex, the European Border and Coast Guard Agency, is an independent institution of the European Union that was established in 2004 to aggregate and manage data on the EU's external borders and migration processes. Because of diffuse responsibilities and complex modes of management, there is a lack of transparency (decision-making in this system is conditioned by many factors) and an ontology of resilience. This system strongly influences the redefinition of EU borders. Borders today can be seen as physical spaces with specific geographic characteristics and also as parts of a complex institution. In the policy and praxis of the borderland, control and surveillance technologies (with their algorithms and IT systems) play important roles in big-data borders and dataveillance.

In the case of migration, the border is also an extraterritorial and transterritorial space. Data collected from remote sensing technologies deterritorializes the notion of a borderland. It is extended to the refugees' countries of origin and narrowed to the space of refugee camps and closed centers for noncitizens. In "Controlling the Crisis," Ian Alan Paul describes the EU border as emanating from a cybernetic system that legitimizes its own existence through ongoing crises (Paul 2020). The existence of this teleological system is based on crisis, leading it to ". . . enact controls to produce metastabilities between the inputs and outputs of a system in an interminable process of regulation that means to minimize the distance between a calibrated ideal and a digitally sensed world" (Paul 2020, 72). The logic of such interdependence leads to cybernetic regimes that produce specific aesthetics. The cybernetic regime develops its aesthetics based on maps visualizing border crises and migrant flows and on reports describing aggregated quantitative data and recommending prospective security—all of which are meant to create a picture of migrant crises in Europe.

In Europe, this complex system of algorithmic migration management is linked to biometric data that is used to record and identify personal identity. It changes the concept and definition of the border so that it is inseparable from the bodies and identities of the people who have crossed it. Certain elements—the designation status (migrant, refugee, asylum seeker), fingerprints, iris scans, biometric facial data, markings of biological sex, race, country of origin—become indelible aspects of postdigital identity. This data can be overwritten but not removed. The complexity of this problem intertwines the production of social identity with the geographic, physical, political, cultural, bodily, and digital. To automate the decision-making process, the characteristics that could prevent entry into digital fortress states must be identified. This might involve the interplay of several characteristics—such as a thirty-year-old male who is Muslim and an economic migrant from Pakistan or a twenty-year-old female who is a single mother and an economic migrant from Niger. Some characteristics of people from the Middle East and Africa tend to be implicitly equated in European culture and popular consciousness with external threats. Young Muslims, for example, represent a "potent marker of otherness," while migrants from West Africa are identified as "exotic" (Loftsdóttir 2018). These categories have often fed xenophobic cultural processes, but the datafication of identity may contribute to new structural forms of technosocial chauvinism. Anyone who is denied entry on the basis of having undesirable characteristics will be labeled with a negative identity that is difficult to erase. This also applies to those who are granted residence permits. Climate refugees, for example (who will increase in number over the next decades), will remain administratively required to identify themselves officially through the prism of climate change, whereas war refugees will be identified with the risk of post-traumatic stress disorder.

The processes of categorization and digital dividuation are fused with systems of social risk assessment and thus produce social identities. "The right to be forgotten"—which was stated in the General Data Protection Regulation, a EU 2016 document that guaranteed the deletion of personal data from the internet and different registers—does not guarantee the deletion of officially collected personal data. It is hard to imagine that European administrations will stop collecting and processing migrant data, since such a decision would subvert the cybernetic regime. The problem of dividuation here is not just that a digital shadow is produced when data is collected about the identity of border crossers. Because this data becomes a tool of biopolitical control and surveillance, it affects the human psychophysical state. As Ian Allan Paul notes, in European neoliberalism, subjectivity is produced through technological dividuation and "itself becomes unthinkable absent either the individualizing force of liberalism or the corresponding set of apparatuses, devices, and mechanisms that materially constitute the cybernetic systems responsible for both producing and dominating individual subjects dividually" (Paul 2020, 80). The paradox of the cyber regime is the mechanism of granting "the right to be dividuated." Some migrants are subjected to violence based primarily on refusal—to be let across the border, to be released from the detention center, or to have their documents recognized. Others clash against the wall of complicated administrative procedures. This level is marked by "the lack of transparency" and "the composite nature of the decision-making procedures" (Tas 2020, 18). Decision-making involves multiple entities, which protracts the time of reaching a final solution and makes it unpredictable. This creates an "administrative vacuum" (Tas 2020, 18). The system was designed in a way that "control and crisis operate together as a singular structure of power that is just as interested in managing crises as it is invested in maintaining them" (Paul 2020, 83).

The society of a cybernetic regime rests on foundations that have many coded biases. Long ago, Seán Cubitt (1998) posed a question concerning the existence of "ethics in a technical device," and that question remains acutely topical in the current migration situation. We should perceive ethical issues as fused in the digital reality with ways of designing specific technological systems, which are not separate from populist and xenophobic policies, pan-European or national legislative processes, or the media culture of the 2010s and 2020s. The problem should be identified at the level of each device, whose physical and digital functionality results from the intertwining of all these factors. Each device, technology, and digital system produces a specific policy and has an inherent ethic. Identifying these transversal issues (ethics, politics, aesthetics, technology, and design) in the device opens possibilities for critical transdisciplinary research that defines the studied object. Only this kind of integral approach can enable the close reading and critique of new border violence.

SMART BORDERS AND SURVEILLANCE SYSTEMS

Since 2013, the EU has been developing a system of automatic monitoring of movement across its borders. This involves collecting biometric data from citizens of European countries (the development of so-called e-citizenship) and from anyone wishing to enter the EU. In 2013, the Smart Borders initiative was announced, and its regulatory proposals and technical solutions were gradually implemented over several years. Solutions relevant to migration processes were put in place in 2022 and 2023 (Smart Borders 2024). The Entry/Exit System (EES) consists of an IT network, databases, and technological autonomous and automated checkpoints at the EU borders. It is "an automated IT system for registering travelers from third-countries . . . each time they cross an EU external border. The system will register the person's name, type of the travel document, biometric data (fingerprints and captured facial images) and the date and place of entry and exit" (Entry/Exit System 2024).

A system of "smart" control was first tested in airports. Automatic "e-gates" autonomously carried out all monitoring activities by identifying passengers, taking a picture of the face, taking fingerprints, and confirming the compliance of the data against a biometric passport. The extension of the system has brought about many new problems. These can be purely technical problems, such as those related to the processing, storing, and management of the so-called big-data border, which are administered by EU states and companies commissioned with the system's operation (Clavell 2017). This arrangement raises many questions related to the security of the data, the forms of access to it, its use, and its transfer to other entities.

Furthermore, dataveillance affects the expansion of the notion of border, which extends into the every possible use of data acquired during the crossing of any border at any point in a person's life: "The physical border is increasingly irrelevant because our rights, privileges, relations, characteristics and risk levels are checked all the time" (Clavell 2017, 34). The digital borderland ceases to be a specific place and becomes a function of monitoring and control of a mediatized society: "In the end, technologies to monitor mobility are political tools. Their aims, design, use, costs, and consequences should be developed and evaluated accordingly" (Dijstelbloem 2017, 32). Interconnected systems of physical borders—with their infrastructure (and their border expression), complex legislation (local and pan-European), smart monitoring and information exchange systems, and administrative procedures—make up a "patchwork of policies" (Dijstelbloem 2017) that are hard to control and are conducive to comprehensive abuses and dissipation of responsibility. They may lead, as Huub Dijstelbloem observes, to what Ulrich Beck called "organized irresponsibility: situations of inadequacy in which it is hard to blame a single actor" (Dijstelbloem 2017, 32).

This diffusion of responsibility for decision-making can be seen in the move toward automating this process, in which a stand-alone technical and algorithmic system will be responsible for decision-making. There has also been a geographical dispersion of decision-making across

Europe: "For example, when the Hellenic Coast Guard spots an unregistered ship in Greek waters, it contacts the national coordination center in Piraeus. The center asks the European Border and Coast Guard Agency in Warsaw to compare the crew's observation with satellite images. On the basis of that combined information, the Hellenic Coast Guard decides what to do" (Dijstelbloem 2017, 33).

Control management systems on the EU's external borders are integrated within the European Border Surveillance System (Eurosur 2024), which is subordinated to Frontex. Monitoring the situation on the border is meant to foster risk analysis and create situational awareness: "Originally a military term, situational awareness involves visualizing critical situations, such as irregular border crossings or emergencies, to assess whether interventions are required" (Dijstelbloem 2017, 33). Data acquired at a higher degree are aggregated to create "situational pictures" that are available to all kinds of governmental and pan-European agencies. Situational pictures are "an aggregation of geo-referenced near-real-time data and information received from different authorities, sensors, platforms and other sources which is transmitted across secured communication and information channels and can be processed and selectively displayed and shared with other relevant authorities in order to achieve situational awareness and support the reaction capability at, along or in the proximity of the external borders and the pre-frontier area" (Eurosur 2021, n.p.). The situation-related access to the data gathered in the Eurosur system may change. This is what happened in the case of the European Asylum Dactyloscopy Database (Eurodac). The fingerprint identification system was intended to prevent the same people from filing many asylum submissions in different countries. However, its functionality was extended, and today the database is used by other governmental agencies, such as Europol, prosecution authorities, and national police. Eurodac has also become a tool for exerting pressure on migrants, making it possible to return them to the countries where their fingerprints were first collected.

All of these systems make up a praxis of EU borders, which generates new decision regimes and systems concerning human lives. As already indicated, the European Border and Coast Guard Agency (Frontex) occupies a special position in the European development of these technologies:

> Frontex extensively surveils, studies, and aggregates information about migration as a means of more effectively policing and controlling it. Profuse amounts of data are routinely captured, aggregated, and analyzed, all of which are then repackaged and published by Frontex in media-rich "Risk Analysis Reports" that advertise new border control technologies and initiatives, present colorful data visualizations and schematic migratory pattern maps, and detail various predictions about the future of migration that together contribute to the constitution of the migrant crisis as an object of cultural concern, security planning, political discourse, and legislative response in the EU. (Paul 2020, 74–75)

A report titled *Artificial Intelligence-Based Capabilities for the European Border and Coast Guard* (Frontex 2021) examines artificial intelligence (AI) systems of information management and decision-making for border and coast guard applications. It details the current state of AI solutions applied in EU border-related infrastructure and defines the goals that should be achieved by future AI solutions in border defense and migration management technologies. The report advocates that systems be developed to automate the work of border controllers in identifying people's identities and making decisions. One of these systems is the surveillance tower. These towers would be fitted with systems that automate object detection and the surveillance of large areas: "It is expected that surveillance towers will provide near real-time analysis of larger areas through fused sensor data from the systems on board. It is also expected that as the capability develops, the surveillance towers will be seamlessly integrated with sensors from other platforms, such as UAS [unmanned aerial system], to provide comprehensive and fully autonomous situational awareness" (Frontex 2021, 33).

RAND Europe, the author of the Frontex report, recommended that AI and machine learning be used in the decision-making process. This should be backed up by deep learning, visual and thermal object recognition, and radar object detection. In the section titled "Technology Adoption Roadmaps," the report indicates specific technologies that should be adopted, their producers, and the research institutes that develop them. This section of the report proposes a vision of a technofuture where Europe's external borders will be "patrolled" and "monitored" by complex sets of drones and robots (including robotic hummingbirds, ravens, pumas, and bat-inspired robots) that will make up a "system which provides a semi-autonomous border surveillance solution with integrated swarms of aerial, water surface, underwater and ground vehicles incorporated directly into the network" (Frontex 2021, 34). According to the report, "the integration of a range of AI technologies . . . will improve drone capabilities and provide real-time situational awareness to border guards, including full-motion video, 'automatic target detection and geolocation.' Improvements are also likely in the ability of sUAS [small unmanned aerial systems] to operate fully autonomously through AI-enabled and computer-vision-based precision landing capability" (Frontex 2021, 35).

The aesthetics of digital border regimes is responsible for the order of perceiving things within border questions and procedures. Its social and political impacts are difficult to determine. If the praxis of the border is subject to digitization and datification and if digital tracking and surveillance procedures extend to migrants in their country of origin from where they begin their journey, then the digital violence that results from the enforcement policies applied at the border is stretched between at least two facts that generate significant conflicts in their ontological nature. There is a clash of concepts between the logic of dataveillance and the physical presence of migrants in frontiers with infrastructures of walls, fences, and militarized space. For this reason, physical migration processes are a policy of motion for the digital projects of the border and the areas within borders. This motion may influence the internal processes that initiate structural change. The greater the risks posed by these processes, the more cybernetic regimes attempt to assert control through stricter regulatory mechanisms.

COUNTERSTRATEGIES AGAINST "LIQUID VIOLENCE"

In line with their aesthetics, cybernetic regimes generate images, messages, visualizations, and datasets to justify the existing crisis management system and the need to acquire and process data. Even as these regimes go through the motions of data and information flow, however, they are focused not on solving a problem but on maintaining a state of quasi-stabilization. In such a situation, an aesthetics of radical truth

(AeRT) can be a counterstrategy for regaining information, locating and situating data, reconstructing the progress of an event, and establishing facts concerning situations of violence. AeRT agglomerates various forms of media practice that together resist procedures of border regimes. Later in this chapter, we list examples of this practice that are a reaction to violence in two types of border zones—a sea border (the Mediterranean Sea) and a natural green border (the forests between Poland and Belarus). While the migratory situation in the Mediterranean has been monitored by many groups and organizations since the 1990s, the migration crisis on the EU's eastern borders began only in 2021. This juxtaposition allows us to show agglomerative processes in two phases. First, counterstructures exist to the violence that people who seek refuge in Europe encounter during and immediately after crossing the Mediterranean and at the eastern borders. Second, agglomeration is working *in situ* and in real time, and media tools and practices are producing its unstable and changing morphological structures.

Forensic Oceanography is a pioneer in collaborative media practices that investigate, reconstruct, and counter violence against migrants in the Mediterranean. The group was founded in 2011 by Lorenzo Pezzani and Charles Heller in response to the policies of violence used against migrants crossing the Mediterranean Sea to reach Europe. The group operates as part of the Forensic Architecture team and tracks crimes against migrants committed on bodies of water, assigns responsibility, and uncovers the mechanisms and forms of what it calls "liquid violence." Its operations are a counterstrategy to the practices of Frontex, the EU government and military agencies responsible for exercising oversight over international and territorial waters. The tools it uses are the same ones used by these agencies to analyze data on the distribution of objects at sea—including satellite imagery, geolocation data, and records of telephone communications. Its strategies are overt and transparent because the goal is to identify violence, share the dataset obtained, involve other research groups and activists in the processes of identifying forms of the weaponization of water, and publish the truth about these forms of violence.

Forensic Oceanography's first project was to investigate a 2011 incident during which a rubber boat with seventy-two migrants left Tripoli,

Libya, and headed toward the small Italian island of Lampedusa, a distance of about 296 kilometers. The boat lost power and was left unassisted for fourteen days. During that time, sixty-three persons died. Forensic Oceanography published a comprehensive report on the incident—*Report on the "Left-to-Die Boat"* (Heller, Pezzani, and SITU Studio 2012)—that identified the maritime boundaries of the jurisdictions of various government and military agencies. The boat left Libyan waters and entered the Maltese search and rescue zone, remaining within the NATO maritime surveillance area at all times. Migrants contacted aid agencies in Italy via satellite phone; the boat's location was known to coastguards in Italy, Malta, and NATO units. Forensic Oceanography analyzed the mechanisms of communication, information, and help requests and the events that led to the deaths. The reconstructed anatomy of this situation illustrates and embodies the mechanisms of the cyber regime. Although people on the boat were in contact with many entities capable of taking direct action, the boat was left adrift. This is how the mechanisms defined above—such as "lack of transparency," "composite nature of the decision-making procedures," and "administrative vacuum"—shift from political violence to direct violence during the "weaponization of water" (figure 4.1). In a 2018 interview with Sophie Hinger, Lorenzo Pezzani said that "distance between the (in-)action of a perpetrator and the fate of a victim, the conversion of water into a deadly weapon, is precisely what has allowed states to present migrants' deaths at sea as tragic events all the while escaping responsibility for them. In a sense, you could think of all our work of the past few years as an attempt to account for and challenge these forms of contactless violence" (Hinger et al. 2018, 196).

Forensic Oceanography has conducted investigations that provide evidence in international litigation against various government agencies and has performed analyses refuting allegations against activists who carried out rescue operations on their own. In 2018, Forensic Oceanography, in cooperation with Forensic Architecture, published evidence (including video footage of the seizure of *The Iuventa*) refuting allegations by Italian authorities against the Jugend Rettet (Youth Rescue), a German group that undertook rescue operations in the Mediterranean (Heller and Pezzani 2018a). The government alleged that, during the group's rescue missions in 2016 and 2017, it colluded with smugglers and assisted with

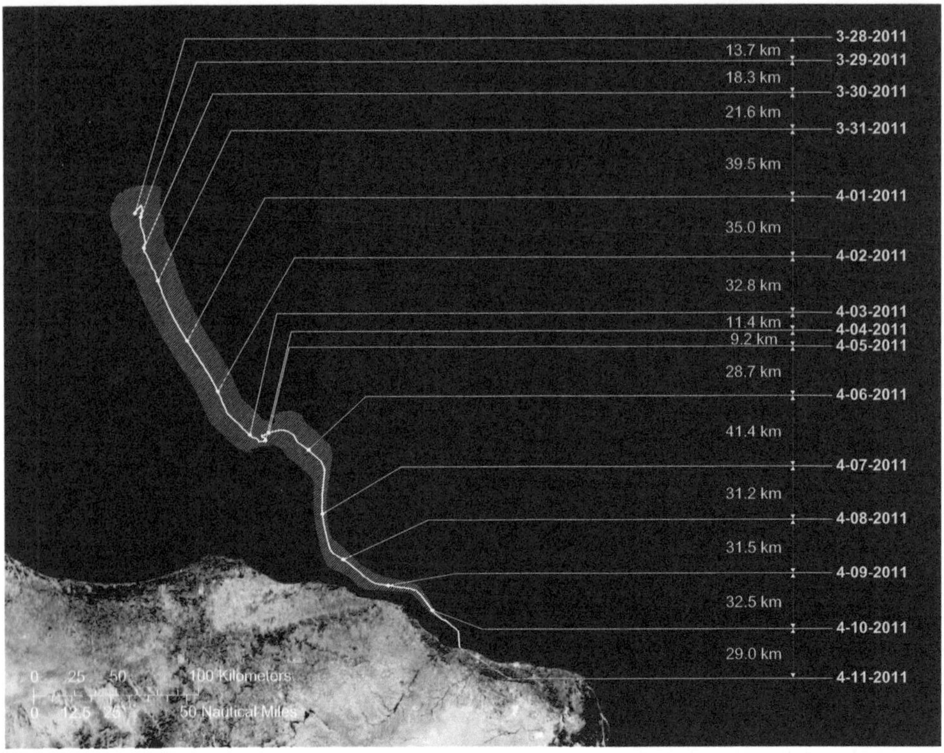

4.1

A drift model showing the hourly positions of the "left-to-die" boat. Over time, the margin of error in the drifting vessel's track decreases as it is constrained by the known position of landing. Forensic Oceanography.

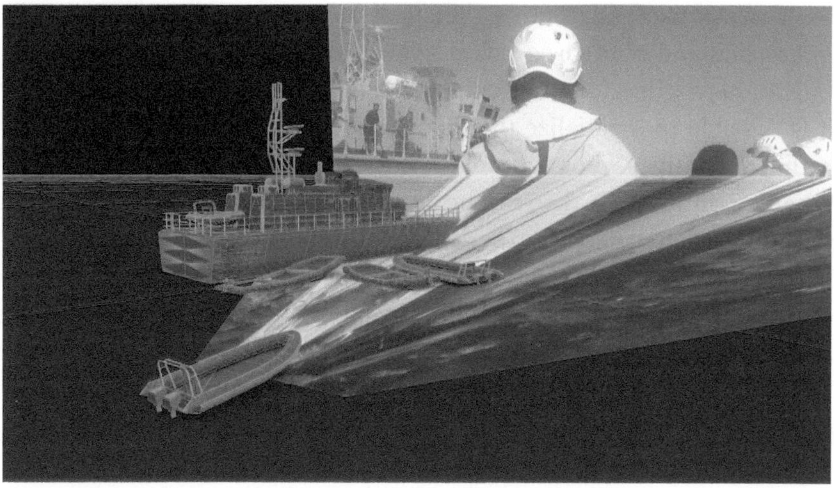

illegal migration. In 2018, Forensic Oceanography and Forensic Architecture[1] published the outcomes of an investigation that revealed the covert policies used by the EU against migrants and activists, which Forensic Oceanography in the project called Mare Clausum (closed sea) (Heller and Pezzani 2018b). This unofficial operation introduced legislation that criminalized aid activities in the Mediterranean and allowed Libyan coast guards to use pull-backs (the practice of forcibly pulling people on the move back, away from the borders they wish to cross) against boats carrying migrants. As a result, Libyan services "operate refoulement by proxy on behalf of Italy and the EU" (Heller and Pezzani 2018b, 7). The report and its video footage revealed outcomes of a rescue intervention carried out by the Sea Watch's boat. The rescue was hindered by the Libyan coast guard, which led to the drowning deaths of some people (figure 4.2).

4.2

Projecting images across digital space within a three-dimensional model allows researchers to determine real-world distances between objects. Forensic Oceanography.

Forensic Oceanography's investigations into how the sea can be militarized and politicized reveal how borders are displaced in hidden migration practices. By analyzing data, documents, and satellite images, it is possible to "spatialize the practices of actors and inscribing them within the political geography of the sea" (Heller and Pezzani 2020b, 104). When migrants cross the sea, the geographical and physical settings of the border matter, and the experience of time becomes critical. When the border regime's area of impact on migrants is stretched, their chances of survival are reduced. Every additional hour spent in a boat that is not assisted threatens the lives of its passengers. Forensic Oceanography uses the same media and technological tools as government and military agencies but reverses their vector of causality. Remote sensing technologies become tools of countersurveillance and provide evidence for violations of the law by governmental agencies instead of migrants: "By corroborating survivors' testimonies with information provided by the vast apparatus of remote sensing technologies that have transformed the contemporary ocean into a digital archive," Forensic Oceanography "assembled a composite image of the events" (Heller and Pezzani 2020b, 102). Via reports, videos, and multimedia installations in cultural and art institutions and in courtrooms, it coproduces and socializes knowledge about the regimes of state borders and the political and social responsibility for the violence they design and inflict. In addition to documenting individual deaths at sea, Forensic Oceanography reveals the politics of "diffuse responsibility" itself. It thus becomes possible to identify those who are direct and indirect perpetrators of "liquid violence" as well as the transformation of "the sea into a central space of political struggle, inventing new strategies and tactics to contest the violence of borders and support migrants' movements" (Heller and Pezzani 2020b, 123).

Counterstrategies to violence experienced by migrants in the Mediterranean Sea are also offered by several organizations that do not investigate and yet act structurally and set up permanent aid networks. The organization Watch the Med monitors and documents cases of power abuse, violence, and death at sea. One of the help tools generated by this organization is a website called Alarm Phone—a "Hotline for boatpeople in distress. No rescue, but Alarm"—that offers information about safe passage across the Mediterranean Sea and an emergency phone number to be used when rescue services fail to act (Alarm Phone 2022). The website offers emergency contacts at coastal services that have jurisdiction over specific sectors of the Mediterranean Sea and videos (in English, French, Arabic, Turkish, and Farsi) that provide vital information about safety and security at sea, including how to use satellite phones in the open sea in places where cellular phones have no reception and how to evaluate weather conditions during sea crossings by using data from Windy.com. Alarm Phone is also an emergency tool and coordination center when local services cannot offer aid to migrants at risk at sea. The activists define their work as follows:

> We ourselves cannot rescue anyone; we are not in the area and do not have boats or helicopters. If you are in distress at sea or are experiencing a pushback, please follow these steps:
>
> - Call the coast guard and tell them about your situation of distress.
> - Call the Alarm Phone. We will make sure that your distress call is acted upon.
> - If you are not promptly rescued by the coast guard, call the Alarm Phone again. We will inform humanitarian organizations and public media to put pressure on the rescue services. (Alarm Phone 2022)

The Alarm Phone website and social profiles also present testimonies of individuals who have been subjected to various forms of administrative pressure after their arrival in Europe, some of which are linked to the collection of biometric data under European legislation on migration policies.

In addition to traveling a dangerous path to Europe, migrants face a legally and procedurally complicated system for refugee administration inside the EU. Various organizations have emerged to help migrants navigate the complicated and ambiguous procedures for granting the right to stay in the EU. These organizations provide advice on how to apply for asylum and how to avoid falling into the traps of the digital administrative system. One organization cocreating agglomerative counterstructures is the online platform Welcome to Europe (w2eu.info available in English, French, Arabic, and Farsi). It disseminates practical legal advice and strategies to use during administrative proceedings for the right to remain in Europe. The group's activists and lawyers provide information about the migration, detention, and deportation procedures in various European countries. The site offers guidelines on how to prepare for and deal with asylum procedures, contact lists of aid and legal organizations that provide support during legal administrative procedures, and procedures for migrants based on forms of electronic information acquisition and exchange between EU countries. These procedures are instrumental for obtaining protection or being deported, for example, under the Dublin Regulation, a law that determines which EU member state is responsible for a particular asylum application and that was signed by all EU member states as well as Iceland, Liechtenstein, Norway, and Switzerland. The rule says that migrants must apply for asylum in the first country where they arrive (acquisition of digital data about a specific person in a given country equals registering their digital presence at this particular place). The w2eu.info website contains information for refuges and migrants in the EU, including information about medical services in various countries, the rights of minors, security at sea, and steps to follow in the case of pushbacks (returns at a border).

Documentation processes also play an important role in creating a counterstructure that agglomerates various activities that have aid, social, and political potential. The Fatal Policies of Fortress Europe project has been ongoing since their 1993 campaign, organized by the international activist network UNITED for Intercultural Action. It documents the patterns of creating a "deathscape" in relation to borders and migration processes (UNITED 2024). Project participants report systemic violence at borders and promote socially sanctioned truths, while applying political pressure and social resistance against a cybernetic regime's policies. This media project involves 560 organizations across 46 European countries, opposing nationalism, racism, and fascism, and supporting migrants and refugees. For over three decades, the network has systematically collected data on the deaths of migrants and refugees from different forms of violence inflicted on them during migration or in their destination countries. The data is updated once a year and made public on June 20 as part of World Refugee Day (established in 2001 by the United Nations General Assembly). As of 2024, the database contained 60,620 records (in 2021 it contained 44,764 records). Each record denotes one person who died due to violence during migration (table 4.1). The "List of Refugee Deaths" is publicly available as a PDF file and in interactive mode (the project's website allows access to data via a world map, and the data covers nearly all continents). The spread of death outside Europe is due to the management of external borders: "What can be seen is that borders are shifting towards the outer parts of Europe where tighter controls are being implemented. The ultimate aim of the 'management of external borders' is to stop victims of persecution, civil war and forced migration even before they reach Europe" (UNITED 2024, n.p.). The "List of Refugee Deaths" is often used in social media campaigns, street protests, and artivism actions. In 2015, for example, the list was presented in Strasbourg during protests outside the European Parliament, and in 2016, the list was presented in New York at an exhibition called *Insecurities: Tracing Displacement and Shelter* (curated by Sean Anderson and Arièle Dionne-Krosnick) at the Museum of Modern Art.

In many antiviolence projects, collecting documents, testimonies, and refugees' phone records represents an important new approach to crisis situations. New technological and digital tools can pinpoint the locations of victims and reconstruct the violence they suffered. The above collaborative projects are only a few of the projects addressing refugee conditions in maritime border zones. As projects and initiatives like these increase, new forms of public engagement are being created that go beyond states and politicians, and a new kind of activism is emerging. At the same time, groups like Forensic Oceanography, Forensic Architecture, Watch the Med (and its Alarm Phone website), and Welcome to Europe and endeavors like the "List of Refugee Deaths" show the Mediterranean Sea as a natural border zone that has become a deathtrap for many migrants. Transborder spaces—like the sea, mountains, rivers, and forests that separate Europe from the rest of the world—become natural archives of violence. They are filled with sensors, remote detectors, and drones and are tracked by satellite imagery. Because of the legislative vagueness of these spaces or the lack of relevant provisions toward migrants and rescue efforts by member states, they have become weaponized landscapes. Therefore, the violence committed at EU borders against asylum-seeking migrants should be seen in a broader perspective. The necropolitics of leaving people to die of exhaustion or exposing them to drowning and

TABLE 4.1
An excerpt from the "List of Refugee Deaths (excerpt)" from the Fatal Policies of Fortress Europe project, 2024

Found dead	No.	name, gender, age	Region of origin	Cause of death	Source
6/8/24	1	n/a	unknown	presumed drowned, rescue organization aircraft discovered body floating off Zawiya (LY)	SeaWatch/ Fanpage
6/7/24	11	n/a (including children; women)	unknown	drowned, rescue organization aircrafts discovered bodies in state of decay floating off Zawiya (LY)	SeaWatch/ Spiegel/ Fanpage
6/6/24	1	n/a (man, ±24)	unknown	died of starvation in hospital in El Hierro (ES) after rescue of boat adrift from Mauritania to Spain; 70 rescued	El Diario
6/6/24	50	n/a (including children; women)	Africa/ Pakistan	died of hunger/thirst, bodies thrown into sea of boat 13 days adrift from Nouakchott (MR) to Spain; 70 rescued	El Diario
6/1/24	1	Nfansou Drame (man, 31)	Senegal	found dead in tent in makeshift camp near Roja river in Ventimiglia (IT); had no access to medical care	Seen/Riviera24
5/31/24	1	n/a	unknown	drowned, boat from Turkey crashed into patrol vessel off Symi (GR), after smuggler jumped off; 18 rescued	NeosKos/ ChinaDaily
5/28/24	1	n/a (baby)	unknown	dead body recovered off Lampedusa (IT) on boat in distress, mother & sister (3) survived; 45 rescued	SOSHumanity/ Angi/Spiegel
5/26/24	7	n/a	Senegal	presumed drowned, Europe bound boat on way from Sfax (TN) capsized; 7 missing, 34 rescued	IOM
5/22/24	8	n/a	unknown	drowned in the Mediterranean Sea off coast of Marsa Deela (LY) on way to Europe; 8 missing, 56 rescued	IOMLibya
5/13/24	1	n/a	unknown	died of exhaustion in hospital in Cabo Verde after rescue from drifting boat on way from Africa to Spain	Expresso
5/13/24	22	n/a	unknown	drowned in the Mediterranean Sea, off coast of Sabratha (Libya) on way to Europe	IOM Lybia
5/13/24	7	n/a	unknown	died of exhaustion on boat drifted to Cape Verdean island on way from Africa to Spain; 7 bf, 6 rescued	Expresso
5/13/24	1	n/a	unknown	died of exhaustion on oil tanker directly after rescue from drifting boat on way from Africa to Spain; 6 rescued	Expresso

TABLE 4.1 (CONTINUED)

Found dead	No.	name, gender, age	Region of origin	Cause of death	Source
5/10/24	26	n/a	Morocco, Sub-Saharan Africa	drowned, rubber boat on way to Canary Islands (ES) capsized off Tan-tan (MA); 11 bf, 15 miss, 36 rescued	Hespress/ NadorCity
5/9/24	1	n/a (man)	Asia	body found near gate in Belarus-Latvia border fence in Braslav district (BY) after push back from Latvia	RIA/Belsat/ SKGovBY/ BelTA
5/9/24	1	n/a (man)	Asia	body found by border guards 40 meters from Belarus-Latvia border fence in Braslav district (BY)	RIA/Belsat/ SKGovBY/ BelTA
5/5/24	34	n/a (including 20 young men)	Tunisia	presumed drowned, boat missing since it left coast of Kairouan (Tunisia) on way to Italy; 34 missing	Mosaique/ TerrePourTous
5/5/24	1	n/a	unknown	died of unknown cause, body found by Belarus border guards on the Belarus-Poland border	GPK/SB.BY/ RIA
5/4/24	1	n/a (man, ±40)	unknown	presumed drowned, body found in canal of Bourbourg in Dunkirk (FR) by skipper who unloaded cargo	MSNcom/ Nieuwsblad/ FranceBleu/ VoixDuNord
5/4/24	23	n/a	Tunisia	presumed drowned, boat missing since it left coast of Korba (Tunisia) on way to Italy; 23 missing	TNnum/ NatGuardTN/ IOMTunisia
5/4/24	25	n/a (25 men)	Guinea	drowned, boat to Canary Islands (ES) sank after onboard fight with smugglers off coast of Senegal; 8 rescued	AfricaGuinee/ TV5/ InfoMigrants
5/4/24	1	Aboubacar Sidiki Touré (man)	Guinea	drowned, boat to Canary Islands (ES) sank after onboard fight with smugglers off coast of Senegal; 8 rescued	AfricaGuinee/ TV5/ InfoMigrants
5/3/24	2	n/a	unknown	died of unknown cause, bodies found by Belarus border guards on the Belarus-Latvian border	GPK/SB.BY/ RIA
5/2/24	36	n/a (2 children; 2 women; 32 men)	Guinea	drowned, boat wrecked off coast of Sfax on way to Lampedusa (Italy); 36 missing, 8 rescued	FricaGuinee

Notes: Instagram: unitedlistofdeath; UNITED for Intercultural Action, European network against nationalism, racism, fascism, and in support of migrants and refugees—Amsterdam refugee campaign secretariat; Postbus 413, NL-1000 AK Amsterdam, Netherlands, phone +31-6-48808808, listofdeaths@unitedagainstracism.org. This UNITED List of Refugee Deaths can be reused, translated, and redistributed; see conditions on UnitedAgainstRefugeeDeaths.eu. By request you can obtain this list with more searchable data in xls format from UNITED.

describing it as "accidental death" reduces human beings to nonhuman entities (Mbembe 2019a, 2019b, 2019c, 2021). They remain nameless victims of the deathscape of the European border zones. Joseph Pugliese describes the creation of new "geocorpographies" as a "violent enmeshment of the flesh and blood of the body within the geopolitics of war, race . . . empire" (Pugliese 2007, n.p.).

The practices of an aesthetics of radical truth that have emerged from collaborative projects and helped to create a policy of solidarity are important because they reconstruct situations of violence, death, and pushback at EU borders despite the difficulties of access to information. This agglomerative structure integrates international formal and informal organizations—local activists, volunteers, researchers, media designers, and border citizens—in creating reports, collecting and sharing evidence, and designing new countermeasures. In natural zones of borders devoid of stable legislation, such practices also require technology to be used in a countersurveillance function so that events can be mapped and reconstructed in time and space. This counteruse of the technologies that create cybersurveillance is itself a reclaiming of the social causality of technologies and raises questions about the ethics of their systemic abuse.

THE BELARUSIAN ROUTE

The migrant situation at the border between Poland and Belarus also is part of the micropolitics of "liquid violence." This border is between an EU country (Poland joined the EU in 2004) and a country that continues the traditions of the Eastern Bloc and the USSR (Belarus gained independence from the Soviet Union in 1991). The reactivation of the Eastern Bloc has proved to be successful for the president of the Russian Federation, Vladimir Putin, who invaded Ukraine in February 2022 and launched a devastating war on its territory. The ghost of the Cold War haunts the Polish government's policy toward refugees on this border. Equally vital is the geography of the border. It is 418 kilometers long and in many places cuts through forests and wetlands. The rivers that mark part of the border are difficult barriers to cross. The border is easy to identify in satellite images, as its shape is highlighted by an undeveloped green belt around one kilometer wide (figure 4.3). Part of the border traverses the Białowieża Forest, one of the largest primeval forests in Europe and a protected area on the UNESCO World Heritage list.

Stefanos Levidis, who has monitored Forensic Architecture's projects reconstructing violence against migrants on EU borders, uses the term "border natures" to define this type of natural green zone and notes that the areas have complex histories of old and new regime policies. In his doctoral dissertation titled "Border Natures: The Environment as Weapon at the Edges of Greece" (Levidis 2021), he analyzes the environmental, historical, political, digital, and monitoring characteristics of the Greek borders as an example of EU external borders. His research and projects carried out by Forensic Architecture have shown that

> the "green border" hints to the ecological, cultural, legislative, and military processes through which the border was demarcated, engineered, emptied, and "wilded." It becomes a crucial theoretical tool that allows us to de-construct the deep histories of original, perpetual border violence and their contemporary hauntings. Spanning large swathes of the external frontiers of the EU, the green border speaks to the intentional rendering of borderlands into "wild spaces," ones that are "naturally" governed by violence. Spaces that at first glance appear to be wild or natural and thus outside the space of civil law, but in reality . . . are very much the result of a "flooding" of the space of the border with violence through law and operational assets. (Levidis 2021, 94)

As Levidis points out, including discourses and studies on violence against migrants at so-called natural borders offers a new perspective on the complexity of border-producing issues. This convergence of discourses on migration, the border, and the environment is evident in the conceptual vocabulary introduced into the research—including "border enforcement collective," "nature-inclusive collective," "hostile terrain," "hostile environments," "landscape as space of moral alibi," "border ecologies," and "ecologies of power"—to "describe the geo-political agency of natural environments and their hybridization and weaponization (not

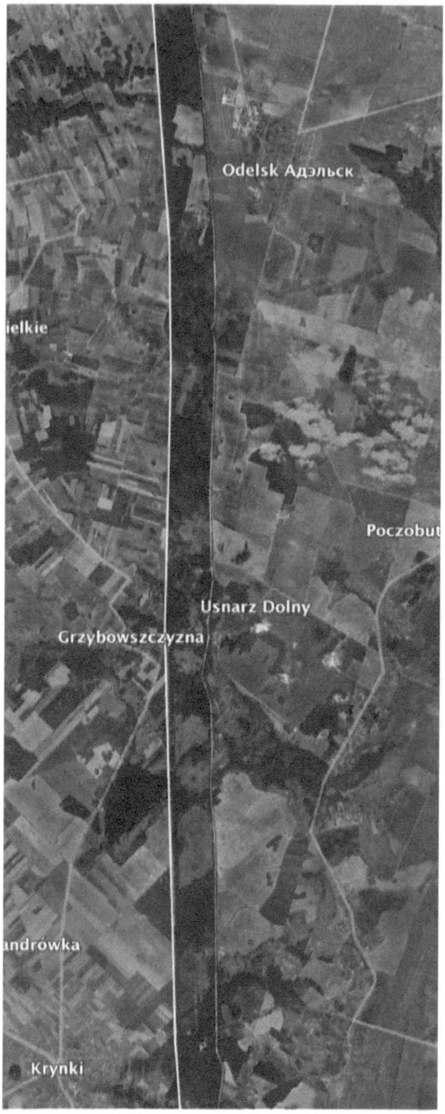

4.3

A green zone at the border between Poland and Belarus. Source: Google Maps, 2022.

exclusively) in border contexts" (Levidis 2021, 20). On the other hand, when Greek border patrols employ the term "natural border," it

> is used to convey the double-entendre of the softer, materially diverse "natural" border infrastructures, where the environment does the work of fencing. Made up of uneven forces and flows, the "green border" expresses the difficulties that the vegetated, hostile terrain poses on border surveillance efforts. At the same time the term is also indirectly mobilized to deflect blame for any deadly "frictions" this terrain imposes on the bodies of migrants, . . . , and with many more who continue to lose their lives during these treacherous . . . crossings. (Levidis 2021, 93)

The hybridization of history and policies and the weaponization of so-called natural borders have also occurred at the Polish-Belarusian border.

As Alicja Fajfer wrote in a report summing up the contemporary migration processes in Central Europe, after the "Mediterranean and Greek routes lost their capacity, the Belarusian route became a viable alternative for undocumented migration from conflict-torn Middle Eastern and African states, such as Afghanistan, Iraq, Syria, and Kongo" (Fajfer 2021, 83). At that time, thousands of migrants from these countries were trying to enter the EU via Belarus.

In the summer of 2021, the political situation in Afghanistan triggered another series of forced migrations. After the United States withdrew its troops from Afghanistan, the Taliban, an Islamic fundamentalist movement, took control of the country. For thousands of Afghans, such a power shift meant that they had to flee the country to avoid the potential punishing actions of a repressive religious regime. This time, migrants and refugees reached the borders of Latvia, Lithuania, and Poland. The tragic situation of those escaping from dangerous home countries to Europe was exploited by the Belarusian president, Aleksandr Lukashenko, who facilitated the arrival of migrants from the Middle East and Africa to his country. A network of Belarusian tourist offices arranged flights to deliver migrants to the EU borders, promising them quick asylum. Belarus granted thousands of tourist visas to citizens of Afghanistan, Iraq, and Syria. Once inside Belarus, however, the migrants were taken to the borders of neighboring EU countries and forced to cross them illegally. An

Amnesty International report compiled on the basis of ethnographic interviews with victims confirms this practice.

> [Migrants] described how they were lured by "attractive travel package" for Belarus, which were widely advertised in their home countries as a safe and easy way to gain access to the EU. Tour operators and others facilitating journeys for a fee told people who arrived in Minsk that they simply had to travel to what is effectively an exclusion zone on Belarus' border with Poland, walk a few kilometers to the Polish border and cross, and then wait for onward transportation to their preferred countries of destination. . . . Once people entered the "zone," often with difficulty crossing the fence and after being forced to pay Belarusian border guards, they had to make their way to the Polish border fences while evading capture by Belarusian border guards who would often forcibly transfer people to "collection sites" where they were violently made to attempt to breach the Polish border in groups. After inevitably being pushed back by Polish border guards and/or captured by Belarusian forces, people were detained in "collection sites" for days or weeks with tens or even hundreds of others without food, water, or shelter, while repeatedly forced to attempt to cross into Poland, often by violent means including beatings, being chased by police dogs and forced to walk through freezing rivers. (Amnesty International 2022, 3)

A report by a Polish organization, Grupa Granica (Border Group), adds that "the humanitarian crisis . . . on the Polish-Belarusian border (as well as on the borders of Belarus with Latvia and Lithuania) is unprecedented in Europe. No country has ever attempted what is people smuggling on such a large scale. Orchestrating migration has become the Belarusian regime's tool to inflict vengeance on the European Union—including on Poland—for their political decisions" (Grupa Granica 2021, 3). As the numbers of people illegally crossing the EU's eastern borders rose, Lithuania, Latvia, and Poland sealed their borders with Belarus (including by building physical barriers such as fences and walls), further aggravating the situation of migrants who found themselves trapped by policies of the Belarusian regime, the Baltic states, and the EU.

The Polish government's first response to this migration crisis was to declare a state of emergency at its border. This banned anyone from staying in the area, which also outlawed civilian relief operations. Later,

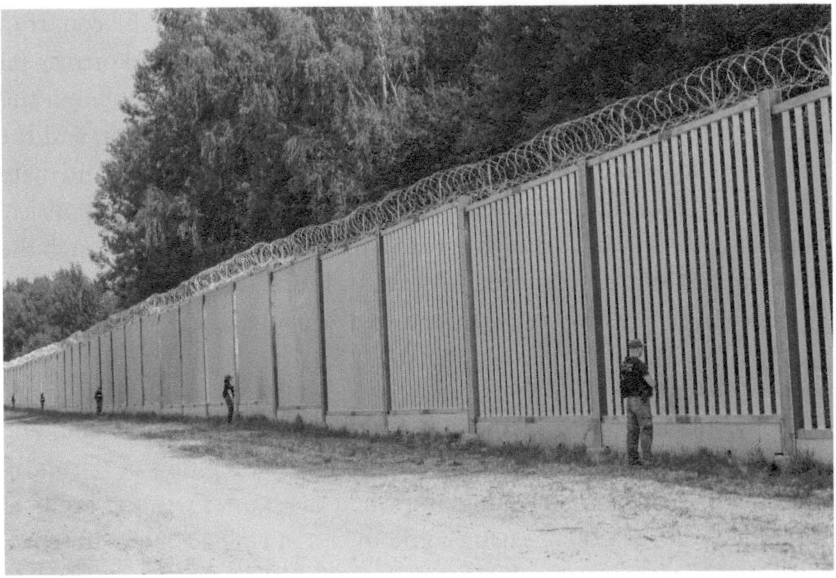

the authorities erected a border wall and installed an electronic infrastructure for monitoring the border area. By the first half of 2022, this architectural and digital barrier included electronic monitoring and a movement-detection system. The structure was built of tall steel spans and was topped by concertina razor wire (figure 4.4). The fence was about six meters high and had deep foundations to prevent tunneling. The electronic system, which the Polish authorities called an "electronic barrier," was an advanced perimetric network of sensors that could detect movement and the presence of objects. It used infrared cameras, visible light band cameras, thermal imaging, microwave barriers that allowed the construction of an invisible field from microwave beams, seismic sensors with self-learning algorithms, and lightweight surveillance drones with daylight and thermal imaging cameras.

4.4

The wall on the border between Poland and Belarus. CC BY 3.0.

The erection of the border barrier in Poland inscribes the country's eastern border into the landscape of the digital regimes of Fortress Europe. Similar fences are being erected on the borders that Lithuania and Latvia share with Belarus. The green border remains, however, and the refugees who become stranded there still need help. The digital and material walls represent how borders can be shifted and redefined for political purposes. At the same time, the green zone militarizes itself through the consumption of detection technologies and surveillance systems as part of a deepening and widening process that weaponizes the landscape.

BREAKING SMARTPHONES

The physical and electronic barriers on the border between Poland and Belarus were under construction when the digital regimes of European border zones were proliferating and when the border was the scene of multiple forms of violence. One common act of violence perpetrated by border services against migrants was seizing their phones, which deprived them of the ability to contact their loved ones, send information about their whereabouts, and record the irregularities and abuses they experienced.

On August 22, 2021, the Polish Hospitality Foundation posted photographs of smashed phones on its Facebook page, showing that the phones' ports were deliberately destroyed by border guards so that they could not be charged (figures 4.5 and 4.6). The pictures were taken by activists in a forest on the border between Poland and Belarus. According to the group's post, the phones belonged to a group of refugees from Afghanistan, Iraq, and Yemen. In response to such destructive practices, various activists and border villagers launched campaigns to collect power banks and smartphones, which were later donated by support groups searching the border forests on the Polish side of the border or left in wrapped packages in the forests to be found by people in need. Telephones were used by activists to contact the groups held up in the forest. The refugees themselves disseminated telephone numbers of Polish organizations that provided support or emergency medical aid. Activists were on duty at the emergency phones, and translators provided support and coordinated emergency responses. Contact by phone became crucial after the state of emergency was imposed. Fundacja Ocalenie (Rescue Foundation) stayed

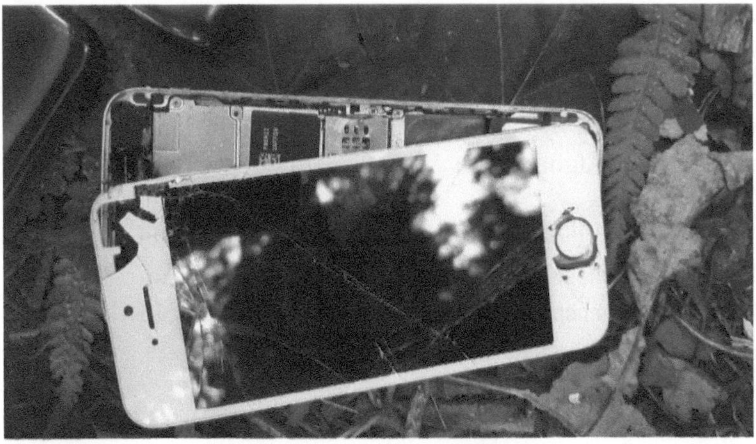

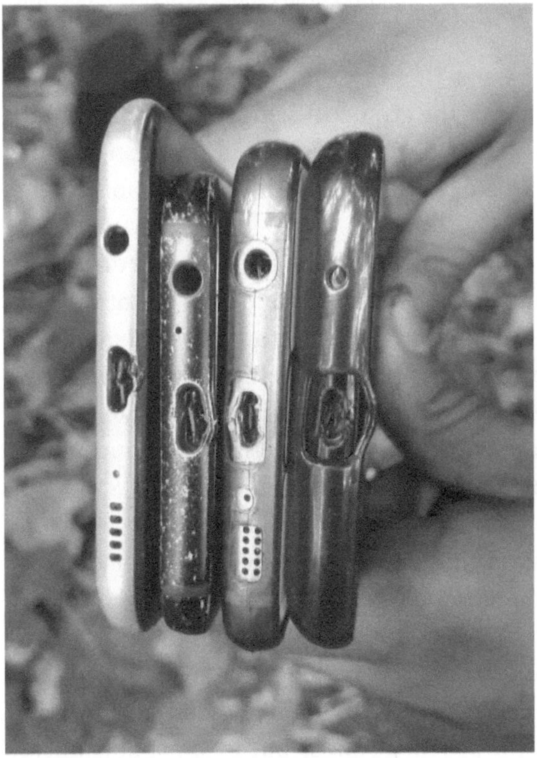

4.5 AND 4.6

Migrants' smashed phones in photographs taken by activists during a humanitarian intervention in the forest. Photo by Chlebem i Solą.

in touch by telephone with groups of refugees who found themselves trapped in the border zone, unable to get to Poland and yet unable to return to Belarus. Some of the conversations, testimonies, and text messages were publicized by activists. One such conversation was with Ms. Gul, a refugee from Afghanistan:

> We are sitting between the barbed wires of Belarus and Poland. What are we going to do, you know whose hands Afghanistan is in. Our country has been taken by the Taliban, and what shall we do? We are surrounded by barbed wire. . . . Take us from here, somewhere inside the country! We only ask this much, save us from death! If you do not want to offer us protection, at least save us from death. If you don't want to protect us, that's not a problem, just save us from death. And then we will do something to return to our country. You all know that we cannot return to our country. If we could, I wouldn't be staying here for a second. (Rescue Foundation 2021)

As the days passed, contact with the groups of refugees wandering in the border zone became increasingly difficult because of the destruction of phones by the border guards of both countries and the inability to recharge phone batteries.

Smartphone damage is one of the more egregious forms of violence inflicted on refugees in vulnerable situations, in foreign countries, with no means of survival, and with no way to return to safety. The practice of depriving people in difficult living conditions of the capacity to communicate freely, use digital maps, and call for help is an example of violence whose genesis and *modus operandi* have both material and digital natures. As Nicos Trimikliniotis, Dimitris Parsanoglou, and Vassilis S. Tsianos observe in *Mobile Commons, Migrant Digitalities and the Right to the City*, people who are in a migration situation are subject to a unique ontology of "mobile commons of migration" (Trimikliniotis et al. 2015) that is produced through a living situation, a current locality, and the policies and mobile digital technologies that make it possible to remain in their own community despite geographic dispersion. Mobile digital technologies, of which smartphones are the primary expression, are an opportunity to communicate and a modern migration toolkit that includes maps, dictionaries, guidebooks, self-help groups, and support groups. They also feature cameras that allow users to photograph their documents and upload them to a virtual drive. This tool allows migrants to document and broadcast in real time the crisis situation in which they may find themselves. Finally, smartphones are also important tools for keeping in touch with loved ones, which often acts as psychological support in crisis situations.

For these reasons, migrants who use smartphones and networked digital services are known as "connected migrants" (Diminescu 2008), the "smart refugee" (Dekker et al. 2018), and the "connected refugee" (Smets 2018). Koen Leurs and Jeffrey Patterson point out that cellular phones used by migrants and refugees make up "digital infrastructures" (Leurs and Patterson 2020) that are the "essentials for survival and transnational communication" (Diminescu 2020). Being a migrant or a refugee is a difficult and dangerous situation. In a refugee situation, smartphones often become the only available infrastructures for communication, contact, reporting to a specific location, and simply survival. The data from phones is also used by the groups and collectives we write about to reconstruct evidence of violence inflicted on refugees as they cross the border.

WEAPONIZATION OF MIGRANTS

Landscape can be weaponized through various techniques and procedures. Sometimes it is enough to functionalize its natural character by using natural barriers in the form of oceans, rivers, lakes, mountain ranges, swamps, and forests. Often, however, the green borders are supplemented with technological infrastructure, such as the electronic barriers and technological monitoring infrastructure along Poland's eastern border. Still, something else is at stake on the Polish-Belarusian border. Not only was the border landscape—consisting mostly of forests, marshes, rivers, and watercourses—subject to weaponization, but this term also began to be used to refer to the refugees themselves. This occurred in a top-down manner within narratives by Polish and EU authorities, condemning migrants to be embedded in the militarized landscape of the border, which from a necropolitical perspective can be viewed as dehumanization and the apartheid policies of Fortress Europe. Since the beginning of the migration crisis and the weaponization of migrants and refugees by the Belarusian regime, individuals and organizations working on the borders of

Belarus with Lithuania, Latvia, and Poland have documented 116 deaths of people trying to cross the EU's eastern border. Another twenty-six deaths have been reported by migrants in testimonies; a few hundred people are considered missing (Pałęcka 2024). This situation at the EU's eastern border has catalyzed the development of independent practices within the aesthetics of radical truth. Artists, researchers, and media designers started to apply open-source intelligence techniques to document and authenticate facts and create a media infrastructure for social justice and the socialization of truth.

One such project in Poland is the video report called *Zone of Hidden Violence* that was drafted by the Border Emergency Collective (2022) (figures 4.7 and 4.8). The research collective collaborated with the Helsinki Foundation for Human Rights, Nomada Association, Forensic Architecture, and Border Group to prepare a video report showing how refugees were instrumentalized when the border between Poland and Belarus was militarized. The video presents evidence collected during a research process that included situated testimonies, geolocation data mapping, audiovisual materials, and three-dimensional reconstructions. The film presents the testimony of two refugees from Syria, Mariam and Hamdi (for the refugees' safety, their identities were anonymized in the report), who identify places where they were detained and experienced various forms of violence at the hands of Polish and Belarusian services. Mariam and Hamdi became victims of the situation we described in an earlier section of this chapter. In Syria, they purchased what they believed would be a trip to Belarus, including tourist visas to that country and a promise that they would be able to cross the green border with Poland. In reality, they were manipulated, repeatedly and illegally detained by Belarusian services, driven from place to place, and forced to wade across a river, wander through the woods, and cut the border fence nets. The two also describe a makeshift camp organized by Belarusian services in the border strip. In the camp, migrants were not allowed to keep cell phones and were beaten for breaching this rule. Miriam and Hamdi experienced multiple pushbacks. Polish services also forced them to sign documents in Polish that they later learned banned them from entering the EU for three years.

On a digitally reconstructed three-dimensional map of the border areas (which included details such as vegetation, brands of border guard

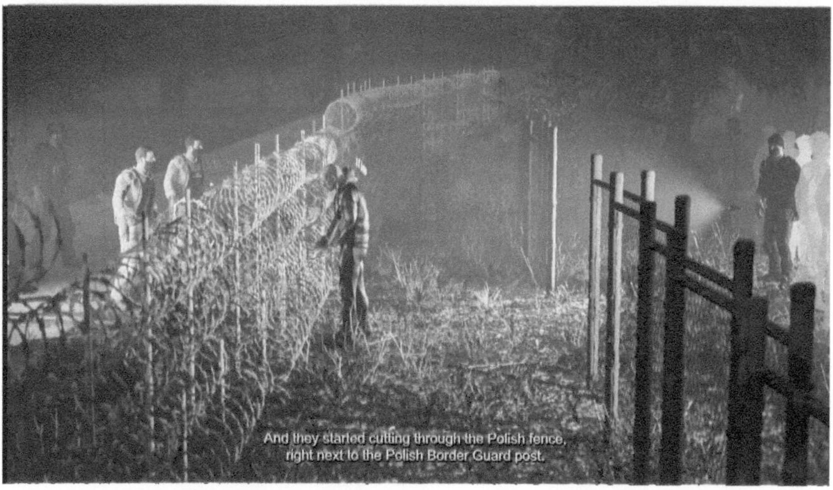

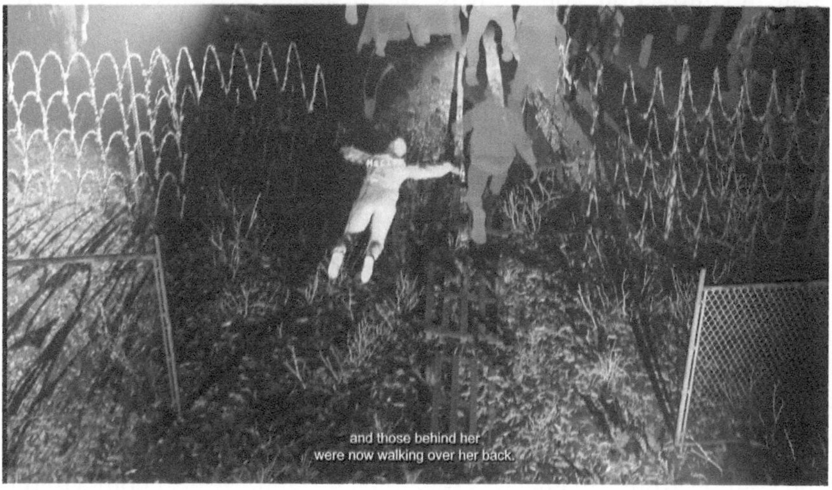

4.7 AND 4.8

Video stills from the Border Emergency Collective's *Zone of Hidden Violence* (2022).

cars, types of terrain, and river landscape), Miriam and Hamdi identified and located the situations they experienced, such as being pushed through a barbed wire fence by Belarusian border services to the Polish side, where an armed cordon of Polish soldiers stood. The materials collected by the groups and organizations that collaborated on this report, along with the situated testimonies of Mariam and Hamdi, are evidence of gross human rights violations and document the instrumentation and use of violence and manipulation against refugees.

The situation on the Polish-Belarusian border illustrates how physical and digital violence operates in the border praxis. It is a necropolitical extension of the European deathscape that now spans the continent. The deathscape is created by the cybernetic regime and the militarization and weaponization of landscape. When defining regimes of contemporary borders, in "Bodies as Borders," Achille Mbembe refers to the expanding "logic of contraction, containment, incarceration and enclosure, whose result is the worldwide erection of all kinds of walls and fortifications, gates and enclaves" (Mbembe 2019a, 5). He sees this as a way to protect territorial borders, seal national identities, impose economic forms of exclusion and exploitation, and manage risks in the modern world: "As a result, borders are no longer merely lines of demarcation separating distinct sovereign entities. Increasingly, they are the name we should use to describe the organized violence that underpins both contemporary capitalism and our world order in general. The border is no longer just a particular point in space, but both a technology and the moving body of undesired masses of population" (Mbembe 2019a, 5). In this text, Mbembe traces various new forms of boundary-setting and wonders why, in a world with ever faster and easier communication, the tendency to cordon off and confine groups in enclaves is gaining ground. He also points to the rapid development of surveillance technologies—sensors, drones, satellites, surveillance robots, infrared detectors, biometric controls, and new forms of chip use—as ways to supervise and manage human bodies and lives. On the other hand, Mbembe notes that borders are increasingly mobile, portable, if ubiquitous realities. This mobility of borders in the face of an attempt to block the mobility of people is aimed at developing regimes of control over speed and movement, so that some can be mobile while others are denied this opportunity. Through this segregation, sorting, and recategorization of people in the name of security, a reclassification of people is carried out to better choose who is who, who should be where, and who should not (Mbembe 2019a, 9).

Viewed and analyzed in this way, the definition of the border includes questions of division, demarcation, and technosurveillance in the contemporary world. Mbembe calls this dangerous process borderization and extends its meaning. It is a process "by which certain spaces are transformed into uncrossable places for certain classes of populations, who thereby undergo a process of racialization; places where speed must be disabled and the lives of a multitude of people judged to be undesirable are meant to be immobilized if not shattered. Whatever the case, the technological transformation of borders is in full swing. In a sense, one of the major consequences of the acceleration of technological innovations has been the creation of a segmented planet of multiple speed regimes" (Mbembe 2019a, 9).

The situations that migrants and refugees face at the EU's borders therefore require a new approach to human rights that calls for action beyond, and in defiance of, the legal and political structures imposed by individual states and global institutions. The politically abused concept of the human must be deconstructed. The human must not cease to be causal in the violence at border zones that have been stripped of legislation or in the mobile border regimes that have been set up to push, segregate, reject, and leave certain individuals in a border deathtrap.

NEW SOLIDARITY

The refugee and migrant situation in many parts of the world is changing the definitions of borders, citizenship, politics of borders, nationality, and affiliation and is generating new forms of violence against those who seek shelter, work, and new lives. Even so, the precarious and ongoing refugee situation in Europe has generated new strategies of collaboration in support of and with these migrants. Nongovernmental organizations are developing ways to integrate and cocreate spaces for migrants to function in new life, legal, social, and cultural situations. In addition, an activist volunteer movement has emerged as "a grassroots mobilization of people of every age, skill and background, who as individuals or small groups responded to a humanitarian crisis that neither governments nor the larger aid agencies seemed willing or able to address" (Clayton 2020, 13). The movement is geographically, culturally, socially, and economically heterogeneous. It is both local and mobile. Residents are helping the migrants who arrive in their neighborhoods, and people who move from different parts of the world to provide aid and assistance are also helping refugees. This assistance involves obtaining various goods for refugees (accommodation, food, clothing, and medicine) and even recharging or organizing phones or internet access so that they can contact their families and begin to find their bearings in their new living conditions. Sometimes legal advice is provided, and guidebooks for getting around a given area are distributed. Protests are conducted against the removal of refugees and their deplorable detention conditions. Refugees themselves provide assistance by preparing places for compatriots, families, and friends who arrive. Each refugee route leading to Europe has different characteristics and requires different ways of cooperation between volunteers and refugees. Different state policies intersect with forms of grassroots assistance.

In her book *New Internationalists: Activist Volunteers in the European Refugee*, Sara Clayton (2020) has collected a few dozen testimonies of activist volunteers. They showcase volunteers' material, legal, civil, and educational aid to migrants, their involvement in the fight for refugee rights and legal status, and support for opening borders for new arrivals. Some of these activities have led to criminal convictions for volunteers. What emerges from the stories gathered in the book is a picture of refugees who are dismantling traditional definitions of politics, the border, the state, and citizenship and of other people who want to create new communities from the bottom up, beyond the state constraints and borders that block opportunities for aid and assistance. Clayton notes that this is a new movement "in which this mobilization is a departure from previous aid or charitable initiatives and can be seen to be a new kind of social intervention, with innovative new forms of organization and effect" (Clayton 2020, 25). Clayton concludes that this new kind of mobilization is developing an international perspective on how to respond to the crisis. A new politics is being generated as a kinetic, mobile, on-the-move grassroots cause. The agglomerative structure of relationships that bind together refugees, volunteer activists, and transdisciplinary research groups creates a dynamic and transversal space for the creation of social, economic, cultural, media, civil, and legal practices.

Clayton's book includes a chapter by Anna-Louise Milne (2020) called "A New Politics of Solidarity?" in which the author looks new possibilities for practicing solidarity in the face of violence and the closing of national borders to those who flee their countries. One possibility is that new mobility policies could lead to a new inclusive definition of citizenship. She cites Michel Foucault—"There exists an international citizenship which as such has its rights and duties, and which is obliged to stand up against all forms of abuse of power, no matter who commits them, no matter who are their victims" (Foucault 1994, 707)—and she implies that we face an important opportunity to change top-down policies for citizenship and refugees. Many of the activists included in Clayton's book indicate that their concepts of the white savior bringing aid to places in need of intervention changed radically after their experiences with refugees. These changes always meant cocreating new forms of cooperation with refugees. Because these forms of mobilization often function outside legal frameworks, activists need to find legal loopholes in legislative state procedures and seek new solutions to migrant problems: "They draw their disruptive and innovative qualities from the fact that they often operate outside the legal framework, turned towards new horizons and unexpected joys, sometimes in overt contempt of law, sometimes in canny negotiation with local or national authorities. The notion that draws these different forms of contemporary radicalism together is solidarity, the watchword of a new international citizenship" (Milne 2020, 430–431). According to Clayton and Milne, this movement could lead to a new polity that can change the face of violent top-down definitions of borders and policies of hostility toward refugees. Many projects are differently opposing border violence, and they involve researchers, designers, artists, activists, volunteers, and, above all, stories, testimonies, recordings, and photos taken by migrants and refugees themselves. These projects need strategies for using the aesthetics of radical truth to agglomerate more people, groups, and organizations. This movement might, in fact, be an embryo of a new solidarity.

Being radical in these circumstances involves solidarity, care, and a politics that goes beyond state patterns of action and beyond recognized aid institutions. The practices of aid groups also need to be redefined in the context of migration changes, digital dividuation, technological acceleration, and economic exclusion. An aesthetics of radical truth can be realized as an aesthetic of kinetic, mobile practices rather than fixed and unchanging practices. AeRT is grassroots causality in action and exists where people track, research, and share knowledge about violence and crimes at the borders. Let us finish this unfinishable chapter with Achille Mbembe's statement about border violence and its deep colonial and extractivist roots:

> We cannot speak about migration without addressing the presence and actions of the West in the rest of the world. Europe and North America cannot possibly go about destroying other people living environments, extracting their oil, gas, timber, diamonds and gold, shipping it all home, leaving nothing behind, turning their cities into rubble, bringing to an end the possibilities of life in faraway places, and expect those affected by such upheavals to survive in the midst of the ruin.
>
> Europe's and America's violence abroad is a key reason why people are forced to run away from places where they were born and raised, but which have become uninhabitable. And I doubt building walls around one's nation-state is the most intelligent way of resolving the many crises we have contributed to fomenting around the world. Instead of marketing fictions and inflaming dark passions and hysteria, we should take seriously the question of the future, reactivate our critical faculties and rehabilitate reason, because if we do not rehabilitate reason, we will not be able to repair the world or learn how to share the planet. (Mbembe 2019a, 16)

5

DIGITAL ARCHIVES FOR EPISTEMIC JUSTICE

This chapter is devoted to the labor of those who gather data and materials about the violence suffered by victims of state regimes, colonized minorities, people of color, indigenous peoples, protesters and the activists. When data recording is agglomerative—collective and commonly shared—archives can resist the kind of institutional control that appropriates memories of historical processes. Instead, new digital archive policies are contingent on shared social justice. Such archives must be open, connective, agglomerative, ecomedial, and distributed. Because the truth that is produced through archival labor and social interaction is multimedia and multisensory and because the work finds narratives and courses of action and compares moments in time, the truth in these archives is never topical but is situated. The agglomerative labor of new archivists and archive users can sidestep direct supervision, deeply ingrained cultural politics of invisibility, regimes that produce historical discourse subordinated to power structures, and the covert colonial and neocolonial systems that capitalize on injustices or relegate minorities to the margins of society. Creating grassroots documentation, narratives, and archives is a practice of resisting regimes of invisibility and reclaiming media identities. This practice arises from a struggle to be seen and understood within a culture that engages in the processes of media documentation and the visual representation of violence.

MEDIA INVISIBILITY AS CULTURAL AND SOCIAL ERASURE

The Twelfth Berlin Biennale for Contemporary Art (curated by Kader Attia in 2022) featured a video installation called *Complexifying Restitution*. Made by Egyptian-born French filmmaker and visual artist Jihan El-Tahir, the work was inspired by the Laval Decree, a law that was adopted by the French government in 1934 and was in force in all French colonies in Africa until 1960 (Genova 2006). The Laval Decree controlled how movies were made in French colonized states. It regulated how films could be made and shown in African countries and prohibited members of colonized communities from filming themselves. This effectively precluded any African filmmakers from recording local culture and identity or using film to promote emancipation. In 1949, a note sent by the French Academy of Colonial Sciences to the Ministry for Overseas France read as follows: "Cinema constitutes, with radio, one of the most powerful weapons of which a nation could make use, in the present period, for its propaganda. . . . Documentary film, in particular, possesses, from this point of view, a capacity and an action infinitely more expansive and more effective than the book or the newspaper, which touches a public much more limited and that does not present any point [of reference] except for the image, [as seen] by its magic and even at times [constitutive of] its undeniable reality, [therefore, documentary film] presents an undeniable value" (Genova 2006, 51–52).

In the postwar years, France tightened its grip over colonial media content even further. Films in Arabic were banned to prevent the promotion of the Arabic language in the French colonies, to curb opportunities for cultural solidarity, and to preclude "potentially subliminal subversive messages that might be lodged in the recesses of meaning within Arabic words and phrases" (Genova 2006, 55). In her film, El-Tahir examines this colonial and media violence and identifies "interstices between official history and memory in an attempt to reinterpret the moments of our history of which no traces have been left behind and to propose a new reading and alternative voice from a Global South perspective" (Al-Tamimi 2022, 108).

Kader Attia calls this kind of colonial violence—which consists in denying the possibility of recording history and independently creating a media representation of one's own identity and culture—a "regime of invisibility and abstraction orchestrated by coloniality, modernity, imperialism, and fascism" (Attia 2022, 30). By aiming to "depoliticize the social subject" and make local cultures "invisible," colonial media violence supervised and controlled possible emancipation processes and rebellions. It also enabled violence that could not be proven in a world that was heavily modernized and mediatized. Violence without material evidence in the media did not exist. As Attia writes: "Invisibility is discourse's preferred weapon of control: always in denial of the crime, the enunciator claims victory while disavowing all responsibility" (Attia 2022, 24).

But media tools and related cultural practices have the potential for agglomeration, which generates political agency—practicing self-determination by using media to represent personal identity and culture, to communicate with others, and to shape equitable media representation. Despite the persistence of colonial empires, agglomeration has infiltrated digital culture and can provide counterstructures to forms of algorithmic governance. As communities explore self-determination of their own social, political, and cultural media representation, Attia asks a question: "Is it possible to achieve emancipation from the latent fascist governances that derive from regimes of invisibility, and from their technological avatar within algorithmic governance? Perhaps—and as paradoxical as this seems—we may do so not by looking at the past or the future but by reappropriating the present" (Attia 2022, 30).

Since new forms of collaborative multimedia archives make up an "endless circulation between different levels, people, networks and locations," Annet Dekker calls them "living archives" (Dekker 2017, 17). Arjun Appadurai also highlights the collaborative nature of media archives, particularly in relation to materials collected by communities affected by violence—forced migrants, refugees, and those living in a diaspora: "We should begin to see all documentation as intervention, and all archiving as part of some sort of collective project. Rather than being the tomb of the trace, the archive is more frequently the product of the anticipation of collective memory" (Appadurai 2003, 16). Appadurai observes that the "deep functions of the archive"—their agglomerative potential and their potential for generating political agency for specific communities—are neutralized by nation states, which see them as a counternarrative for top-down forms that homogenize history to subject it to the political interests of these states. Archives can be hazardous in that they are more than just a record and distribution of memory. They are a form of "shared narratives and practices," and given the communicative potential of the digital media, they can generate a "diasporic public sphere" (Appadurai 2003, 21–22).

Wolfgang Ernst, who adopted a category called a "dynarchive" to describe the ontology of media archives, opens up a path to studying unstable documents, something that "lies between the archival and the anarchival spheres" (Ernst 2016, 10). As a media archeologist, Ernst points to the infrastructural meaning of traditional archives (both analogue and digitized by institutions). Their procedures, structures, collections, and institutions affect the way we preserve and store documents that identify the past and the ways these infrastructures produce a memory of the past.

Achille Mbembe says in "Decolonizing Knowledge and the Question of the Archive" that to grasp anew the archiving process requires rejecting its epistemic foundations by demythologizing "whiteness": "Whiteness is about entrapment. Whiteness is at its best when it turns into a myth. It is the most corrosive and the most lethal when it makes us believe that it is everywhere, that everything originates from it and that it has no outside" (Mbembe 2015 n.p.). Archives have continued to be tools of the dominant historical discourse of whiteness. They produce knowledge that is subordinated to a prevailing political agenda and ideology. Western culture honed these strategies under colonialism. As Mbembe sees it, each museum is an epistemic space, and archives also constitute epistemic practices. This is because dominating in global north models of archiving is an extension of the westernalized model of knowledge production and dissemination. When they are decolonized, a new epistemic practice will emerge: "Our capacity to make systematic forays beyond our current knowledge horizons will be hampered if we rely exclusively on those aspects of Western archive that disregard other epistemic traditions" (Mbembe 2015, n.p.).

For J. J. Ghaddar and Michelle Caswell, "effective decolonization requires a radical transformation that can only be realized through a radical praxis" (Ghaddar and Caswell 2019, 71). Archives related to the colonized are a kind of "afterlife of slavery," and decolonizing archival records and generating documents to be stored in archives are matters not of discourse but of radical praxis. Ghaddar and Caswell invoke one of the earliest critical post- and decolonial concepts, Aimé Césaire's radicalism. This refers to the generation of colonial knowledge, which is important from the perspective of archivism. Colonization means "thingification," as Césaire calls the process (Césaire et al. 2000). When the right to generate archival knowledge is regained, the people who were enclosed and enslaved in the cataloguing procedures are empowered. This is because archives embody the fundamental logic of colonial subordination, as Césaire observed many years ago: "No human contact, but relations of domination and submission which turn the colonizing man into a classroom monitor, an army sergeant, a prison guard, a slave driver, and the indigenous man into an instrument of production. My turn to state an equation: colonization = 'thingification.' I hear the storm. They talk to me about progress, about 'achievements,' diseases cured, improved standards of living" (Césaire et al. 2000, 42).

The archives and media repositories discussed in this chapter are examples of radical praxis. They restore the truth of the documents and generate and agglomerate tools and strategies that enable everyone to document reality, deconstruct discourses on the correctness of the archives produced in white and Western epistemology, and denounce discourses of violence in identifying and interpreting archival records. As Ghaddar and Caswell observe: "radical refers to a research and practice approach that goes to the root cause of social, cultural, economic and political phenomena; that reflects on and is transparent about the assumptions and positionalities of those producing and disseminating knowledge; and that is committed to dismantling structures and systems of oppression and domination. It is change-oriented and future-minded insofar as it helps us imagine both a different way of archiving and a different world to be archived" (Ghaddar and Caswell 2019, 72). Within this methodological horizon, the traditionally understood notion of archive must be distorted and opened to new modes of epistemic praxis.

From these perspectives, we describe the distribution of information through Arab archives that document various forms of protest and resistance to state regimes—the first protests of the 2010 Arab Spring in Egypt, the repression and military violence during the war in Syria, and the resistance in Lebanon. We explore the significance of projects such as the 858: An Archive of Resistance (repository of video footage of violence committed by security forces in Egypt from 2010 to 2013), the Syrian Archive (documentation of human rights violence committed by all parties to the conflicts in Syria since 2011), and the Alsaha Archive (documentation of protests against the Lebanese government since 2019). The second part of the chapter looks at the media representation of structural violence against African Americans. Here, we analyze the Police Brutality at the Black Lives Matter Protests project (Forensic Architecture and Bellingcat 2020), a living archive that documents a systemic culture of violence against protesters. It illustrates how the media record is neutralized by the violence of the dominant media and cultural discourse. Finally, we look at an experimental form of the Quipu Project archive that combines open modes of mediascapes, interactive online documentary and forensic investigation, and the memories of violence against indigenous and rural people in Peru.

THE ARAB ARCHIVES OF UPRISINGS

One of the first grassroots and most geographically extensive archive projects recording acts of revolution against national leadership and violence against protesters are the Arab Spring archives. They cover several Arab countries—Tunisia, Libya, Egypt, Yemen, Syria, and Bahrain—where between 2010 and 2012 civilians tried to regain liberties and rights. The platforms, tools, and repositories of data from the social revolution that emerged at the time are important within the new design of digital living archives. Some archives continue the labor of data gathering, collecting a broad perspective of viewpoints and analyzing the social, political, and cultural consequences of the protests, especially in situations of military conflict and harm to civilians in Arab countries. These archives are the result of the grassroots practices of various groups and organizations that identified where protesters were cut off from free access to information. In practice, access to certain sites on the internet has been restricted, and governments have attempted to cut off their citizens from internet access. On the third day of protests in Egypt, the country went completely offline, which became one of the iconic moments of the Arab Spring. The situation strongly coupled physical and digital spaces and showed that the internet is not merely a digital place but also a new realm of physical space dedicated to information and communication. In this new topology of (especially urban) space, one aspect of modern infrastructure was taken away top-down, leading to many acts of self-reconstruction and the recovery of the digital and material dimensions of reality. Cutting off Egyptian citizens from the internet did not end their protests. On the contrary, they urgently sought ways of recording the violence perpetrated by the regime against the protesters and of distributing those recordings globally. People continued to gather in large numbers and remained in city squares and streets—demonstrating, blocking traffic, and establishing new grassroots access points to the telecommunications network and the internet.

This wave of social and political resistance sparked novel grassroots strategies for archiving protests and for circumventing restrictions. One of these was the Alkasir app developed by Yemeni software developer Walid al-Saqaf. Al-Saqaf himself was a victim of violence when his YemenPortal.net was blocked by the Yemeni regime in 2008 (Al-Saqaf 2014, 23). Blocking access to information did not deter activists from creating independent content and disseminating knowledge about the violence of these regimes. As Al-Saqaf observes in his book *Breaking Digital Firewalls. Analyzing Internet Censorship and Circumvention in the Arab World*:

> The Internet is not centrally located and cannot be directly controlled by any state. This created a weak spot that some Arab activists have noticed and effectively exploited by taking advantage of governments' ill preparations for such a major paradigm shift in the way information is shared and people communicate. . . . activists have started developing an understanding of how to overcome Internet filtering using technique called censorship circumvention and effectively overcame a major technical hurdle set by the government. By using proxy websites or other circumvention tools, and with a little experimentation, those activists were able to end governments' information monopoly by getting around censorship and continuing to publish sensitive and dissident content freely. (Al-Saqaf 2014, 24–25)

The archives of the Arab Spring document these events and generate resistance by producing an independent media infrastructure for disseminating the news and building a global visibility strategy on the web. In doing so, they become independent of local regimes and the structures of postcolonial surveillance that are continued by technocapitalism and algorithmic platform censorship.

THE 858 ARCHIVE

858: An Archive of Resistance is an online repository documenting the 2011 protests in Egypt against police brutality under Hosni Mubarak's presidency and for increased civil rights. The website's name indicates the number of hours of video footage available in the archive when it went online publicly in 2018. Since then, the archive, founded by an anonymous volunteer media activist collective called Mosireen, which was formed during the Egyptian revolution, has been expanded and updated. The collective documented the uprising by arranging and broadcasting media actions that matched what was taking place on the streets of Egyptian cities and thereby became strategies of protest and resistance. Members of the collective made their own recordings during the revolution, gathered recordings from others, and secured materials removed from the public space of the media by official broadcasters.

In the first phase of its operations, 2011 to 2014, Mosireen focused on making recordings and posting them online. The 250 videos produced during this time were intended to show street politics, state violence, and labor rights. In addition, members of the group organized screenings and educational workshops in public spaces. As the collective points out, its committed work "on the streets" was significantly reduced after August 14, 2013, when Cairo police killed hundreds of supporters of deposed President Mohamed Morsi who were staging a weeks-long sit-in at Cairo's Rabaa al-Adawiyya square and al-Nahda square. According to various sources, large groups of police removed peacefully demonstrating protesters from these squares, killing from between a few hundred to more than a thousand people (Human Rights Watch 2014). After this event, the collective worked to collect video evidence of the sit-ins in an open archive. According to the group's website: "858 is, of course, just one archive of the revolution. It is not, and can never be, *the archive.* It is one collection of memories, one set of tools we can all use to fight the narratives of the counter-revolution, to pry loose the state's grip on history, to keep building new histories for the future" (858 Archive 2018).

The 858: An Archive of Resistance is available in Arabic and English, and videos can be filtered by date, place, event, and keywords. The location of the filming of specific videos can be shown on a map of Egypt. All materials in the archive are available under Creative Commons licenses. The archive was built on the open-source software Pad.ma (Public Access Digital Media Archive), which facilitates the creation of online public repositories and an agglomeration of users around them. The tools help users browse the video materials, create other collections, annotate materials, make comments, make keywords, export the materials into various formats, and upload them to other locations. Its functionality allows Pad.ma to serve as an effective tool for collaborative work with archival material (figure 5.1).

On its website, the Mosireen collective has also published a do-it-yourself kit that explains (in Arabic) the key technical aspects of video making and editing in the context of protests and a long text (in English and Arabic) that addresses the archiving process and its historical, media, and cultural significance. "858: No Archive Is Innocent: On the Attempt of Archiving Revolt" (mosireen_soursar 2020) is an archivist manifesto signed by an activist group member called "mosireen_soursar." The manifesto acknowledges the importance of labor in the archive process—determining what is to be archived, how much care should be spent on the process, and what the significance of the decolonization strategies is. This leads to a desire to avoid the patterns that are engrained in Western archives and that determine what to show, how to catalog it, and what a single record is. As the manifesto declares:

> The act of archiving is . . . complicated. Behind every category, every naming, the use of language, title, date, lies a decision which appears to have been simple when seen in its finalized form. Every one of those decisions is a choice to participate in the game of power.
>
> . . . what matters, is having bodies on the street. . . . Let us not over-celebrate archives. Archiving revolt is a critical act, but it is a secondary one. First and

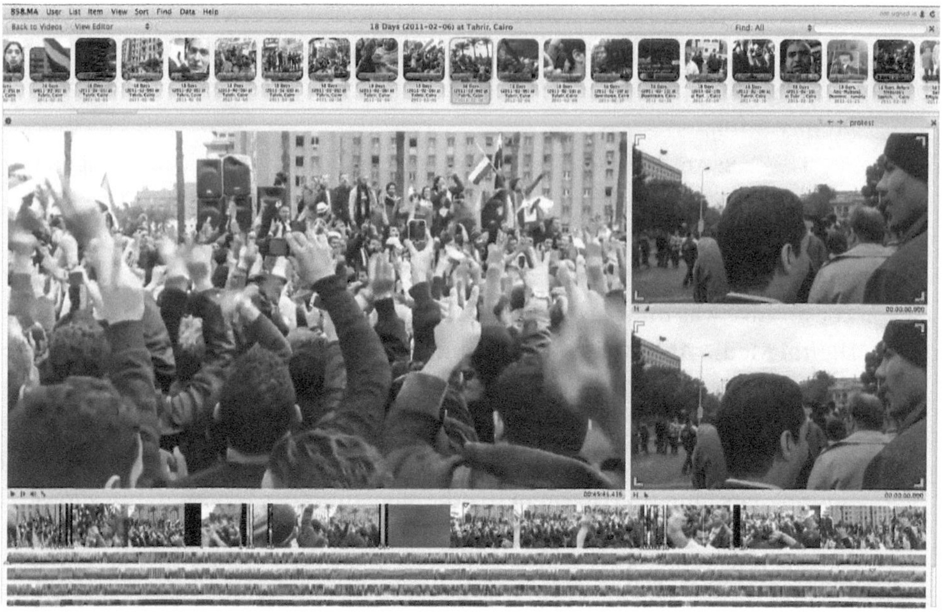

> foremost comes the revolt, taking the risk, confronting state violence, the pain of loss, the sleepless nights, and facing your own fears. . . .
>
> Every archived moment entails the lack of a lot of others that aren't. We could not access the torture chambers, we could not lay bare the military tribunals, nor can any archive relay the effect of years of economic policies that privileged a few at the expense of the majority, this invisible thing we call neocolonialism that keeps re-inventing itself in the most brutal of ways. (mosireen_soursar 2020, n.p.)

The manifesto addresses both the complex process of decolonizing archives and a policy of providing visibility for those who were excluded,

5.1

Video editing and annotation tools on a page from the 858 Archive.

repressed, negated, and destroyed by violent regimes. According to the members of the collective themselves:

> We started 858,
>
> because the narrative of events is day by day being written by the media outlets, through school curricula, through new laws, through the continuous incarceration of those who dare to speak out, through the writing of books and the speaking of speeches of the tyrants in power and their "democratic" partners across the globe who engage in trade and diplomacy and general statist performances, because the narrative is thereby taken from those who shouted "we want the downfall of the system."
>
> because there are lessons to be found in those chants, in the tactics, in the battles won, in the things people spoke in front of or behind a camera or audio recorder in the time of revolt.
>
> because there are traces of the solidarity that existed between cities, between struggles, as well as evidence of a lack thereof, both of which are critical to reflect on for the coming uprisings.
>
> because we must learn our lesson from the tactics of the counter-revolution that attacked and subverted a vibrant revolt.
>
> because the archive has the potential to shape our ideas and move our emotions, to act as a reminder, to prepare for what is to come. (mosireen_soursar 2020, n.p.)

The 858 Archive is deliberately open and multisensory. So is the attendant, radically situated truth about uprisings. One more major question is addressed by Donatella Della Ratta in *Shooting a Revolution: Visual Media and Warfare in Syria* (Della Ratta 2018). Those who record or want to record the violence of the regime with a smartphone, camera, or video camera risk their own freedom and the lives of many others. These risks to the documentalists' lives cannot be disregarded when analyzing and reconstructing the origins of documents preserved in the archives of the Arab Spring. The term that Della Ratta uses—the "shooting revolution"—has the double implication of taking pictures and being shot at. As the author observed in an interview related to the book: "It addresses the aesthetic and material implications of the act of 'shooting' as a practice of everyday life, as a mundane activity carried on among other life activities. A life activity that, yet, becomes labor within the infrastructure of the networks where both unpaid and under-paid work, whether produced by peaceful activists or by jihadis, indifferently becomes part of the 'sharing' economy of platform capitalism" (Della Ratta 2019, n.p.). That is why selecting documents and carefully preserving them in the archive are crucial. They preserve both the situational memory of the event and the act of recording.

As indicated above, over time, attempts were made to remove many documents from social media and publicly available digital platforms—in effect, to eliminate the essential elements necessary for reconstructing the situation. According to mosireen_soursar's archivist manifesto:

> On March 16, 2018, the private Egyptian TV channel OnTV removed from its YouTube channel the archive of four programs that ran during the time of revolution.
>
> Google's fourth quarter report of 2017 announced the company removed over 8 million videos with "a machine-learning-based algorithm to flag videos for terms of service (ToS)-related violations . . . to expedite the removal of propaganda videos." We know that countless videos of the non-violent protests that began the Syrian uprising were purged during this time. No other copies of many of these exist. From these consequences, we can judge the political intentions behind such an "algorithm."
>
> The collective didn't want an algorithm, government or company to decide for us which traces to preserve and which to delete. . . .
>
> With 858, we are trying with care to disseminate copies of the archive on servers worldwide so that they remain accessible even after a potential attack or blocking of any one server.
>
> These are attempts to undermine the hegemony of ownership. (mosireen_soursar 2020)

THE SYRIAN ARCHIVE

The Syrian Archive was started by archivist and activist Hadi Al Khatib (2020), and it is now managed by Mnemonic, an organization he founded. The archive's holdings contain over fifteen years' worth of materials documenting events from the Arab protests in 2011 to civil and human rights violations in Syria by all the parties to the ongoing conflict. As the founders of the archive note: "In the Syrian conflict, there are more hours of videos documenting the conflict than there have been hours in the conflict itself" (Syrian Archive 2025, n.p.). Agglomerative mechanisms are needed for the archive, as the documents dispersed through social media make up an "accidental" archive (Syrian Archive 2025, n.p.). As the authors of the archive observe, the internet "allows anyone in the world to witness a conflict for the first time in history, practically in real time" (Syrian Archive 2025, n.p.). The breadth and accessibility of the materials provide opportunities for a precise, multisite documentation of violence, but this huge influx of media materials may overlook tiny facts of enormous importance. Another problem is the memory structures of these events, which during media dispersion can take on an undetermined, incidental, and fluid character.

The Syrian Archive is one of the Digital Lost and Found Item projects that copy and secure online data that is often later removed from social media by moderators or algorithms. Another project, (Re-)Humanization of the Syrian Digital Memory, gathers multisource digital testimonies and digital copies of everyday lives during war. The archive's website states that via "autobiographical-narrative interviews with Syrian digital content producers, we aim to contextualise and re-humanise the digital memories of the Syrian uprising and conflict through the everyday, social, individual and collective memories of their producers, as surviving eyewitnesses of atrocities" (Syrian Archive 2025, n.p.).

To date, the Syrian Archive has gathered over three million records, but it publishes only those verified through a standard methodology that authenticates data and safeguards against revictimization. The archive uses English and Arabic, but most of the texts and source materials are available only in Arabic. The records can be filtered through many designations, such as time, type of event, and type of data, and a map can be used to locate the events related to the records. Investigations are another important part of the archive. They are an example of the application of the material collected in the archive. Using open-source intelligence techniques, archivists analyze and compile materials into datasets and post multimedia reports online. For example, the investigation "Targeting Health: Attacks against Medical Facilities in Syria" (Syrian Archive 2021) identified and documented 410 assaults on 270 medical facilities between

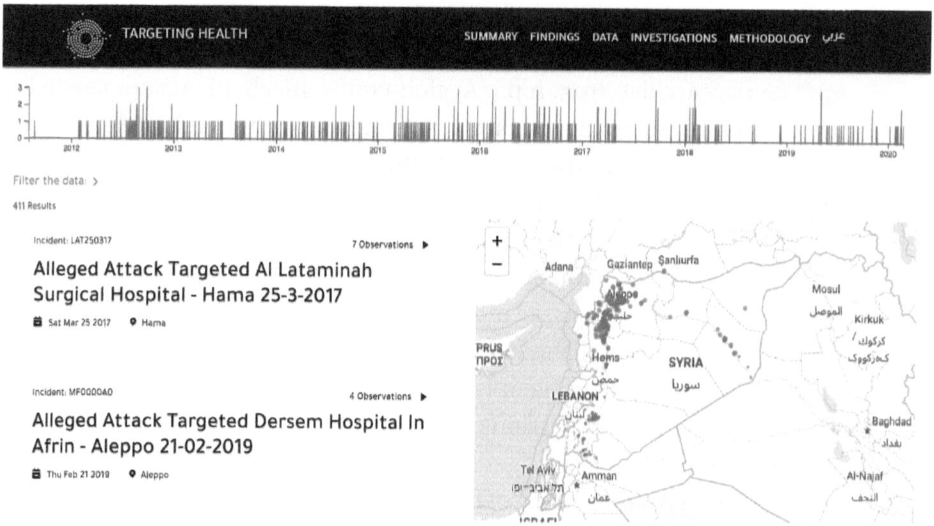

2011 and 2020. The investigation depicts the systemic and intentional nature of these attacks, whose consequences targeted civilians (figure 5.2).

THE ALSAHA ARCHIVE

The Alsaha Archive is an online repository of documents that is published solely in Arabic. The project is led by the Akhbar Al-Saha Digital Observatory. It documents violence perpetrated by Lebanese authorities against citizens and disseminates information on the injustices experienced by minorities like refugees, foreign workers, homosexuals, and trans people. According to the group's website: "There is no social justice without equal distribution of wealth, and fighting masculinity, capitalism, sectarianism, classism, racism, and the systematic starvation system against all people residing in Lebanon" (Alsaha Archive 2025, n.p.). The archive began

5.2

A webpage from the Syrian Archive's investigation called "Targeting Health: Attacks against Medical Facilities in Syria."

during the 17 October Protests that took place in Lebanon in 2019 as part of the Second Arab Spring. The protests were against additional taxes on gasoline and on VoIP (voice over internet protocol) calls on apps such as WhatsApp but primarily condemned sectarian rule. Unlike earlier protests, the 2019 demonstrations extended beyond large cities like Beirut and involved a variety of groups.

The Alsaha Archive agglomerates crucial evidence that documents events from the perspective of the protesters on the streets. This material has great medial and cultural potential because it provides *in situ* evidence about the nature and microdynamics of the protests. The collected materials also reveal the violence used by the government against rebellious Lebanese citizens. Navigation through the archive is done by tags that allow browsing by type of record (text, photos, videos, or posters), geographic location (figure 5.3), keywords, temporal chronology, shouts and chants of the protesters, people associated with politics and protests, and source of the materials (such as names of press outlets or publishers). Equally important are the media materials collected in the Beirut Walls catalog, including photos and videos documenting protest graffiti, murals, and other forms of visual interventions in the urban and architectural structure of Beirut (Talking Walls 2019). The archive documents forms of artivism, street art, tactical media, and strategies of urban critique and countersurvivalence.

The materials collected in the archive are heterogeneous. They document political events and bear witness to microhistories, narratives, and personal testimonies about the protests against systemic violence in Lebanon. The media archive documents the Lebanese protest movement using visuals, sounds, and art to show the political and cultural everyday lives of protesters and the media ethnographic and urban digital infrastructures.

LIVING ARCHIVES OF RESISTANCE

Arab archives are examples of multisite, bottom-up, open, and transparent practices of documenting both the uprisings against brutal regimes and the violence inflicted on the protesters. Most the secured media documents, data, and records never made it to the government archives of the Arab states or the archives of the countries supporting the Arab

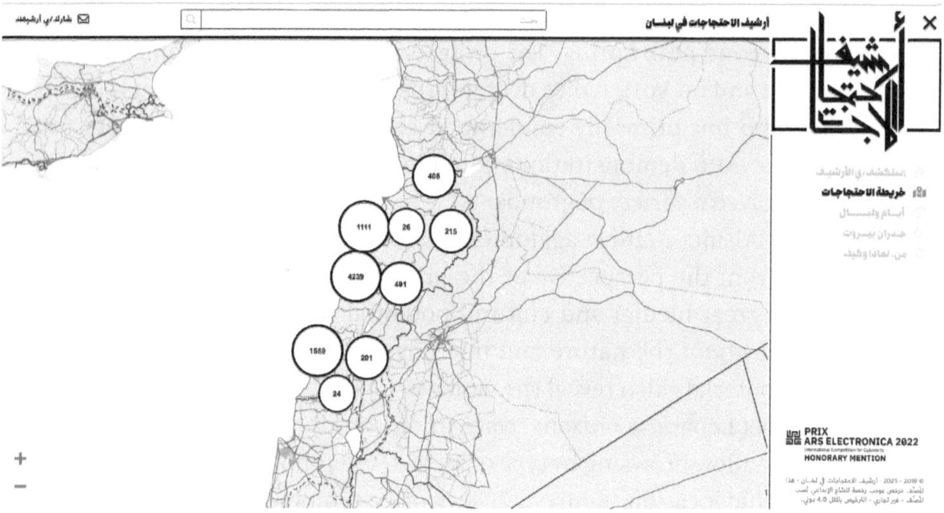

revolution. As the authors of the 858 archive note, "archiving isn't an innocent activity and in its most routine manifestation is wrapped up in the institution of the state. It is deeply violent" (858 Archive, n.p.). Therefore, a grassroots effort was needed, and it was on the ground, in a specific situation, and often at the risk of the archivist's life. Individuals, groups, and associations worked to create tools and strategies for archiving and navigating the collected documents. These are digital living archives and can be read individually or together, and each time a different interweaving of situations and events becomes evident. The aesthetics of arranging and compiling documents here are transparent and open, so that understanding and getting to the truth are agglomerative work for the audience, future researchers, activists, and journalists. This is why the multisite

5.3

A webpage from the Alsaha Archive website that enables users to browse records based on a geographical location.

Arab archives are mediascapes (Appudarai 2003) that reach a large group of recipients. They give voice and opportunities to be seen to those who were previously denied such opportunities.

Archives documenting civil resistance are a vital complement to documents that bear witness to the violence of state regimes, such as the publicized photographs of prisoners tortured by the Syrian regime between 2011 and 2013. Surreptitiously taken out of Syria in 2013 by a former officer in the Syrian military police, the photos were later exhibited in Europe in 2016 as *Codename: Caesar. Syrian Prisoners Victims of Torture*. The exhibition shocked visitors with its unequivocal evidence of extreme violence committed against political prisoners by the Syrian government. The grassroots archives created by participants in the protests do not allow us to forget that violence directly affects bodies and also penetrates the structures of reality by becoming a condition of everyday life.

Violence is a structural force that is used by regimes to suppress democratic uprisings, but the documents do not take a straightforward path to become publicly available to reveal the multilevel nature of violence. Documentation is made on the street, goes online to social media, and is subjected to the mechanisms of digital surveillance of platform capitalism. Unless photos and videos documenting violence are collected and archived—via agglomerative processes that form larger collections and bring together people to work on their meaning and perpetuation—they often are deleted or lost in a plethora of other content. This was the precedent-setting case in 2018 when YouTube identified thirty-three million videos as "terrorist propaganda" and deleted them (Della Ratta 2020, 105). The deleted materials included those shared by independent media activists as evidence of the violence committed against civilians by authorities in Syria, Egypt, and Lebanon. Therefore, the archives we describe have their own independent or open-source platforms where it is possible to agglomerate various materials, data, and narratives and thus document violence and counter the false narratives created by state regimes. This strategy of media independence is linked to "operational aesthetics," which Christoph Brunner defines as "the conception of commons as an affective and aesthetic politics of sense/making" (Brunner 2021, 243).

VISUALIZING A RACIST EPISTEME

The frozen image is automatically subject to the rules of culturally trained perception. Perhaps this is why the defense attorneys for the police officers who were charged with beating Rodney King decided, in preparing their arguments for the court, to freeze video images. Their goal was to disrupt the referentiality of the image to the event recorded on videotape, to extract images from the collection of systemic violence to manipulate their interpretation, and to create an alternative version of the event based on social and cultural biases. Rodney King was observed speeding in Los Angeles in 1991 and was arrested after a high-speed chase on a highway and through residential streets. He was severely beaten by a group of white police officers. A nearby resident, George Holliday, who was testing his new video camera on the terrace of his apartment, recorded the beating. Holliday told local police about his video recording but was never asked to submit it, and it was not admitted as evidence in the inquiry. Holliday then gave the video cassette to a local television station. Portions of the recording were televised several times, and it sparked a wave of video activism and a bottom-up movement that began to use videos as tools for documenting exclusion and systemic violence against various social groups (Stuart 2011). Although the public perception was that the videotape of King's beating spoke for itself, when it was incorporated into the legal proceedings, its impartiality was neutralized when prosecutors created a web of doubt about the incident. They stopped the processual nature of the videotape and reframed the stopped images, drawing attention to details that were given a false context. The gesture of the victim raising his hand to defend himself was reconstructed as the gesture of an aggressor who wanted to attack a representative of law enforcement.

Such a narrative fueled what Judith Butler, after analyzing the video that showed King being beaten, called the "racist episteme" (Butler 1993, 19) and what was later dubbed "anti-epistemology" by Matthew Fuller and Eyal Weizman, who extended the context and mechanism of functioning of post-truth strategies in the media in the 2010s (Fuller and Weizman 2021, 18). Both of these perspectives reveal a cultural, social, and political (linked to practices of power preservation) mechanism for reversing the causality of evidence and building a false view of the referentiality of the video image and reality. During the trial, the police officers who committed the violence were acquitted, and the authenticity of the video that documented the incident was neutralized. In this case, the neutralization procedure consisted in setting the video in false contexts and in generating an "alternative, police-friendly interpretation" (Stuart 2011, 327) and "alternative truths" (Kim 2016, 83).

Butler points to the practice of "victimizing the victimizers" (Butler 1993, 19), a reverse logic based on a deep-seated racism that creates oppressive stereotypes of black men as perpetrators of violence (Fanon 2008). In a culture infected with a racist episteme, any visual proof may be negated or changed to benefit "white paranoia" (Butler 1993, 19): "That it was achieved is not the consequence of ignoring the video, but, rather, of reproducing the video within a racially saturated field of visibility. If racism pervades white perception, structuring what can and cannot appear within the horizon of white perception, then to what extent does it interpret in advance 'visual evidence'? And how, then, does such 'evidence' have to be read, and read publicly, against the racist disposition of the visible which will prepare and achieve its own inverted perceptions under the rubric of 'what is seen'"? (Butler 1993, 15). In this case, white paranoia consists in a fallacious (and subconscious, a consequence of the cultural praxis) conviction that Rodney King must have been the actual agent of violence. What is present here is not simply an act of perception but "the racial production of the visible, the workings of racial constraints on what it means to 'see'" (Butler 1993, 16). The cultural matrix of perception determines the classification of what is or what can become visual evidence of violence. Even though the violence perpetrated against people of color is documented on various media, it becomes invisible to white perception and the white system of justice: "it is in some cases impossible to establish the 'truth' of racist brutality through recourse to visual evidence" (Butler 1993, 17). The prosecutors' use of the video documenting violence against King is seen by Butler as a "violent decontextualiztion and violent recontextualization" (Butler 1993, 15). The manipulation of a media document (for example, by removing a video's soundtrack or by magnifying details on frozen video frames) created a narrative that did not prove the truth but instead justified the use of violence and the brutality of the perpetrators.

The video of Rodney King's beating did not find a real place in the public administration responsible for the execution of justice. The document was edged out of social reality and became a document index shown in the realm of art, where it started to agglomerate people and evidence in the labor of proving the truth.

In 1993, George Holliday's video showing the brutal beating of Rodney King was screened at the Whitney Museum of American Art in New York City at the museum's Biennial Exhibition (curated by Thelma Golden, John G. Hanhardt, Lisa Phillips, and Elisabeth Sussman). In his text "Media Art Worlds: New Expressions in Film and Video 1991–93," published in the exhibition catalogue, John G. Hanhardt wrote the following:

> Probably the most well-known home video is that of George Holliday, whose camcorder memorialized the beating of Rodney King by officers of the Los Angeles Police Department. Perhaps this now-infamous videotape prefigures a new form of documentary. Holliday's determined effort to record what he saw was, unconsciously, the result of complicated series of decisions on his part. Implicit in this video is an act of intention, an effort to make empirical and real by recording on videotape what was happening in front of him. This pattern of police brutality, often referred to but never "seen," was brought to light for public scrutiny. (Hanhardt 1993, 46)

What was missing from interpretations of the King beating video was any reference of this case to other such incidents and to the possibility of invoking the social practice of identifying violence in a media documentary. In fact, when evidence is collected extensively and reveals a pattern of violence in different places with its location (geolocation and chronolocation but also cultural, social, economic, and political place), it becomes part of the socially shared knowledge of systemic oppression.

In 2020, when social media showed videos documenting the killings of Breonna Taylor and then George Floyd at the hands of white police officers, mass protests swept across the United States, inspiring the Black Lives Matter movement. Forensic Architecture and Bellingcat secured the online media footage of the protests and data related to unlawful forms of the coercion and violence used by the police against the protesters. All the data was collected in the digital archive called Police Brutality at the Black

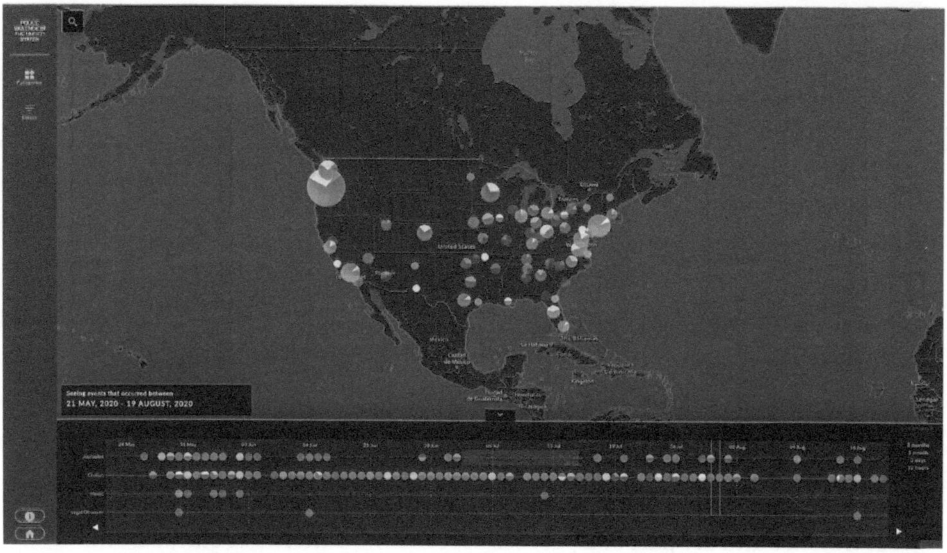

Lives Matter Protests project (figure 5.4). By using Timemap, Forensic Architecture's open-source software, the archivists amassed media evidence of violence and abuse of power against protesters, journalists, medics, and legal observers. The archive includes photos and videos whose authenticity has been verified and chrono- and geolocalized. The interactive archive contains evidence related to the misuse of tear gas, pepper spray, and various forms of physical violence and illegal practices used by the police—such as hiding their identities, tolerating aggressive behavior by counterprotesters coming from far-right backgrounds, and using kettling (corralling large groups of people to restrict their movement). In

5.4

A page from Forensic Architecture and Bellingcat's Police Brutality at the Black Lives Matter Protests archive. Users can select multiple filters to compare violations across time and space.

the interactive archive, documents reveal nontransparent relationships between police officers and far-right militia groups (such as police officers and militia members posing for joint photos) and situations in which police officers gave advice to self-organized far-right movements on how to behave when confronting demonstrators during protests.

Unlike the Los Angeles police officers who attacked Rodney King in 1991, the Minneapolis police officer who killed George Floyd in 2020 was found guilty of murder and sentenced to prison in 2021. The other Minneapolis police officers who took part in the incident also were sentenced for violating George Floyd's civil rights. The Louisville, Kentucky, police officers who were responsible for Breonna Taylor's death in 2020 when they forced entry into her apartment with a no-knock search warrant were found guilty of violating her civil rights in 2024.

Archives such as Police Brutality at the Black Lives Matter Protests reveal violence and are part of a process of revealing patterns of cultural and political violence deeply embedded in historical archives designed within the Western knowledge model. Through their agglomerative nature, the tools and infrastructures that produce these new digital archives decolonize historical phenomena. They show us that the tools used in designing archives (such as the types of media, software, and graphics) significantly shape the memory of violence.

Ramon Amaro, in his book *The Black Technical Object: On Machine Learning and the Aspiration of Black Being* (2023), expands on the decolonizing concepts of Frantz Fanon, where, under white cultural and colonial pressure, black subjects are seen as nonexisting—as objects. They are either absent, fused with the background, or used as visual objects. Amaro writes about the history of racism as evolving with machines and technologies. During this coupled process, hierarchical technical values were established. There is no neutral technology; each has an inherent idea of perceiving the other. Amaro devotes a good deal of space to machine learning strategies, which in their first iterations either excluded black subjects as invisible or, in urban monitoring systems, pointed to black individuals as likely criminals.

The Police Brutality at the Black Lives Matter Protests archive designed by Forensic Architecture and Bellingcat deconstructs and decolonizes the models of thinking and the technologies and control tools. To some extent, this approach implements the concept of Wolfgang Ernst's dyanarchives, a project in which the archive is not limited but is open to social interaction: "Dynarchives lies between the archival and the anarchival spheres" (Ernst 2016, 10). Such collections open up to and call for the agglomerative labor of the recipients—their involvement, their responsibility, and a reevaluation of their views and epistemic schemes: "By becoming electronically accessible 'online,' the archive is being deprived of its traditional power. As long as the archive has been distanced from public discourse, archival knowledge has been an internal privilege of governmental agencies" (Ernst 2016, 15).

Because the archives of the Black Lives Matter protests enable users to pursue and identify patterns of violent and racist behavior and lay out facts in relation to other facts, they cease to be a collection of incidental events—which would be the neutralizing narrative of the old colonial cultural order. Doing independent work with the archives—finding materials on the timeline and identifying events—becomes an agglomerative tool that produces knowledge of historical and present-day truth. As dynarchives, Police Brutality at the Black Lives Matter Protests becomes a platform of resistance—a digital counterinfrastructure that is dynamic and open and subject to a continuous process of cultural, technological, and epistemic decolonization. The platform can serve as a way to use digital media documents to collect, record, preserve, distribute, redistribute, discuss, and research what we remember. While the traditional administrative archive has immutable tectonics that create only one possible (controlled) form of memory (read-only memory) (Ernst 2016, 10), the new digital archive enables open agglomerative processes where memory is produced through multistate collaboration and socialization. The counternarratives that are produced can refute hegemonic state-imposed, white historiographies. The morphological structure of such archives also exposes the structure of violence. The documentation and exposure of structural violence is done by media counterinfrastructures that are designed for this purpose—open and agglomerating audiences. These archives are both a collection of evidence and a creation of a shared, socially decolonized narrative of violence.

Between 1996 and 2000, about 300,000 people, including over 270,000 women, were sterilized in Peru under the rule of President Alberto Fujimori (Carranza Ko 2023, quoting Amnesty International). The program was called the Programa de Salud Reproductiva y Planificación Familiar (PSRPF) (Reproductive Health and Family Planning Program). Most of the people who were sterilized were from poor and rural places, mainly indigenous Peruvians who spoke the Quechua language. At least seventeen people (fifteen women and two men) died as a result of surgical sterilization, and another six women suffered serious complications such as paralysis of limbs and heart failure (Caranza Ko 2023, citing Defensoría del Pueblo). As Ñusta Carranza Ko, a researcher who focused on this question, writes in a text published years after the events: "Recent studies conclude this to be a case of genocide, with the state systematically subjecting an ethnic minority population—the Indigenous peoples—to a coercive sterilization campaign that sought to eliminate in whole or in part Andean and Amazonian Indigenous communities" (Carranza Ko 2023, 11).

On September 15, 1996, President Alberto Fujimori spoke in Beijing before the Fourth United Nations World Conference on Women. Portraying himself as a progressive statesman, he announced a law prohibiting violence against women in Peru and a "right" to tubal ligation and vasectomy, which he claimed formerly had been performed illegally (Fujimori 1995). His address was seen introducing a modern health system in which Peruvians could make their own reproductive decisions. Fujimori's speech was met with thunderous applause. Few suspected that the speech was not intended to expand human rights but instead to enact an agenda of systemic violence against Peru's indigenous peoples. It soon was revealed that Fujimori was proclaiming that the state would impose forced sterilization on men and women, primarily indigenous and poor Peruvians. As early as 1997, the Defensoría del Pueblo, the Peruvian ombudsman's office, started receiving reports from women "who had been sterilized through fallopian tube ligation without their consent. . . . These included cases without signing any authorization, women who were not treated for complications arising from surgical interventions, a woman who was sterilized a day after giving birth without any medical follow-up, and a woman who died of internal bleeding as a consequence of surgical interventions" (Brown and Tucker 2017, 3–4, citing Defensoria del Pueblo).

The ombudsman's office investigated these violations of the government's sterilization program, and its investigation was joined by human rights organizations that were fighting for women's rights. The Fujimori government dismissed the complaints for lack of conclusive evidence (Carranza Ko 2021). According to Matthew Brown and Karen Tucker, "The Ministry of Health has neither acknowledged the violations of rights that took place nor established a mechanism to compensate those affected, and within the Peruvian state more broadly, the issue of unconsented sterilizations has generally been ignored" (Brown and Tucker 2017, 4). After new studies were carried out and new evidence was collected, it became apparent that many of the affected women were too afraid to provide official testimony: "They were lied to, pressurized, and in some cases, physically forced to undergo sterilization, often in unhygienic conditions and with little attempt to provide suitable aftercare. Many were illiterate or educated only to primary level, most of them were women, most of them were Indigenous or mestiza, and most of them lived in rural Andean communities, far from centers of power in Peru" (Brown and Tucker 2017, 4, citing Defensoria del Pueblo). The women belonged to an ethnic minority that was a marginalized social minority in Peru, and they had no administrative emergency support and no tools to communicate their suffering and to find the truth.

On April 7, 2009, Fujimori, the former president of Peru, was tried for crimes against humanity. He was found guilty of the disappearance and unlawful execution of nine students and one professor from La Cantuta University on July 18, 1992; the massacre of fifteen civilians in Barrios Altos on November 3, 1991; and the kidnapping of journalist Gustavo Gorriti and businessman Samuel Dyer in April 1992 (Carranza Ko 2021, 57). His sentence did not mention the forced sterilization of women and men or the seventeen people who died as a direct consequence of this practice. Eventually, his sentence was reduced. Subsequent Peruvian presidents "discussed Fujimori's amnesty on health grounds, submitted considerations for a pardon, and tested the public's opinion on this matter. Within this political narrative, on December 24, 2017, Fujimori finally received a humanitarian presidential pardon from President Kuczynski" (Carranza Ko 2021, 58).

Peru's forced sterilization program has not been recognized as a crime by successive governments, despite the efforts of many NGOs, activist groups, and women who have protested in the streets of Lima. Therefore, it was necessary to look for other ways to disseminate the truth about these crimes. One such project is the participatory digital archive called the Quipu Project, which collects testimonies from women who were forced to be sterilized. The project began in 2013 in Huancabamba, a village in the Peruvian Andes, and then spread to Ayacucha and Cusco. There a team of researchers, media designers, and volunteers contacted the Asociación de Mujeres Afectadas por Esterilizaciones Forzadas (AMAEF) (Association of Women Affected by Forced Sterilization). This organization raises awareness about the issue and represents more than thirteen hundred women who were forcibly sterilized (Bertha Foundation 2025, n.p.). The team included consultants from the University of Bristol (including Matthew Brown, Magde Dresser, Bill Thompson, and Karen Tucker), founders of the Chaka Studio (Maria Court and Rosemarie Lerner), and a network of internationals volunteers. All of the group's activities, especially creating an interactive archive and launching a media campaign to expand social impact, were intended to "respond to the desire of activists and community leaders in Peru to document and record the experiences of those who were sterilized without their consent, and was developed in close collaboration with Peruvian partner organizations. . . . Quipu was designed in a way to ensure participants retained as much power and control over the research process and output as possible" (Brown and Tucker 2017, 6).

To create an archive together with the victims, an unprecedented technology was used. A phoneline allowed callers to tell their story in their own terms, "and it gives access to all the data generated to anyone who calls, thereby allowing those same participants to analyze and extract meaning from the archived material" (Brown and Tucker 2017, 6). It was patterned after WeFarm, a peer-to-peer service where farmers can contribute to and access crowd-sourced information without the internet (Bertha Foundation 2025). The line was advertised in the local press, radio, and on posters hung in various smaller towns. Of great significance, too were the workshops and talks involving various relief organizations in Huancabamba and Cusco: "Workshops were organized to discuss the project and its method, where it might lead (increased national and cross-national knowledge of their cases, for example) and what it may or may not bring about (extra resources from the state, reparations, legal justice). All of the first calls were made after these workshops" (Tucker and Brown 2017, 9).

These meetings and activities did not yield the expected result, however, as very few women called the designated number to tell their stories: "The subject did not lend itself to a public phone call—from a phone booth located in a public square or municipal offices, which is where most telephones are located in these areas, rather than in private homes" (Brown and Tucker 2017, 9). Only when the group decided to distribute cellphones to women from cooperating Peruvian partner organizations did the situation change. The women traveled from village to village, talking to other women and explaining the meaning of their testimonies. They handed out analogue cellphones to enable those who wanted to use them to share their memories and experiences. In addition, women who wanted to tell their stories could use the phones to listen to the stories of other women that were recorded in the archive. This simple interaction through other people's prerecorded anonymous testimonies helped women feel less alone in their trauma. They could hear other women's voices, and this often was the deciding factor, as they took the phone in hand to record their story. This was a watershed moment for the project. This situation is also documented in a film accompanying the Quipu Project titled *Calls for Justice*. The film was commissioned by the Bertha Foundation and *The Guardian* newspaper and was coproduced by Lucida Media (Peru), Mucha Media (Chile), and Sandelion Productions (Colombia). To ensure that technology would not be an obstacle to participation, the Quipu Project used simple cell phones. Additionally, a media campaign on local radio explained that testimonies could be submitted in the Quechua language, not in Spanish, and the content of the testimonies would not be changed.

After being recorded, the women's histories were translated into Spanish and English and deposited into an interactive archive. The testimonies (over a hundred hours so far) are divided into four thematic sections—the government's sterilization program, the physical sterilization operation, the physical and emotional consequences of the sterilization, and the campaign for justice. The interface of interaction archives evokes the Inca knotted cords, which were a script called *quipu* (figure 5.5). According to researchers who have studied this ancient writing, the quipus were woven from intertwining strands of different colors. Their meaning was influenced by the color, the arrangement of the strands, and the knots that appear on them. Each strand was a record of data and preserved it. It was an archive of data and facts that was readable in precolonial culture and tradition. The project goes beyond the archive structures ascribed to white Western epistemology by annexing the Inca model of recording and producing knowledge as equivalent to Western knowledge: "The work has developed through an iterative process, constantly being added to with new material, knots shifting to reflect new realities" (Brown and Tucker 2017, 7). Each colored thread represents something worth recording and remembering and also provides a reference to other threads. This is how the collected stories of violence and trauma work. The quipu writing pattern has become a viable method for labor with personal narratives, "for the way in which the project is producing complex, interwoven, multivocal knowledge of the unconsented sterilization that took place in Peru" (Brown and Tucker 2017, 2).

The Quipu Project's advisory ethics board, appointed in 2014, recommended that given names and surnames be removed from the testimonies and that participants should provide their testimonials anonymously. This was to ensure a safe environment, as those giving testimony could face retaliation from the authorities. Concerns were also raised about health care workers who could be exposed to attacks.

The use of simple technology and Inca writing as a model to navigate a digital archive shows that an ecological approach to technology is possible, as observed by Cajetan Iheka in his book *African Ecomedia: Network Forms, Planetary Politics* (2021). Such technologies serve those who make testimonies and are tailored to them so that the truth that emerges from

5.5

An interactive page from the Quipu Project archive, showing an interface for listening to audio testimonies.

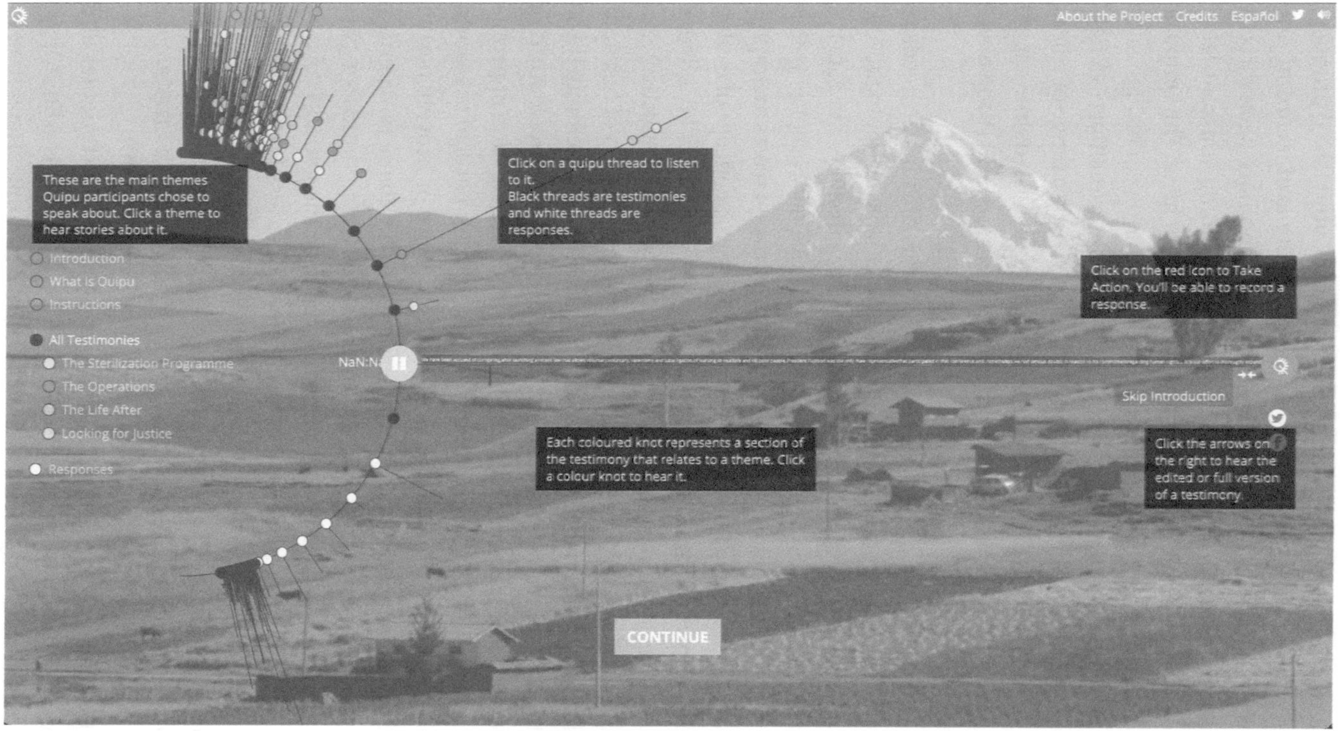

About the Project
Credits
Español
These are the main themes Quipu participants chose to speak about. Click a theme to hear stories about it.
Introduction
What is Quipu
Instructions
All Testimonies
The Sterilization Programme
The Operations
The Life After
Looking for Justice
Responses
Click on a quipu thread to listen to it.
Black threads are testimonies and white threads are responses.
NaN:Na
Click on the red Icon to Take Action. You'll be able to record a response.
Skip Introduction
Each coloured knot represents a section of the testimony that relates to a theme. Click a colour knot to hear it.
Click the arrows on the right to hear the edited or full version of a testimony.
CONTINUE

them can exist as ecological in the sense that Seán Cubitt (2023) proposes. The truth can be open, situated, and based on methods of recording and distribution that are most appropriate for those who have been directly affected by the violence. A radical truth demands doing constant labor, continuously acquiring data, and establishing further facts. The Quipu archive is therefore adapted to incorporate new testimonies. Through such activities: "Quipu facilitates the production of counter-memory—a field of discourse that . . . is inherently diverse, incorporating a range of voices, memories and perspectives that have been marginalized in dominant cultural memory . . .—in relation to Peru's authoritarian past" (Brown and Tucker 2017, 5).

The Quipu Project shows that recording stories of violence needs to be collaborative and archived by the community. Its use of analogue and digital tools and methods throughout the archive's design—the data collected *in situ* and distributed through an interactive network, the voices of witnesses, and the physical suffering of the victims—creates an impressive viewing experience. Its platform, embedded in the concept of ecological media, allows for the sharing and shaping of grassroots knowledge about forced sterilization in Peru, where "digitality is not a substitute, in other words, for the communicative and human dimensions of research. It is, rather, an additional terrain on which to pursue and facilitate these encounters" (Brown and Tucker 2017, 13). The agglomerative nature of the ecological aesthetics of this archive allows the participation of people who have been affected by a similar problem in other parts of the world and those who can extract evidence from this archive or provide participatory knowledge about this systemic violence in the name of restoring justice. According to the Bertha Foundation's website, "human rights organizations in Peru have also been tapping into the Quipu Project's archive in their legal and advocacy work to secure redress for the women affected, namely the Estudio para la Defensa de los Derechos de la Mujer (Office for the Defense of Women's Rights) and the Instituto de Defensa Legal (Institute for Legal Defense), as well as in Amnesty International's Against Their Will campaign" (Bertha Foundation 2025, n.p.).

On October 30, 2024, after it examined hundreds of testimonies and reviewed a joint communication submitted by five victims who in 1996 and 1997 were forcibly sterilized within the state birth control laws in Peru, the United Nations Committee on the Elimination of Discrimination against Women (CEDAW) published a decision (United Nations Office of the High Commissioner for Human Rights 2024). As a committee member, Leticia Bonifaz, noted: "The victims described a consistent pattern of being coerced, pressured, or deceived into undergoing sterilizations at clinics lacking proper infrastructure or trained personnel. . . . Forced sterilizations were carried out as part of a systematic and generalized attack against rural and Indigenous women, and the policy resulted in the nullification and substitution of their reproductive autonomy" (United Nations Office of the High Commissioner for Human Rights 2024, n.p.). These words about systemic violence were momentous in the struggle for justice for the people of Peru and could be the basis for recognizing these actions as crimes against humanity under the Rome Statute (the founding document of the International Criminal Court, effective as of July 1, 2002). CEDAW urged Peru to speed up and expand investigations, provide financial compensation and psychological support, and implement a comprehensive reparations program for the victims (United Nations Office of the High Commissioner for Human Rights 2024, n.p.).

Via experimental media practices, the Quipu Project deconstructs and decolonizes the notion of an archive, thereby revealing its covert forms of violence related to cataloging, structuring, and valorizing. In these archives, the violence done to people and the environment is brought out of the "realm of issues without solution" and social and political "invisibility" and becomes visible through contemporary digital media as forms of memory are recorded and remembered and presented as documents, evidence, or forms of "material witness" (Schuppli 2020).

RADICALLY SITUATED AND GLOBALLY DISTRIBUTED EVIDENCE OF VIOLENCE

Digital archives emerge as a new form of distributed knowledge of violence. These archives agglomerate people who have experienced violence, who have narrated and recorded it using media, who have prepared platforms to house them, and who can interact with these digital environments and media documents. This archived memory is a human memory but also a media memory. Its ontology is linked to the media that record violence and the network structures that arrange, display, and share them. In all these cases, the archive is contingent on openness, sensitivity, and an ethics of care toward people who have experienced violence. The archivists discussed in this chapter built their own counterstructures—which are open, inclusive, and sensitive to abuse—to bear witness to violence more broadly and responsibly and to bring in audiences as affective participants. The documents are embedded in a media environment that allows relational and morphological analysis of the linkages of data and events. They are created with care and therefore with attentiveness to the victims, the data concerning them, the documents, and the testimonies they deposited. The Latin word *cura* ("care") is the origin of the English words *curation* and *curating*, and this can lead to a rethinking and redesigning of the entire process—from the acquisition of archival data to the designs for the environment in which it is deposited: "an archival approach marked by radical empathy would require archives to make survivors and implicated communities not just a target group of users, but central focal points in all aspects of the archival endeavour, from appraisal to description to provision of access. In this case, an ethics of care would transform the reading room space from a cold, elitist, institutional environment to an affective, user-oriented, community-centred service space" (Caswell and Cifor 2016, 24).

Radical empathy throughout the archival process can produce epistemic justice, giving the rights to be seen and heard to those who have been denied them. Epistemic justice requires going beyond top-down defined processes of documentation and archiving. It requires moving beyond institutional procedures that, in many cases, have been premised on the foundations of social and cultural exclusion, consciously or unconsciously perpetuating neocolonial and exploitative regimes. Each memory has its own geographic, cultural, and historical locations, its own media record, and its own networked presence. In these cases, an aesthetics of radical truth is realized with new forms of radically situating but globally displaying and distributing memories of violence. Archives must be connective and ecological and must produce multimedia and multisensory environments. Archives must generate active engagement and induce agglomerative labor for epistemic justice.

EPILOGUE

TOWARD AN AGGLOMERATIVE AESTHETICS OF RADICAL TRUTH

The practices of producing an aesthetics of radical truth (AeRT) discussed in this book are hybrid and agglomerative in nature. They are geographically, culturally, and thematically diverse. They use a range of tools, practices, and methodologies for exposing violence, but they all approach aesthetics as a way to use media to trace and gather data, facts, stories, and images of violence and to collaborate in socializing and sharing the process of establishing truth. This aesthetics enables "a frame of visibility and intelligibility that puts things or practices together under the same meaning, which shapes thereby a certain sense of community. A community of sense is a certain cutting out of space and time that binds together practices, forms of visibility, and patterns of intelligibility" (Rancière 2009, 31).

In addition to what Jacques Rancière wrote about aesthetics as a work of creating communities, two other issues are important in the projects discussed in this book. One issue is the recovery of the notion of radical truth in investigating, revealing, proving, and countering violence. Radicality becomes a return to the root (*radix*) of the production of consistent, collective, collaborative, and most often bottom-up practices against violence. Truth is seen as an agglomerative process based on transparent inquiry and shared understanding of the causes of violence. These are primarily bottom-up practices, producing their own counterinfrastructures against violence in specific places on the planet and using media tools as the binding agents of these practices. The tools become an object as event and are the mediating binders of an aesthetics of radical truth. A second issue is that all practices share values and ethics that are based on care for the victims of violence and on acting to rectify injustice against people and the environment. The relationship of a shared, situated set of values has been described by Bruno Latour: "We might be more connected to each other by our worries, our matters of concern, the issues we care for, than by any other set of values, opinions, attitudes or principles" (Latour 2005, 14). Ethics becomes here more of a care for and response to victims of situated violence. It is a shift from a set of projected ethics to action, where care becomes "practice and value" (Held 2006, 39). This is the radicalness of these groups, labs, associations, and teams that seek to disclose violence and look for ways to socialize evidence, data, the entire process, and all the tools that serve these practices.

This new trend began in the 2010s and is continuing in the 2020s, and it is made up of diverse phenomena and practices that are underpinned by care as a value, by ways of producing knowledge based on an aesthetics of radical truth, and by new forms of commitment to tracing, recording, and disclosing injustice. Researchers and academics used to consider such a phenomenon in the contexts of international movements or political forces, but the trends we are writing about transcend both these categories. They create counterinfrastructures for actions and practices on a different level of knowledge formation. They are not a homogeneous movement but rather a dispersed set of situated phenomena that often agglomerate with one another yet remain in the realm of solving specific problems in specific places in the world. There is an exchange of experiences, tools, practices, but the focus remains on specific problems and situations of emergence and actions of situated violence. In many of these cases, new definitions of politicity as social labor and new practices against violence are also emerging, moving between new concepts, theories, and strategies of social sharing and engagement.

In this context, it might be worth evoking Jacques Derrida's significant text *The Specters of Marx: The State of the Debt, the Work of Mourning and the New International* (Derrida 2011). It is based on a lecture Derrida delivered in 1993 at an international conference at the University of California in Riverside. Derrida was delivering his lecture after the fall of the Berlin Wall, which highlighted the failure of communism, devastated by the Soviet Union's totalitarian system. His lecture also came after the bloody repression of the attempted revolt in Tiananmen Square in Beijing in 1989, the cruelty and violence that prevailed after the dismantling of the old Yugoslavia, the civil war and ethnic cleansing there since 1992, the ethnic wars in African countries fueled by Western countries, and, as he repeatedly emphasized, apartheid and racism everywhere. For Derrida, these events demonstrated a global crisis of political systems and of the concept and construction of the state and the nation. The philosopher is proposing the need to deconstruct the type of politics that has been appropriated by states or regimes in various parts of the world. His objectives seem to be twofold. The first one was to critique racism and apartheid as ongoing systems of power in many states, and to connect them historically to capitalism as a form of economic new slavery. In this context, he revisited Marx's thought so that it might be used for new sociopolitical practices. What was at stake here was mainly the power of critique and the foundation of deconstruction that Derrida identified in Marx's texts. Derrida's main aim was to offer theoretical, critical reflection and emphasize the capacity of deconstruction to work in the specter of Marx's critique of capital and its unjust use of workers' labor.

His second objective was linked to the proclamation of the "New International"—an alliance of people who are inspired by Marx's ideas about politics and the state. This was to be a spectral concept that links the past to the future and that results in a new phenomenon capable of producing extrasystemic forms and practices of action "without link, without status, without title and without public, . . . without coordination, without party, without country, without national community . . . without co-citizenship, without common belonging to a class" (Derrida 2011, 107).

Derrida's need to redefine politics meant underwriting new social practices based on an ethic of care. The renewed power of critique and deconstruction were to empower "one [to] try to liberate from any dogmatics and even from any metaphysico-religious determination, from any messianism" (Derrida 2011, 111). The New International was not to remain in the field of spectrology and abstraction. It was to appear as a new divergent, nondogmatic, nonstate, and extrainstitutional force to "produce events, new effective forms of action, practice, organization, and so forth. To break with the 'party form' or with some form of the State or the International does not mean to give up every form of practical or effective organization. It is exactly the contrary that matters to us here" (Derrida 2011, 112).

In many of his texts, Derrida stressed the need to shift away from outdated state and national structures and toward de- and reconstructed notions of hospitality, care, and guest in relation to the growing migrant crisis caused by violence in various parts of the world. He supported the actions of Nelson Mandela, the right to migrate, and the need for legislative changes in refugee laws in Europe (he rejected the notion of illegal migration). Derrida understood institutional political violence also from his own experiences. He was born in Algiers to a family of Sephardic Jews. As a result of the antisemitic school quotas of the French Vichy government, he was expelled from his school at the age of twelve and for a year refused to attend Jewish schools. Eventually, he became one of the most frequently read and commented on philosophers of the second half of the twentieth century. As Benoit Peeters writes, however, his biography is "the story of a fragile and tormented man who, to the end of his life, continued to see himself as 'rejected' by the French university system" (Peeters 2013, 3). The demand for extrastate and extrasituational actions is thus articulated by an internal migrant, a philosopher of deconstruction who has never felt at home. These interwoven strands of his biography—the critique of the political system from the inside and the expressed need to build counterinfrastructures, collective practices of resistance, and cooperation—make his words about the New International take on a deeper meaning regarding the new practices examined in this book. Scattered in different parts of the planet, these practices do not form a homogeneous group or a one-sided political tendency. They are always situated and agglomerated in a specific situation of resistance to violence which they reveal.

In the early twenty-first century, another philosopher of postcolonial thought sought community and collaborative action for the sake of environmental and human justice. Edward Said was a Palestinian American who was born in Mandatory Palestine as a perennial outsider, which is what he calls himself in his memoir titled *Out of Place*. In his 2003 article "Orientalism," published in *Counterpunch* magazine shortly before his death, Said envisaged a new trend of resistance to the top-down politics of violence: "we are today abetted by the enormously encouraging democratic field of cyberspace, open to all users in ways undreamt of by earlier generations either of tyrants or of orthodoxies. The world-wide protests. . . . would not have been possible were it not for the existence of alternative communities all across the world, informed by alternative information, and keenly aware of the environmental, human rights, and libertarian impulses that bind us together in this tiny planet" (Said 2003, n.p.).

Said believed in the capabilities of the internet, which quickly showed its duplicity. Nevertheless, he saw the potential of new media practices; the power of bottom-up, extrastate, extranational action; and associations of people committed to regaining their own rights and demanding environmental justice. Said also pointed to a need for a broader postcolonial view of violence as long-lasting and as manifesting itself in various forms of human and environmental destruction, social and economic exclusion, racism, and land grabbing. This is why he emphasized the need to develop bottom-up, situated, and historically and socially context-sensitive practices of resistance to violence.

The practices described in this book agglomerate academic discourse and prompt us to reconstruct philosophical thought and humanist and social texts on ethics, justice, and truth. We invoke and agglomerate the concepts of many people involved in this collaborative vision of truth, including Foucault, Latour, Cubitt, Weizman, Fuller, Nixon, Mbembe, Césaire, Dekker, Barad, Haraway, Schuppli, Derrida, Said, Rancière and many others. All their concepts call for reconstituting viewpoints and recognizing new practices to discover today's collaborative and agglomerative truth.

This approach to deconstructing and seeking ideas in ingrained paradigms of thought can also be found in a significant book by Chela Sandoval, a feminist, postcolonial activist and scholar. As she writes in the introduction to her *Methodology of the Oppressed*: "the methodology of the oppressed is a deregulating system: it represents a lapse in the sovereignty, training, and laws that regulate disciplines" (Sandoval 2000, 9). In this collection of texts on Western philosophy, Sandoval shows how important it is to revisit humanist thought, especially poststructuralist ideas, to extract new concepts and to decolonize them to recover their social causality. And by "the expediencies of this examination, we will discover new ways of reading, thinking, behaving, hoping, imagining, from the simplest activity . . . to the most obtuse, understanding the differential form of oppositional consciousness and social movement as the methodology of the oppressed" (Sandoval 2000, 10).

Derrida's New International, Said's alternative communities, and Sandoval's methodologies of the oppressed are just examples of many concepts that are conceptually ingrained in the outliers in twentieth-century models of human and environmental rights. They all focus on thinking and practicing resistance to violence and reasserting the truth for those who are marginalized, weak, and excluded. They also serve as an important impulse for seeking new approaches to law for countering such crimes and practicing new forms of collective and anti-systemic stances against violence. The engaged practices we describe could be said to constitute counterinfrastructures, experimental methods, and methodologies for exposing violence and for recovering the strategies of knowledge production. They are united not by politics or ideology but by ethics as labor and action in a situation of ever-new humanitarian and refugee crises, wars, and violence perpetrated against humans and the environment in both physical and digital realities.

These practices are not identical to the forms and strategies of large organizations furthering human rights, which have long-standing traditions and ways of operation. These groups are mainly oriented toward direct action in crisis situations and usually do not build environments around them based on sharing practices, data, information, and community knowledge creation with local communities. However, this situation has been changing in recent years. Some media practices and tools (for example, open-source intelligence techniques or forms of evidence preservation) are infiltrating these organizations, as is pointed out in earlier chapters. These organizations often work on projects with the teams and groups discussed in this book and can provide the necessary infrastructure and experience in the modus operandi they have developed. Cases in point are the environmental defenders in the Amazon or the Polish informal Emergency Border Collective, which brings together NGOs, creative and activist associations, and many volunteers and was created in response to the humanitarian crisis on the border between Poland and Belarus.

The problem we present here is not so much about having NGOs fulfill specific functions in tracking down violence but about revising the concept of human rights itself, which again connotes specific forms of hidden violence. It unlocks multiple semantic fields. This complex situation was described by Rancière in his article "The Ethical Turn of Aesthetics and Politics":

> Human rights had been the weapon of dissidents who were opposing another people to the one their governments pretended to incarnate. They then became the rights of populations who were the victims of the new ethnic wars, the rights of individuals driven away from their destroyed homes, of women raped and men massacred. They became the specific rights of those who were unable to exercise those rights. As a result, the following alternative presented itself: either these human rights no longer meant anything, or they became the absolute rights of those without rights, that is to say rights demanding a response which was itself absolute, beyond all formal, juridical norms. (Rancière 2006, 7–8)

The need to redefine and deconstruct the notion of human rights was also recognized by Jean-François Lyotard in a 1993 article titled "The Other's Rights" (Lyotard 1993). He was responding to a question posed by Amnesty International: What do human rights become in the context of humanitarian intervention? In his answer, Lyotard gave "the other's rights" a significance that sheds light on the meaning of ethics and the ethical turn. He said that human rights cannot be the rights of man as man, the rights of the nude man. The argument in its essence is not new. Lyotard himself recalled that it was used by Karl Marx (1994) and Hannah Arendt (1973), who both showed that the naked human, the apolitical human, has no rights. Humans must be something other than human to have rights. Historically, the other than human was called a citizen. The duality of human and citizen has historically influenced two things—the critique of the duality of these rights (which are always located elsewhere than they should be) and the political actions that introduce various forms of discord into the gap they produce between man and citizen—as Costas Douzinas, a lawyer who has researched the formulation and political use of the standardized concept of human rights, observes in the book *The Radical Philosophy of Rights* (2019). That is why Douzinas expresses his radicality as the "reference to 'humanity' in human rights introduces an element of normative universality into the law. But the history of humanity since the adoption of the Universal Declaration [of Human Rights] indicates that there is no common or accepted conception of what it means to be human. Some people are fully human, others less so, and a large part of humanity has been excluded from the protections of law. The fate of refugees and migrants trying to enter Europe or North America shows this gradation of humanity" (Douzinas, 2019, ix).

The notion of human rights was born in the legal and philosophical discourse of the global north and therefore should be deconstructed there, among the researchers and practitioners who work with these rights. Being aware of the injustices that can occur when legal and conceptual constructs are universalized and normativized, the archivists who participated in the projects we describe here identified specific victims and witnesses who were situated in injustices and violence at a given time and place. Each situation produces the need for different forms of evidence gathering, for the naming the perpetrators of a given act of violence, and for the sharing practices of resistance. This is borne out by the examples of violence that involve migrants and victims of war as well as political violence.

The same deconstructive task must be performed with the environment. There is no single environment and no single environmental justice. Problems that affect specific places on earth should be considered as embedded in those contexts, as we indicate in the indigenous militant digital cartographies in Indonesia and the Amazon. Environmental violence reveals colonial roots in these cases but can also, through practices of resistance, be the beginning of a new media deconstruction of the memory of violence and a reconstruction of the relationship between people and the environment.

Media structures, such as appropriately designed online platforms, can enable more people (volunteers and practitioners alike) to support and agglomerate this type of action. Just as the agglomerate itself, being a geological structure, is susceptible to change due to external and internal factors, collaborating and developing more new counterinfrastructures will show further possibilities to recover the truth about violence in the twenty-first century. In this book, we have presented only a selection of practices and projects exposing and opposing violence and social and environmental injustice from among the growing number of such activities emerging in different places around the globe. We hope that this is the beginning of a significant bottom-up change.

Above all, we must today reclaim the notion and meaning of truth. New online conspiracy-based practices seek to implement a dark epistemic. The groups and projects we write about show that it is possible to reclaim the truth through constant labor to make it transparent and open rather than hidden and contained. Today we face new challenges from the rapid development of artificial intelligence. AI is not necessarily negative in itself, but the wrong corporations, ruling politicians, or extremist groups can create fake news and deep-fake strategies that perform a work that is the opposite of what we write about.

Truth—collaborative, open, shared, and thus radical—is essential today. We have only begun to embark on this labor. As Frantz Fanon said this years ago in his 1961 book *The Wretched of the Earth* in context of ongoing structural racist and colonial violence, "Nobody has a monopoly on truth, neither the leader nor the militant. The search for truth in local situations is the responsibility of the community" (Fanon 2004, 139). Radical truth must be generated within a community by its own labor, and there is no single model or a toolbox for it. There is no one procedure for working with data, archival records, and testimonies, just as there is no one form of digital records of memory of violence. What we really need are open procedures for analyzing and verification of objects as events, shared tools, public engagement, shared knowledge about the process and radical care as resistance to dark epistemology.

APPENDIX

This is a list of groups, organizations, projects, and media tools discussed in the book.

GROUPS AND ORGANIZATIONS

Alarm Phone, https://alarmphone.org/en/
Amnesty International, https://www.amnesty.org
Bellingcat, https://www.bellingcat.com
Bertha Foundation, https://berthafoundation.org
Coordinator of Indigenous Organizations of the Amazon River Basin (Coordinadora de las Organizaciones Indígenas de la Cuenca Amazónica) (COICA), https://coicamazonia.org
Digital Democracy, https://www.digital-democracy.org
Forensic Architecture (and Forensic Oceanography), https://forensic-architecture.org
Global Land Analysis and Discovery (GLAD), Department of Geographical Sciences, University of Maryland, https://glad.umd.edu
Interethnic Association for the Development of the Peruvian Rainforest (Asociación Interétnica de Desarrollo de la Selva Peruana) (AIDESEP), https://aidesep.org.pe
Jus Talionis Reconstruction Lab, https://talio.org/en
Louisiana Bucket Brigade, https://labucketbrigade.org
Moisireen Collective, https://www.mosireen.com
Public Laboratory for Open Technology and Science (Public Lab), https://static.publiclab.org
Rainforest Foundation US, https://rainforestfoundation.org
Safecast, https://safecast.org
SITU Research, https://situ.nyc/research
UNITED for Intercultural Action, https://unitedagainstrefugeedeaths.eu

Watch the Med, https://watchthemed.net
Welcome to Europe, https://w2eu.info/en

PROJECTS: INVESTIGATIONS, ONLINE REPOSITORIES, ARCHIVES, INTERACTIVE REPORTS

Alsaha Archive (2019), https://akhbaralsaha.com/archive/

Amnesty International and Forensic Architecture
Black Friday (2014), https://blackfriday.amnesty.org

Bellingcat
Geolocation of Werfalli Execution Site (2017), https://www.bellingcat.com/news/mena/2017/10/03/how-an-execution-site-was-geolocated/
Mapping Civilian Harm in Ukraine (2022), https://ukraine.bellingcat.com

Border Emergency Collective
Zone of Hidden Violence (2022), https://archiwum.hfhr.pl/en/visual-report-zone-of-hidden-violence-3d-reconstruction-documenting-violations-of-human-rights-and-pushbacks-in-the-polish-belarusian-border-area/index.html

858: An Archive of Resistance (2011), https://858.ma

Forensic Architecture
Cloud Studies (2020), https://critical-zones.zkm.de/#!/detail:cloud-studies; https://forensic-architecture.org/investigation/cloudstudies
The Bombing of Rafah (2015), https://forensic-architecture.org/investigation/the-bombing-of-rafah

Forensic Architecture and Bellingcat
Police Brutality at the Black Lives Matter Protests (2020), https://forensic-architecture.org/investigation/police-brutality-at-the-black-lives-matter-protests

Forensic Architecture, SITU Research
The Use of White Phosphorus Munitions in Urban Environments (2012), https://forensic-architecture.org/investigation/white-phosphorus-in-urban-environments

Forensic Oceanography
Sea Watch vs. the Libyan Coastguard (2018), https://forensic-architecture.org/investigation/seawatch-vs-the-libyan-coastguard
The Seizure of *The Iuventa* (2018), https://forensic-architecture.org/investigation/the-seizure-of-the-iuventa

Forensic Oceanography and SITU Research
Left-to-Die Boat (2012), https://forensic-architecture.org/investigation/the-left-to-die-boat

Jennifer Gabrys
Citizen Sense (2013), https://citizensense.net

Public Laboratory for Open Technology (Public Lab)
BP Oil Spill (2010), https://publiclab.org/wiki/gulf-coast

Quipu Project (2013), https://interactive.quipu-project.com
Quipu: Calls for Justice (2017), documentary film, https://www.youtube.com/watch?v=LcYNOoZmPwY

Rainforest Foundation US
How Satellites and Drones Help Indigenous Peoples Protect the Amazon Forest (2019), https://rainforestfoundation.org/video-how-satellites-and-drones-help-indigenous-peoples-protect-the-amazon-forest/

Safecast
Global Radiation Map (2011), https://map.safecast.org

SITU Research
Euromaidan Event Reconstruction (2018), https://situ.nyc/research/projects/euromaidan-event-reconstruction; http://maidan.situplatform.com

Syrian Archive (2014), https://syrianarchive.org

UNITED for Intercultural Action
List of Refugee Deaths (since 1993), https://unitedagainstrefugeedeaths.eu/about-the-campaign/about-the-united-list-of-deaths/

MEDIA TOOLS: SOFTWARE AND HARDWARE

Alkasir: https://github.com/alkasir/alkasir
Bento Geiger counter (bGeiger nano) (Safecast): https://safecast.org/devices/bgeigie-nano/
Codec (SITU Research): https://situ.nyc/research/projects/codec-collaborative-tool
Global Forest Watcher: https://forestwatcher.globalforestwatch.org
Map Knitter (Public Lab): https://publiclab.github.io/Leaflet.DistortableImage/examples/archive.html
Pad.ma (public access digital media archive): https://pad.ma/
Timemap (Forensic Architecture): https://forensic-architecture.org/investigation/timemap-for-cartographic-platforms
Ushahidi: https://www.ushahidi.com

ABBREVIATIONS

AERT: aesthetics of radical truth

AIDESEP: Asociación Interétnica de Desarrollo de la Selva Peruana (Interethnic Association for the Development of the Peruvian Rainforest)

AMAEF: Asociación de Mujeres Afectadas por Esterilizaciones Forzadas (Association of Women Affected by Forced Sterilizations)

BLM: Black Lives Matter

CBPR: community-based participatory research

CCTV: closed-circuit television

CEDAW: United Nations Committee on the Elimination of Discrimination against Women

CHRS: Carnegie Mellon University's Center for Human Rights Science

COICA: Coordinadora de las Organizaciones Indígenas de la Cuenca Amazónica (Coordinator of the Indigenous Organizations of the Amazon Basin)

DEDA: decentralized data

DOE: United States Department of Energy

EES: Entry/Exit System

EU: European Union

EURODAC: European Asylum Dactyloscopy Database

EUROSUR: European Border Surveillance System

FRONTEX: European Border and Coast Guard Agency

FEMINIST STS: feminist science and technology studies

GIS: geographic information systems

GLAD: Global Land Analysis and Discovery laboratory, Department of Geographical Sciences, University of Maryland

ICC: International Criminal Court

INES: International Nuclear and Radiological Event Scale

ISIS: Islamic State of Iraq and Syria

IT: information technology

LABB: Louisiana Bucket Brigade

NGO: nongovernmental organization

NNSA: United States National Nuclear Security Administration

OHCHR: United Nations Office of the High Commissioner for Human Rights

OOD: object-oriented democracy

OOP: object-oriented programming

OSI: open-source investigation

OSINT: open-source intelligence techniques

PSRPF: Programa de Salud Reproductiva y Planificación Familiar (Reproductive Health and Family Planning Program)

STS: science and technology studies

TEK: traditional ecological knowledge

TEPCO: Tokyo Electric Power Company

UAD: unmanned aerial devices

UAS: unmanned aerial system

UNESCO: United Nations Educational, Scientific, and Cultural Organization

UNHCR: United Nations High Commissioner for Refugees

UNRWA: United Nations Relief and Works Agency for Palestine Refugees in the Near East

WMO: World Meteorological Organization

ZKM: Zentrum für Kunst und Medien in Karsruhe (Center for Art and Media in Karsruhe, Germany)

NOTES

PREFACE

1. Awards and honorable mentions have been earned by the following projects: Alsaha Archive (Digital Communities, Honorary Mention, 2022); Bellingcat (Digital Communities, Golden Nica, 2018); 858. An Archive of Resistance (Digital Communities, Honorary Mention, 2018); Forensic Architecture, Cloud Studies (Artificial Intelligence & Life Art, Golden Nica, 2021); Quipu Project (Digital Communities, Honorary Mention, 2016); and Syrian Archive (Digital Communities, Honorary Mention, 2021).

ACKNOWLEDGMENTS

1. This task was also supported by a grant from the ID-UB program at Adam Mickiewicz University, Poznań, Poland (no. 124/08/POB5/0008).
2. This book is the result of research conducted under the auspices of a grant from the Polish National Science Centre, entitled "Art as Laboratory of New Society: The Cultural Consequences of the Post-technological Turn" (no. UMO-2014/13/B/HS2/00508).

CHAPTER 1

1. The name of a special-purpose police detachment in Belarus.
2. From the perspective of the phenomena we address in this book, the activities of hacking groups and whistleblowers are important, but they are not directly related to the origin of the practices we are interested in. Some of the groups, like Bellingcat, are skeptical of the information published as part of hacking activities, believing that the anonymity of the hackers and the acquisition mechanisms makes it is difficult to assess credibility. The methods of acquisition should not raise doubts, however, if the information is disseminated socially and evidence is provided in the process of revealing the truth. From the perspective of the history of media, hacking movements belong to a different tradition in which the sources are closed groups and subcultures of experts with special and unique competencies. The activities of the groups we write about in this book are entirely overt, as are their methods, strategies, and tools.

CHAPTER 2

1. The exhibition *Making Things Public: Atmospheres of Democracy* was held in in 2005 in Karlsruhe, Germany, at the Center for Art and Media. Curated by Bruno Latour and Peter Weibel, it focused on representation in politics. The show was a response to the notion of politics and political practice in terms of its social efficacy.
2. Forensic Architecture also used Timemap in its investigations into earlier forms of violence by Russia against Ukraine. In 2019, Forensic Architecture published a platform in which Timemap was used to prove the presence of Russian troops during operations in eastern Ukraine that were carried out by so-called separatists. In fact, as the evidence collected by the Forensic Architecture shows, Russian Federation troops took part in operations in Donetsk in 2014 in addition to pro-Russian separatists.

CHAPTER 3

1. Louisiana Bucket Brigade collaborates with local communities in Louisiana to help victims of community violence. The group was started in 2000 by Dorothy Jenkins, Shonda Lee, Margie Richard, and Anne Rolfes. They were inspired by Anne Rolfes's work in Benin in West Africa when she helped document the history of Nigerians who were resisting local community violence. Crude oil and natural gas extraction were responsible for the forced resettlement and economic and community migration of many inhabitants of the Niger River Delta in Nigeria.
2. According to estimates presented by Daniel Nguen (2013), around forty thousand Americans of Vietnamese origin employed in the fish processing industry, and around ten thousand fishermen in the Gulf of Mexico were directly affected by the economic impact of the disaster. In total, about a third of seafood-based products in the US market was contaminated.
3. Ushahidi is an African open-source platform for crowdsourcing the acquisition of information. The primary purpose of the software is to enable the reporting and mapping of violence and crime in a specific area. Usahidi was developed in 2007, and the software was first used in 2007 and 2008 in Kenya to report on violence on the local population after the presidential election. The word *ushahidi* in Swahili means "testimony" (see Rotich 2017).

CHAPTER 4

1. Forensic Architecture also conducted multiple land border investigations, such as the series of cases of pushbacks across the Evros/Meriç River, which included investigations of pushback cases from 2016 to 2020. These projects grew out of the group's collaboration with Stefanos Levidis, whose methodologies for

investigating border violence are discussed later in this chapter. Also analyzed were cases of gunfire and deaths of migrants during the escalation of violence on the border between Greece and Turkey on March 4, 2020. The Killing of Muhammad Gulzar project was run in cooperation with Bellingcat and Lighthouse Reports. Forensic Architecture analyzed violence on the border between Spain and Morocco, as well as systemic forms of violence used by Israel in the Occupied Palestinian Territories. The findings of all Forensic Architecture investigations into border violence can be viewed at https://forensic-architecture.org/category/borders.

REFERENCES

Abe, Yasuhito. 2014. “Safecast or the Production of Collective Intelligence on Radiation Risks after 3.11.” *Asia-Pacific Journal* 12, issue 7, no. 5. https://www.cambridge.org/core/journals/asia-pacific-journal/article/safecast-or-the-production-of-collective-intelligence-on-radiation-risks-after-311/B4EEE47B63CBC3CF4894E143EFBA5185.

Alarm Phone. 2022. Homepage. https://alarmphone.org/en/.

Al Khatib, Hadi. 2020. “Corporations Erasing History: The Case of the Syrian Archive.” In *The Arab Archive: Mediated Memories and Digital Flows*, edited by Donatella Della Ratta, Kay Dickinson, and Sune Haugbolle, 89–98. Amsterdam: Institute of Network Cultures.

Alsaha Archive. 2025. “About the Archive.” https://akhbaralsaha.com/archive/about/.

Al-Saqaf, Walid. 2014. *Breaking Digital Firewalls: Analyzing Internet Censorship and Circumvention in the Arab World*. Örebro: Örebro University.

Al-Tamimi, Joud Halawani. 2022. “Jihan El-Tahri.” In *Still Present!*, edited by Kader Attia, Gabriele Horn, and Iris Ströbel. Berlin: KW Institute for Contemporary Art and Kunst-Werke Berlin.

Amaro, Ramon. 2023. *The Black Technical Object: On Machine Learning and the Aspiration of Black Being*. London: Sternberg Press.

Amnesty International. 2009. “Israel/Gaza: Operation ‘Cast Lead’: 22 Days of Death and Destruction.” July 2. https://www.amnesty.org/en/documents/mde15/015/2009/en/.

Amnesty International. 2022. “Poland: Cruelty Not Compassion, at Europe’s Other Borders.” April 11. https://www.amnesty.org/en/wp-content/uploads/2022/04/EUR3754602022ENGLISH.pdf.

Amnesty International and Forensic Architecture. 2014. “‘Black Friday’: Carnage in Rafah.” https://blackfriday.amnesty.org/report.php.

Appadurai, Arjun. 2003. “Archive and Aspiration.” In *Information Is Alive*, edited by Joke Brouwer, Arjen Mulder, Susan Charlton, and V2. Rotterdam: V2/NAi Publishers and D.A.P./Distributed Art Publishers.

Arendt, Hannah. 1973. *The Origins of Totalitarianism*. New York: Harcourt Brace Jovanovich.

Aronson, Jay D., McKenna Cole, Alex Hauptmann, Dan Miller, and Bradley Samuels. 2018. “Reconstructing Human Rights Violations Using Large Eyewitness Video Collections: The Case of Euromaidan Protester Deaths.” *Journal of Human Rights Practice* 10, no. 1 (February 1): 159–178. https://doi.org/10.1093/jhuman/huy005.

Atkinson, Ti-Grace. 1969. *Radical Feminism.*

Atoui, Farah. 2020. "The Calais Crisis: Real Refugees Welcome, Migrants 'Do Not Come.'" In *Moving Images: Mediating Migration as Crisis*, edited by Krista Lymes, Tyler Morgenstern, and Ian Alan Paul, 211–228. Bielefeld: Transcript.

Attia, Kader. 2022. "Introduction: Still Present!" In *Still Present!*, edited by Kader Attia, Gabriele Horn, and Iris Ströbel, 21–41. Berlin: Kunst-Werke Berlin.

Azoulay, Ariella Aisha. 2015. *Civil Imagination: A Political Ontology of Photography*. London: Verso.

Bal, Mieke. 2002. *Travelling Concepts in the Humanities: A Rough Guide*. Toronto: University of Toronto Press.

Barad, Karen Michelle. 2007. *Meeting the Universe Halfway: Quantum Physics and the Entanglement of Matter and Meaning*. Durham, NC: Duke University Press.

Basdeo, Sahadeo. 1997. "The 'Radical' Movement towards Decolonization in the British Caribbean in the Thirties." *Canadian Journal of Latin American and Caribbean Studies* 22, no. 44 (January): 127–146. https://doi.org/10.1080/08263663.1997.10816756.

Baumgarten, Alexander Gottlieb. 2013. *Metaphysics: A Critical Translation with Kant's Elucidations, Selected Notes, and Related Materials*. Translated and edited by Courtney D. Fugate and John Hymers. New York: Bloomsbury.

Bazalgette, Felix, and Eyal Weizman. 2018. "The Whole Truth and Nothing but the Truth." *Elephant*, March 14. https://elephant.art/the-whole-truth-and-nothing-but-the-truth/.

Bellingcat. 2017. "How a Werfalli Execution Site Was Geolocated." October 2. https://www.bellingcat.com/news/mena/2017/10/03/how-an-execution-site-was-geolocated/.

Bellingcat. 2022. "Hospitals Bombed and Apartments Destroyed: Mapping Incidents of Civilian Harm in Ukraine." March 17. https://www.bellingcat.com/news/2022/03/17/hospitals-bombed-and-apartments-destroyed-mapping-incidents-of-civilian-harm-in-ukraine/.

Bennett, Jane. 2010. *Vibrant Matter: A Political Ecology of Things*. Durham, NC: Duke University Press.

Bertha Foundation. 2025. "Quipu Project in Peru: Using Technology and Film to Mobilize Communities Affected by Forced Sterilizations." https://berthafoundation.org/story/quipu-project-in-peru/.

Biber, Katherine, and Trish Luker, eds. 2017. *Evidence and the Archive: Ethics, Aesthetics and Emotion*. London: Routledge.

Bonney, Rick. 1996. "Citizen Science: A Lab Tradition." *Living Bird* 15, no. 4: 7–15.

Border Emergency Collective. 2022. *Zone of Hidden Violence*. Video. https://archiwum.hfhr.pl/en/visual-report-zone-of-hidden-violence-3d-reconstruction-documenting-violations-of-human-rights-and-pushbacks-in-the-polish-belarusian-border-area/index.html.

Bourriaud, Nicolas. 1998. *Relational Aesthetics*. Translated by Simon Pleasance, Fronza Woods, Mathieu Copeland, Dijon: Les Presses du Réel.

Bradshaw, Elizabeth A. 2012. "Deepwater, Deep Ties, Deep Trouble: A State-Corporate Environmental Crime Analysis of the 2010 Gulf of Mexico Oil Spill." PhD diss., Western Michigan University. https://scholarworks.wmich.edu/dissertations/53.

Bradshaw, Elizabeth A. 2015. "'Obviously, We're All Oil Industry': The Criminogenic Structure of the Offshore Oil Industry." *Theoretical Criminology* 19, no. 3 (August): 376–395. https://doi.org/10.1177/1362480614553521.

Breen, Jessica, Shannon Dosemagen, Jeffrey Warren, and Mathew Lippincott. 2015. "Mapping Grassroots: Geodata and the Structure of Community-Led Open Environmental Science." *ACME: An International Journal for Critical Geographies* 14, no. 3: 849–873. https://acme-journal.org/index.php/acme/article/view/1236.

Brown, Azby, Pieter Franken, Sean Bonner, Nick Dolezal, and Joe Moross. 2016. "Safecast: Successful Citizen-Science for Radiation Measurement and Communication after Fukushima." *Journal of Radiological Protection* 36, no. 2 (June): S82–S101. https://doi.org/10.1088/0952-4746/36/2/S82.

Brown, Matthew, and Karen Tucker. 2017. "Unconsented Sterilisation, Participatory Story-Telling, and Digital Counter-Memory in Peru." *Antipode* 49, no. 5: 1186–1203. https://doi.org/10.1111/anti.12316.

Brunner, Christoph. 2021. "Concatenated Commons and Operational Aesthetics." In *Aesthetics of the Commons*, edited by Felix Stadler, Cornelia Sollfrank, and Shusha Niederberger, 241–269. Zurich: Diaphanes.

Burke, Edmund, and L. G. Mitchell. 2009. *Reflections on the Revolution in France*. New York: Oxford University Press.

Butler, Judith. 1993. "Endangered/Endangering: Schematic Racism and White Paranoia." In *Reading Rodney King/Reading Urban Uprising*, edited by Robert Gooding-Williams. New York: Routledge.

Carranza Ko, Ñusta. 2021. *Truth, Justice, and Reparations in Peru, Uruguay, and South Korea: The Clash of Advocacy and Politics*. Singapore: Springer Singapore. https://doi.org/10.1007/978-981-33-4939-1.

Carranza Ko, Ñusta. 2023. "Unacknowledged Genocide: Coercive Sterilization of Indigenous Women in Peru." *Violence: An International Journal* 4, no. 1–2: 11–29. https://doi.org/10.1177/26330024231210306.

Caswell, Michelle, and Marika Cifor. 2016. "From Human Rights to Feminist Ethics: Radical Empathy in the Archives." *Archivaria* 81 (May): 23–43. https://archivaria.ca/index.php/archivaria/article/view/13557.

Césaire, Aimé, Robin D. G. Kelley, and Aimé Césaire. 2000. *Discourse on Colonialism*. New York: Monthly Review Press.

Clavell, Gemma Galdon. 2017. "Protect Rights at Automated Borders." *Nature* 543, no. 7643 (March): 34–36. https://doi.org/10.1038/543034a.

Clayton, Sue. 2020. *The New Internationalists: Activist Volunteers in the European Refugee Crisis*. London: Goldsmiths Press.

Code, Lorraine. 1993. "Taking Subjectivity in Account." In *Feminist Epistemologies*, edited by Linda Alcoff and Elizabeth Potter, 15-47. London: Routledge.

Coletti, Mark, Carolynne Hultquist, William G. Kennedy, and Guido Cervone. 2017. "Validating Safecast Data by Comparisons to a U.S. Department of Energy Fukushima Prefecture Aerial Survey." *Journal of Environmental Radioactivity* 171 (May): 9–20. https://doi.org/10.1016/j.jenvrad.2017.01.005.

Couldry, Nick. 2015. "The Myth of 'Us': Digital Networks, Political Change and the Production of Collectivity." *Information, Communication & Society* 18, no. 6 (June 3): 608–626. https://doi.org/10.1080/1369118X.2014.979216.

Couldry, Nick, and Andreas Hepp. 2017. *The Mediated Construction of Reality*. Cambridge: Polity Press.

Crasnow, Sharon L., and Kristen Intemann, eds. 2021. *The Routledge Handbook of Feminist Philosophy of Science*. New York: Routledge.

Cubitt, Seán. 1998. *Digital Aesthetics*. Thousand Oaks, CA: Sage.

Cubitt, Seán. 2005. *EcoMedia*. Amsterdam: Rodopi.

Cubitt, Seán. 2014. *The Practice of Light: A Genealogy of Visual Technologies from Prints to Pixels*. Cambridge, MA: MIT Press.

Cubitt, Seán. 2015. "Data Visualization and the Subject of Political Aesthetics." In *Postdigital Aesthetics*, edited by David M. Berry and Michael Dieter, 179–190. London: Palgrave Macmillan, https://doi.org/10.1057/9781137437204_14.

Cubitt, Seán. 2018. "Truth (Preliminary Note)." http://seancubitt.blogspot.com/2018/08/truth-preliminary-note.html.

Cubitt, Seán. 2023. *Truth: Aesthetic Politics*. London: Goldsmiths Press.

Davies, Thom. 2022. "Slow Violence and Toxic Geographies: 'Out of Sight' to Whom?" *Environment and Planning C: Politics and Space* 40, no. 2 (March): 409–427. https://doi.org/10.1177/2399654419841063.

De Genova, Nicholas. 2013. "Spectacles of Migrant 'Illegality': The Scene of Exclusion, the Obscene of Inclusion." *Ethnic and Racial Studies* 36, no. 7 (July): 1180–1198. https://doi.org/10.1080/01419870.2013.783710.

De Genova, Nicholas, ed. 2017. *The Borders of "Europe": Autonomy of Migration, Tactics of Bordering*. Durham, NC: Duke University Press.

Dekker, Annet, ed. 2017. *Lost and Living (in) Archives: Collectively Shaping New Memories*. Amsterdam: Valiz.

Dekker, Rianne, Godfried Engbersen, Jeanine Klaver, and Hanna Vonk. 2018. "Smart Refugees: How Syrian Asylum Migrants Use Social Media Information in Migration

Decision-Making." *Social Media + Society* 4, no. 1 (January): 205630511876443. https://doi.org/10.1177/2056305118764439.

DeLanda, Manuel. 1997. "The Machinic Phylum." *TechnoMorphica*. https://v2.nl/archive/articles/the-machinic-phylum.

Deleuze, Gilles, and Félix Guattari. 2004. *A Thousand Plateaus: Capitalism and Schizophrenia*. Translated by Brian Massumi. London: Bloomsbury Academic.

Della Ratta, Donatella. 2018. *Shooting a Revolution: Visual Media and Warfare in Syria*. London: Pluto Press.

Della Ratta, Donatella. 2019. "Donatella Della Ratta, Shooting a Revolution: Visual Media and Warfare in Syria (interview)." *Jadaliyya*, March 25. https://www.jadaliyya.com/Details/38497.

Della Ratta, Donatella. 2020. "Why the Syrian Archive is no Longer (only)About Syria." In *The Arab Archive: Mediated Memories and Digital Flows*, edited by Donatella Della Ratta, Kay Dickinson, and Sune Haugbolle, 101-116. Amsterdam: Institute for Network Cultures.

Derrida, Jacques. 2011. *Specters of Marx: The State of the Debt, the Work of Mourning and the New International*. Translated by Peggy Kamut. London: Routledge. Originally published in 1993.

Dersley, Stephen. 2025. *Thought Collectives and Cultural Change: Applying Ludwik Fleck's Theory of Thought Collectives to the Study of Cultural Transformations*. Cham: Springer Nature.

Dijstelbloem, Huub. 2017. "Migration Tracking Is a Mess." *Nature* 543, no. 7643 (March): 32–34. https://doi.org/10.1038/543032a.

Diminescu, Dana. 2008. "The Connected Migrant: An Epistemological Manifesto." *Social Science Information* 47, no. 4 (December): 565–579. https://doi.org/10.1177/0539018408096447.

Diminescu, Dana. 2020. "Reaching the Connected Migrant." In *The Sage Handbook of Media and Migration*, edited by Kevin Smets, Leurs Koen, Georgiu Myria, Witteborn Saskia, and Gajjala Radhika, 74–78. Thousand Oaks, CA: Sage.

Dosemagen, Shannon, and Jeffrey Yoo Warren. 2011. "Leftovers." https://publiclab.org/wiki/leftovers.

Douzinas, Costas. 2019. *The Radical Philosophy of Rights*. Abingdon, UK: Routledge.

Dubberley, Sam, Alexa Koenig, and Daragh Murray, eds. 2020. *Digital Witness: Using Open Source Information for Human Rights Investigation, Documentation, and Accountability*. Oxford: Oxford University Press.

858 Archive. 2018. "An Archive of Resistance: What Is This?" https://858.ma.

Entry/Exit System. 2024. "Entry/Exit System." European Commission. https://home-affairs.ec.europa.eu/policies/schengen-borders-and-visa/smart-borders/entry-exit-system_en.

Ernst, Wolfgang. 2013. *Digital Memory and the Archive*, edited by Jussi Parikka. Minneapolis: University of Minnesota Press, 2013.

Ernst, Wolfgang. 2016. “Radically De-Historicising the Archive: Decolonising Archival Memory from the Supremacy of Historical Discourse.” In *Decolonising Archives*, edited by L'Internationale Online and Rado Ištok, 9–16. https://www.internationaleonline.org/library/#decolonising_archives.

Ernst, Wolfgang. 2021. *Technológos in Being: Radical Media Archaeology and the Computational Machine*. New York: Bloomsbury Academic.

European Border Surveillance System. 2021. “On the Situational Pictures of the European Border Surveillance System (EUROSUR).” https://eur-lex.europa.eu/legal-content/EN/TXT/?uri=CELEX:32021R0581&qid=1618306409753.

European Border Surveillance System. 2024. “EUROSUR.” https://home-affairs.ec.europa.eu/policies/schengen-borders-and-visa/border-crossing/eurosur_en.

Fairhead, James, Melissa Leach, and Ian Scoones. 2012. “Green Grabbing: A New Appropriation of Nature?” *Journal of Peasant Studies* 39, no. 2 (April): 237–261. https://doi.org/10.1080/03066150.2012.671770.

Fajfer, Alicja. 2021. “The Costs of Deterring Migration on the Polish-Belarusian Border in 2021.” In *Cross-Border Review. Yearbook 2021*, edited by James W. Scott, 82–89, Budapest. https://dspace.uzhnu.edu.ua/jspui/bitstream/lib/39131/1/CBR_Y2021.pdf#page=81.

Fanon, Frantz. 2004. *The Wretched of the Earth*. Translated by Richard Philcox. New York: Grove Press. Originally published in 1961.

Fanon, Frantz. 2008. *Black Skin, White Masks*. Translated by Richard Philcox. New York: Grove/Atlantic. Originally published in 1952.

Fleck, Ludwik. 2008. *Genesis and Development of a Scientific Fact*. Translated by Fred Bradley and Thaddeus J. Trenn. Chicago: University of Chicago Press. Originally published in 1935.

Fleck, Ludwik. 2011. “Scientific Observation and Perception in General.” In *Cognition and Fact: Materials on Ludwik Fleck*, edited by Robert S. Cohen and Thomas Schnelle. Dordrecht: D. Reidel. Originally published in 1935.

Forensic Architecture. 2014. *Forensis: The Architecture of Public Truth*. Berlin: Sternberg Press.

Forensic Architecture. 2020. “Cloud Studies.” https://forensic-architecture.org/investigation/cloudstudies.

Forensic Architecture and Bellingcat. 2020. “Police Brutality at the Black Lives Matter Protests.” https://forensic-architecture.org/investigation/police-brutality-at-the-black-lives-matter-protests.

Forensic Architecture and SITU Research. 2012. “The Use of White Phosphorus Munitions in Urban Environments: An Effects-Based Analysis.” https://content.forensic

-architecture.org/wp-content/uploads/2018/08/Report-The-Use-of-White-Phosphorus.pdf.

Fortun, Kim, and Alli Morgan. 2015. "Thinking across Disaster." In *Mental Health and Social Issues Following a Nuclear Accident: The Case of Fukushima*, edited by J. Shigemura, R. K. Chhem, and H. Yabe, 55–64. Japan: Springer.

Foth, Marcus, and Greg Hearn. 2007. "Networked Individualism of Urban Residents: Discovering the Communicative Ecology in Inner-City Apartment Buildings." *Information, Communication & Society* 10, no. 5 (October): 749–772. https://doi.org/10.1080/13691180701658095.

Foucault, Michel. 1994. *Dits et écrits 1954–1988 IV*. Paris: Gallimard.

Foucault, Michel. 2011. *The Courage of Truth (the Government of Self and Others II): Lectures at the Collège de France, 1983–1984*. Translated by Graham Burchell. New York: Picador.

Franken, Pieter. 2021. "The Future of Trust = Decentralized Data." TEDxOgikubo. https://www.youtube.com/watch?v=lRdCMwgXpag.

Franzoni, Chiara, and Henry Sauermann. 2014. "Crowd Science: The Organization of Scientific Research in Open Collaborative Projects." *Research Policy* 43, no. 1 (February): 1–20. https://doi.org/10.1016/j.respol.2013.07.005.

Frontex. 2021. *Artificial Intelligence-Based Capabilities for the European Border and Coast Guard: Final Report*. https://www.frontex.europa.eu/publications/artificial-intelligence-based-capabilities-for-the-european-border-and-coast-guard-final-report-CYyjoe.

Fujimori, Albero. 1995. "Speech Given by the President of the Republic Peru before the IV World Conference on Women." Beijing, China, September 15. https://www.un.org/esa/gopher-data/conf/fwcw/conf/gov/950915131946.txt.

Fuller, Matthew. 2005. *Media Ecologies: Materialist Energies in Art and Technoculture*. Cambridge, MA: MIT Press.

Fuller, Matthew, and Eyal Weizman. 2021. *Investigative Aesthetics: Conflicts and Commons in the Politics of Truth*. Brooklyn: Verso Books.

Funabashi, Yoichi, and Kay Kitazawa. 2012. "Fukushima in Review: A Complex Disaster, a Disastrous Response." *Bulletin of the Atomic Scientists* 68, no. 2 (March): 9–21. https://doi.org/10.1177/0096340212440359.

Gabrys, Jennifer. 2019. *How to Do Things with Sensors*. Minneapolis: University of Minnesota Press.

Galtung, John. 1969. "Violence, Peace, and Peace Research." *Journal of Peace Research* 6, no. 3: 167–191. http://www.jstor.org/stable/422690.

General Data Protection Regulation. 2016. "Right to Be Forgotten." https://gdpr-info.eu/issues/right-to-be-forgotten/.

Genova, James E. 2006. "Cinema and the Struggle to (De)Colonize the Mind in French/ Francophone West Africa (1950s–1960s)." *Journal of the Midwest Modern Language Association* 39, no. 1 (April 1): 50. https://doi.org/10.2307/20464156.

Ghaddar, J. J., and Michelle Caswell. 2019. "'To Go Beyond': Towards a Decolonial Archival Praxis." *Archival Science* 19, no. 2 (May): 71–85. https://doi.org/10.1007/s10502-019-09311-1.

Global Witness. 2021. *Last Line of Defence: The Industries Causing the Climate Crisis and Attacks against Land and Environmental Defenders*. London: Global Witness. https://www.globalwitness.org/en/campaigns/environmental-activists/last-line-defence/.

Golan, Jacob, Simone Athayde, Elizabeth Anne Olson, and Alex McAlvay. 2019. "Intellectual Property Rights and Ethnobiology: An Update on Posey's Call to Action." *Journal of Ethnobiology* 39, no. 1 (April 3): 90. https://doi.org/10.2993/0278-0771-39.1.90.

Grindon, Gavin, ed. 2008. *Aesthetics and Radical Politics*. Newcastle, UK: Cambridge Scholars Publishing.

Grupa Granica. 2021. "Humanitiarian Crisis at the Polish-Belarusian Border." December. https://www.grupagranica.pl/files/Grupa-Granica-Report-Humanitarian-crisis-at-the-Polish-Belarusian-border.pdf.

Grusin, Richard. 2015. "Radical Mediation." *Critical Inquiry* 42, no. 1 (September): 124–148. https://doi.org/10.1086/682998.

Hage, Ghassan. 2015. *Alter-Politics: Critical Anthropology and the Radical Imagination*. Carlton, Victoria: Melbourne University Press.

Hanhardt, John G. 1993. "Media Art Worlds: New Expressions in Film and Video 1991–93." In *1993 Biennal Exhibition*, edited by John G. Hanhardt, Lisa Phillips, and Elisabeth Sussman, 36–51. New York: Whitney Museum of American Art.

Haraway, Donna. 1988. "Situated Knowledges: The Science Question in Feminism and the Privilege of Partial Perspective." *Feminist Studies* 14, no. 3 (1988): 575. https://doi.org/10.2307/3178066.

Haraway, Donna. 2003. *The Companion Species Manifesto: Dogs, People, and Significant Otherness*. Chicago: Prickly Paradigm Press.

Haraway, Donna. 2016. *Staying with the Trouble: Making Kin in the Chthulucene*. Durham, NC: Duke University Press.

Harcourt, Bernard E. 2016. "Introducing the Courage of Truth." Michel Foucault's Collège de France Lectures (1970–1984) at Columbia University. https://blogs.law.columbia.edu/foucault1313/2016/04/07/introducing-the-courage-of-truth/.

Harding, Sandra G. 1991. *Whose Science? Whose Knowledge? Thinking from Women's Lives*. Ithaca, NY: Cornell University Press.

Held, Virginia. 2006. *The Ethics of Care: Personal, Political, and Global*. Oxford: Oxford University Press.

Heller, Charles, and Lorenzo Pezzani. 2018a. *Blaming the Rescuers: Criminalising Solidarity, Re-enforcing Deterrence*. Forensic Oceanography. https://content.forensic-architecture.org/wp-content/uploads/2023/04/2017_Report_Blaming-The-Rescuers.pdf.

Heller, Charles, and Lorenzo Pezzani. 2018b. *Mare Clausum: Italy and the EU's Undeclared Operation to Stem Migration across the Mediterranean*. Forensic Oceanography. https://content.forensic-architecture.org/wp-content/uploads/2019/05/2018-05-07-FO-Mare-Clausum-full-EN.pdf.

Heller, Charles, and Lorenzo Pezzani. 2020a. "Forensic Oceanography: Tracing Violence within and against the Mediterranean Frontier's Aesthetic Regime." In *Moving Images: Mediating Migration as Crisis*, edited by Krista Lymes, Tyler Morgenstern, and Ian Alan Paul, 95–125. Bielefeld, Germany: Transcript.

Heller, Charles, and Lorenzo Pezzani. 2020b. "Intervention: Forensic Oceanography: Tracing Violence within and against the Mediterranean Frontier's Aesthetic Regime." In *The Handbook of Displacement*, edited by Peter Adey, Janet C. Bowstead, Katherine Brickell, Vandana Desai, Mike Dolton, Alasdair Pinkerton, and Ayesha Siddiqi, 453–458. Cham, Switzerland: Palgrave Macmillan.

Heller, Charles, Lorenzo Pezzani, and SITU Studio. 2012 2011. *Report on the 'Left-to-Die Boat.'*" Forensic Oceanography. https://content.forensic-architecture.org/wp-content/uploads/2019/06/FO-report.pdf.

Hemming, John. 2006. "Romance and Reality: The First European Vision of Brazilian Indians." In *Human Impacts on Amazonia: The Role of Traditional Ecological Knowledge in Conservation and Development*, edited by Darrell Addison Posey and Michael J. Balick, 5–16. New York: Columbia University Press.

Herb, Guntram H., Jouni Häkli, Mark W. Corson, Nicole Mellow, Sebastian Cobarrubias, and Maribel Casas-Cortes. 2009. "Intervention: Mapping Is Critical!" *Political Geography* 28, no. 6 (August): 332–342. https://doi.org/10.1016/j.polgeo.2009.09.005.

Higgins, Eliot. 2021. *We Are Bellingcat: An Intelligence Agency for the People*. London: Bloomsbury.

Higginson, John. 2015. *Collective Violence and the Agrarian Origins of South African Apartheid, 1900–1948*. New York: Cambridge University Press.

Hinger, Sophie, Charles Heller, and Lorenzo Pezzani. 2018. "Transformative Trajectories: The Shifting Mediterranean Border Regime and the Challenges of Critical Knowledge Production. An Interview with Charles Heller and Lorenzo Pezzani." *Movement. Journal for Critical Migration and Border Regime Studies* 4, no. 1: 193–208. https://movements-journal.org/issues/06.wissen/12.hinger--transformative-trajectories-the-shifting-mediterranean-border-regime-and-the-challenges-of-critical-knowledge-production-charles-heller-lorenzo-pezzani.html.

Hobart, Hi'ilei, Julia Kawehipuaakahaopulani, and Tamara Kneese. 2020. "Radical Care." *Social Text* 38, no. 1 (March 1): 1–16. https://doi.org/10.1215/01642472-7971067.

Human Rights Watch, ed. 2014. *All According to Plan: The Rab'a Massacre and Mass Killings of Protesters in Egypt*. New York: Human Rights Watch.

Hyde, Carrie, and Joseph Rezek. 2014. "Introduction: The Aesthetics of Archival Difference." *J19: The Journal of Nineteenth-Century Americanists* 2, no. 1: 155–162. https://doi.org/10.1353/jnc.2014.0011.

Iheka, Cajetan. 2021. *African Ecomedia: Network Forms, Planetary Politics*. Durham, NC: Duke University Press. https://doi.org/10.1215/9781478022046.

Ingraham, Chris. 2020. "The Present as Platform." *Media Theory* 4, no. 2: 115–138. http://journalcontent.mediatheoryjournal.org/index.php/mt/article/view/121.

Irwin, Alan. 1995. *Citizen Science: A Study of People, Expertise, and Sustainable Development*. London: Routledge.

Jelewska, Agnieszka, and Michal Krawczak. 2014. "The Difficult Relations between Art, Science and Technology in Poland." In *Art and Technology in Poland: From Cybercommunism to the Culture of Makers*, edited by Agnieszka Jelewska. Poznań, Poland: Adam Mickiewicz University Press.

Jelewska, Agnieszka, and Michał Krawczak. 2018. "The Spectrality of Nuclear Catastrophe: The Case of Chernobyl." Paper presented at the conference on Politics of the Machines: Art and After, Aalborg University, Copenhagen, May 15–17. https://doi.org/10.14236/ewic/EVAC18.30.

Jelewska, Agnieszka, and Michal Krawczak. 2025. *Nuclear Gaia: Media Archives of Planetary Harm*. Bristol, UK: Intellect, distributed by the University of Chicago Press.

Jelewska, Agnieszka, Michał Krawczak, and Julian Reid. 2024. "New Ways of Gathering and Practicing in Times of Crises." In *Postcollectivity: Situated Knowledge and Practice*, edited by Agnieszka Jelewska, Michał Krawczak, and Julian Reid, 1–12. Leiden, Netherlands: Brill. https://doi.org/10.1163/9789004694880.

Jones, David Houston. 2022. *Visual Culture and the Forensic: Culture, Memory, Ethics*. New York: Routledge.

Kahn, Peter H. 1999. *The Human Relationship with Nature: Development and Culture*. Cambridge, MA: MIT Press.

Kahn, Peter H. 2011. *Technological Nature: Adaptation and the Future of Human Life*. Cambridge, MA: MIT Press.

Kaufman, Asher. 2014. "Thinking beyond Direct Violence." *International Journal of Middle East Studies* 46, no. 2 (May): 441–444. https://doi.org/10.1017/S0020743814000427.

Kautzer, Chad. 2015. *Radical Philosophy: An Introduction*. Boulder, CO: Paradigm.

Keenan, Thomas, and Eyal Weizman. 2012. *Mengele's Skull: The Advent of a Forensic Aesthetics*. Berlin: Sternberg Press / Portikus.

Keller, Evelyn Fox. 1995. *Reflections on Gender and Science*. New Haven, CT: Yale University Press.

Kim, Soyeon. 2016. "Alternative Truths: The Construction of Narratives in the Rodney King Trial." *Elements* 12, no. 2. https://doi.org/10.6017/eurj.v12i2.9453.

Kitchin, Rob, and Martin Dodge. 2007. "Rethinking Maps." *Progress in Human Geography* 31, no. 3 (June): 331–344. https://doi.org/10.1177/0309132507077082.

Kitchin, Rob, and Martin Dodge. 2011. *Code, Space: Software and Everyday Life*. Cambridge, MA: MIT Press.

Kittler, Friedrich A. 1999. *Gramophone, Film, Typewriter*. Stanford, CA: Stanford University Press.

Knorr-Cetina, K. 1999. *Epistemic Cultures: How the Sciences Make Knowledge*. Cambridge, MA: Harvard University Press.

Koedt, Anne, Ellen Levine, and Anita Rapone, eds. 1973. *Radical Feminism*. New York: Quadrangle Books.

Kurgan, Laura. 2013. *Close Up at a Distance: Mapping, Technology, and Politics*. Brooklyn, NY: Zone Books, https://doi.org/10.2307/j.ctt14bs159.

Latour, Bruno. 1983. "Give Me a Laboratory and I Will Raise the World." In *Science Observed: Perspectives on the Social Study of Science*, edited by Karin Knorr-Cetina and Michael Mulkay, 141–170. Beverly Hills, CA: Sage.

Latour, Bruno. 1993. *We Have Never Been Modern*. Cambridge, MA: Harvard University Press.

Latour, Bruno. 2004. "Why Has Critique Run Out of Steam? From Matters of Fact to Matters of Concern." *Critical Inquiry* 30, no. 2 (January): 225–248. https://doi.org/10.1086/421123.

Latour, Bruno. 2005. "From Realpolitik to Dingpolitik or How Make Things Public." In *Making Things Public: Atmospheres of Democracy*, edited by Bruno Latour and Peter Weibel, 14–43. Cambridge, MA: MIT Press.

Latour, Bruno. 2007. *Reassembling the Social: An Introduction to Actor-Network-Theory*. Oxford: Oxford University Press.

Latour, Bruno. 2017. *Facing Gaia: Eight Lectures on the New Climatic Regime*. Cambridge: Polity.

Latour, Bruno, and Dipesh Chakrabarty. 2020. "Conflicts of Planetary Proportion: A Conversation." *Journal of the Philosophy of History* 14, no. 3: 419–454. https://doi.org/10.1163/18722636-12341450.

Latour, Bruno, and Francis Halsall. 2012. "An Aesthetics of Proof: A Conversation between Bruno Latour and Francis Halsall on Art and Inquiry." *Environment and Planning D: Society and Space* 30, no. 6 (December): 963–970. https://doi.org/10.1068/d3005int.

Leurs Koen, and Patterson Jeffrey. 2020. "Smartphones: Digital Infrastructures of the Displaced." In *The Handbook of Displacement*, edited by Peter Adey, Janet C. Bowstead,

Katherine Brickell, Vandana Desai, Mike Dolton, Alasdair Pinkerton, and Ayesha Siddiqi, 583–597. Cham, Switzerland: Palgrave Macmillan.

Levidis, Stefanos. 2021. "Border Natures: The Environment as Weapon at the Edges of Greece." PdD diss., Goldsmiths, University of London. https://research.gold.ac.uk/id/eprint/30506/.

Loftsdóttir, Kristín. 2018. "Global Citizens, Exotic Others, and Unwanted Migrants: Mobilities in and of Europe." *Identities* 25, no. 3 (May 4): 302–319. https://doi.org/10.1080/1070289X.2016.1233879.

Longino, Helen E. 1990. *Science as Social Knowledge: Values and Objectivity in Scientific Inquiry*. Princeton, NJ: Princeton University Press.

Loukissas, Yanni A. 2019. *All Data Are Local: Thinking Critically in a Data-Driven Society*. Cambridge, MA: MIT Press.

Lovink, Geert. 2002. *Dark Fiber: Tracking Critical Internet Culture*. Cambridge, MA: MIT Press.

Lymes, Krista, Tyler Morgenstern, and Ian Alan Paul, eds. 2020. *Moving Images: Mediating Migration as Crisis*. Bielefeld, Germany: Transcript.

Lyotard, Jean-François. 1993. "The Other's Rights." In *On Human Rights*, edited by Stephen Shute and Susan Hurley, 135–148. New York: Basic Books.

Marino, Sara. 2021. *Mediating the Refugee Crisis: Digital Solidarity, Humanitarian Technologies and Border Regimes*. Cham, Switzerland: Palgrave Macmillan.

Marx, Karl. 1994. "On the Jewish Question." In *Marx: Early Political Writings*, 28–56. Cambridge: Cambridge University Press. Originally published in 1844. https://doi.org/10.1017/CBO9781139168007.006.

Massumi, Brian. 2015. *Politics of Affect*. Cambridge: Polity.

Mbembe, Achille. 2001. *On the Postcolony*. Berkeley: University of California Press.

Mbembe, Achille. 2003. "Necropolitics." *Public Culture* 15, no. 1 (January 1): 11–40. https://doi.org/10.1215/08992363-15-1-11.

Mbembe, Achille. 2015. "Decolonizing Knowledge and the Question of the Archive." Paper presented at the University of Witwatersrand in Johannesburg, University of Cape Town, and University of Stellenbosch. https://wiser.wits.ac.za/system/files/Achille%20Mbembe%20-%20Decolonizing%20Knowledge%20and%20the%20Question%20of%20the%20Archive.pdf.

Mbembe, Achille. 2019a. "Bodies as Borders." *From the European South* 4: 5–18. https://www.fesjournal.eu/numeri/africas-planetary-futures/#bodies-as-borders_283.

Mbembe, Achille. 2019b. "If We Don't Rehabilitate Reason, We Will Not Be Able to Fix Our Broken World." *Mail & Guardian*, May 9. https://mg.co.za/article/2019-05-09-if-we-dont-rehabilitate-reason-we-will-not-be-able-to-fix-our-broken-world/.

Mbembe, Achille. 2019c. *Necropolitics*. Durham, NC: Duke University Press.

Mbembe, Achille. 2021. *Out of the Dark Night: Essays on Decolonization*. New York: Columbia University Press.

McIntyre, Lee C. 2018. *Post-truth*. Cambridge, MA: MIT Press.

McNutt, Marcia K., Rich Camilli, Timothy J. Crone, George D. Guthrie, Paul A. Hsieh, Thomas B. Ryerson, Omer Savas, and Frank Shaffer. 2012. "Review of Flow Rate Estimates of the *Deepwater Horizon* Oil Spill." *Proceedings of the National Academy of Sciences* 109, no. 50 (December 11): 20260–20267. https://doi.org/10.1073/pnas.1112139108.

Meiners, Joan. 2020. "Ten Years Later, BP Oil Spill Continues to Harm Wildlife." *National Geographic*, July 17. https://www.nationalgeographic.com/animals/2020/04/how-is-wildlife-doing-now--ten-years-after-the-deepwater-horizon/.

Milne, Anna-Louise. 2020. "A New Politics of Solidarity?" In *The New Internationalists: Activist Volunteers in the European Refugee Crisis*, edited by Sue Clayton, 349–378. London: Goldsmiths Press.

mosireen_soursar. 2020. "858: No Archive Is Innocent. On the Attempt of Archiving Revolt." https://www.mosireen.com/-no-archive-is-innocent.

Murillo, Luis Felipe, and Shannon Dosemagen. 2022. "Collaborative Climate Futures? Envisioning the Role of Open Data Infrastructures for Collaborative Socio-Environmental Research." *Commonplace*, April 28. https://doi.org/10.21428/6ffd8432.8f2f6a1d.

Nail, Thomas. 2020. "Migrant Images." In *Moving Images: Mediating Migration as Crisis*, edited by Krista Lymes, Tyler Morgenstern, and Ian Alan Paul, 147–164. Bielefeld, Germany: Transcript.

Nakamura, Akira, and Masao Kikuchi. 2011. "What We Know, and What We Have Not Yet Learned: Triple Disasters and the Fukushima Nuclear Fiasco in Japan." *Public Administration Review* 71, no. 6: 893–899. http://www.jstor.org/stable/41317388.

Nardi, Bonnie A., and Vicki O'Day. 1999. *Information Ecologies: Using Technology with Heart*. Cambridge, MA: MIT Press.

Nguyen, Daniel. 2013. "Daniel Nguyen of MQVN Discusses Best Practices for Citizen Science during the BP Oil Disaster." Blog post, February 1. Public Lab. https://publiclab.org/notes/eustatic/2-1-2013/daniel-nguyen-mqvn-discusses-best-practices-citizen-science-during-bp-oil-di.

Nielsen, Michael A. 2014. *Reinventing Discovery: The New Era of Networked Science*. Princeton, NJ: Princeton University Press.

Nixon, Rob. 2011. *Slow Violence and the Environmentalism of the Poor*. Cambridge, MA: Harvard University Press.

Norgaard, Kari Marie. 2011. *Living in Denial: Climate Change, Emotions, and Everyday Life*. Cambridge, MA: MIT Press.

Novak, Paolo. 2017. "Back to Borders." *Critical Sociology* 43, no. 6 (September): 847–864. https://doi.org/10.1177/0896920516644034.

O'Lear, Shannon, ed. 2021. *A Research Agenda for Geographies of Slow Violence: Making Social and Environmental Injustice Visible*. Cheltenham, UK: Edward Elgar Publishing.

Palacin, Victoria, Sarah Gilbert, Shane Orchard, Angela Eaton, Maria Angela Ferrario, and Ari Happonen. 2020. "Drivers of Participation in Digital Citizen Science: Case Studies on Järviwiki and Safecast." *Citizen Science: Theory and Practice* 5, no. 1 (October 12): 22. https://doi.org/10.5334/cstp.290.

Pałęcka, Alicja, ed. 2024. *No Safe Passage: Migrants' Deaths at the European Union-Belarusian Border*. Warsaw: Fundacja Ocalenie, 2024.

Paneque-Gálvez, Jaime, Irene Pérez-Llorente, Ana Catarina Luz, Maximilien Guèze, Jean-François Mas, Manuel J. Macía, Martí Orta-Martínez, and Victoria Reyes-García. 2018. "High Overlap between Traditional Ecological Knowledge and Forest Conservation Found in the Bolivian Amazon." *Ambio* 47, no. 8 (December): 908–923. https://doi.org/10.1007/s13280-018-1040-0.

Paneque-Gálvez, Jaime, Nicolás Vargas-Ramírez, Brian Napoletano, and Anthony Cummings. 2017. "Grassroots Innovation Using Drones for Indigenous Mapping and Monitoring." *Land* 6, no. 4 (December 7): 86. https://doi.org/10.3390/land6040086.

Parikka, Jussi. 2011. *Medianatures: The Materiality of Information Technology and Electronic Waste*. London: Open Humanities Press.

Parikka, Jussi. 2015. *A Geology of Media*. Minneapolis: University of Minnesota Press, 2015.

Parikka, Jussi. 2018. "Medianatures." In *Posthuman Glossary*, edited by Rosi Braidotti, and Maria Hlavajova, 251–253. London: Bloomsbury Academic.

Parks, Lisa, and Nicole Starosielski. 2015. "Introduction." In *Signal Traffic: Critical Studies of Media Infrastructures*, edited by Lisa Parks and Nicole Starosielski, 1–38. Urbana: University of Illinois Press.

Paul, Ian Allan. 2020. "Controlling the Crisis." In *Moving Images: Mediating Migration as Crisis*, edited by Krista Lymes, Tyler Morgenstern, and Ian Alan Paul, 71–94. Bielefeld, Germany: Transcript.

Peeters, Benoît. 2013. *Derrida: A Biography*. Translated by Andrew Brown. Cambridge: Polity Press.

Peluso, Nancy Lee. 2008. "A Political Ecology of Violence and Territory in West Kalimantan." *Asia Pacific Viewpoint* 49, no. 1 (April): 48–67. https://doi.org/10.1111/j.1467-8373.2008.00360.x.

Posey, Darrell Addison. 1985. "Indigenous Management of Tropical Forest Ecosystems: The Case of the Kayap Indians of the Brazilian Amazon." *Agroforestry Systems* 3, no. 2: 139–158. https://doi.org/10.1007/BF00122640.

Posey, Darrell Addison. 1990. "Intellectual Property Rights: And Just Compensation for Indigenous Knowledge." *Anthropology Today* 6, no. 4 (August): 13. https://doi.org/10.2307/3032735.

Posey, Darrell Addison, and Michael J. Balick, eds. 2006. *Human Impacts on Amazonia: The Role of Traditional Ecological Knowledge in Conservation and Development.* New York: Columbia University Press.

Postman, Neil. 1998. "Five Things We Need to Know about Technological Change." Paper delivered at the conference on New Tech, Denver, CO, March 28. https://web.cs.ucdavis.edu/~rogaway/classes/188/materials/postman.pdf.

Pugliese, Joseph. 2007. "Geocorpographies of Torture." *ACRAWSA* 3, no. 1. https://www.researchgate.net/publication/228684336_Geocorpographies_of_Torture.

Puig de la Bellacasa, María. 2017. *Matters of Care: Speculative Ethics in More than Human Worlds.* Minneapolis: University of Minnesota Press.

Pye, Oliver, and Irendra Radjawali. 2017. "Land Grabs and the River: Eco-Social Transformations along the Kapuas, Indonesia." *Canadian Journal of Development Studies / Revue Canadienne d'études du développement* 38, no. 3 (July 3): 378–394. https://doi.org/10.1080/02255189.2017.1298518.

Rabaka, Reiland. 2010. *Forms of Fanonism: Frantz Fanon's Critical Theory and the Dialectics of Decolonization.* Lanham, MD: Lexington Books.

Radjawali, Irendra, and Oliver Pye. 2017. "Drones for Justice: Inclusive Technology and River-Related Action Research along the Kapuas." *Geographica Helvetica* 72, no. 1 (January 177): 17–27. https://doi.org/10.5194/gh-72-17-2017.

Raley, Rita. 2009. *Tactical Media.* Minneapolis: University of Minnesota Press.

Rancière, Jacques. 2004. *The Politics of Aesthetics: The Distribution of the Sensible.* Edited and translated by Gabriel Rockhill. London: Continuum.

Rancière, Jacques. 2006. "The Ethical Turn of Aesthetics and Politics." *Critical Horizons* 7, no. 1 (February 21): 1–20. https://doi.org/10.1163/156851606779308242.

Rancière, Jacques. 2009. "Contemporary Art and the Politics of Aesthetics." In *Communities of Sense: Rethinking Aesthetics and Politics*, edited by Beth Hinderliter, Vered Maimon, Jaleh Mansoor, and Seth McCormick, 31–49. Durham, NC: Duke University Press.

Rancière, Jacques. 2016. *Dissensus: On Politics and Aesthetics.* Translated by Steven Corcoran. London: Bloomsbury Academic.

Reardon, Jenny, Jacob Metcalf, Martha Kenney, and Karen Barad. 2015. "Science and Justice: The Trouble and the Promise." *Catalyst* 1, no. 1. https://doi.org/10.28968/cftt.v1i1.28817.

Reinberger, Hans-Jörg. 2014. "Generating Experimental Knowledge: Experimental Systems, Concept Formation and the Pivotal Role of Error." Max Planck Institute for the History of Science. https://www.mpiwg-berlin.mpg.de/research/projects/GeneratingExperimentalKnowledge.

Rescue Foundation (Fundacja Ocalenie). 2021. *Wiadomość z Usnarza od Pani Gul (A message from Usnarz from Mrs. Gul).* Video. YouTube. https://www.youtube.com/watch?v=zbqaCY4jNh4.

Rodriguez-Lonebear, Desi. 2016. "Building a Data Revolution in Indian Country." In *Indigenous Data Sovereignty: Toward an Agenda*, edited by T. Kukutai and J. Taylor, 253–272. Canberra: Australian National University Press. http://www.jstor.org/stable/j.ctt1q1crgf.21.

Ross, David A. 2003. "Radical Software Redux." Radical Software. https://www.radicalsoftware.org/e/ross.html.

Rotich, Juliana. 2017. "Ushahidi: Empowering Citizens through Crowdsourcing and Digital Data Collection." *Field Actions Science Reports*, special issue 16 on Smart Cities at the Crossroads, 36–38. https://journals.openedition.org/factsreports/4316.

Rugoff, Ralph. 1997. *Scene of the Crime*. With contributions by Anthony Vidler and Peter Wollen. Cambridge, MA: MIT Press.

Rylko-Bauer, Barbara, and Paul Farmer. 2016. "Structural Violence, Poverty, and Social Suffering." In *The Oxford Handbook of the Social Science of Poverty*, edited by David Brady and Linda Burton, 47–74. New York, Oxford University Press.

Safecast. 2023. "200 Million Datapoints!" https://safecast.org/200-million-datapoints/#.

Said, Edward. 2003. "Orientalism." *Counterpunch*, August 5. https://www.counterpunch.org/2003/08/05/orientalism/.

Saker, Michael, and Jordan Frith. 2019. "From Hybrid Space to Dislocated Space: Mobile Virtual Reality and a Third Stage of Mobile Media Theory." *New Media & Society* 21, no. 1 (January): 214–228. https://doi.org/10.1177/1461444818792407.

Sandoval, Chela. 2000. *Methodology of the Oppressed*. Minneapolis: University of Minnesota Press.

Schatzki, Theodore R., K. Knorr-Cetina, and Eike von Savigny, eds. 2001 *The Practice Turn in Contemporary Theory*. New York: Routledge.

Schnabel, Landon, Lindsey Breitweiser, and Amelia Hawbaker. 2016. "Subjectivity in Feminist Science and Technology Studies: Implications and Applications for Sociological Research." *Sociology Compass*, 10, no. 4, 318–329. https://doi.org/10.1111/soc4.12364.

Schuppli, Susan. 2020. *MATERIAL WITNESS: Media, Forensics, Evidence*. Cambridge, MA: MIT Press.

Scolari, Carlos A. 2012. "Media Ecology: Exploring the Metaphor to Expand the Theory." *Communication Theory* 22, no. 2 (May): 204–225. https://doi.org/10.1111/j.1468-2885.2012.01404.x.

Simondon, Gilbert. 2017. *On the Mode of Existence of Technical Objects*. Translated by Cécile Malaspina and John Rogove. Minneapolis, MN: Univocal Publishing.

Simpson, Leanne. 2017. *As We Have Always Done: Indigenous Freedom through Radical Resistance*. Minneapolis: University of Minnesota Press.

Singh, Priyanka, and Vipin K. Singh. 2010. *What and Why They Are: A Peep into Feminism*. Central Milton Keynes, UK: AuthorHouse.

SITU Research. 2022. "Codec." GitHub repository. https://github.com/SITU-Research/codec?tab=readme-ov-file#readme.

Smart Borders. 2024. "Smart Borders." European Commission. https://home-affairs.ec.europa.eu/policies/schengen-borders-and-visa/smart-borders_en.

Smets, Kevin. 2018. "The Way Syrian Refugees in Turkey Use Media: Understanding 'Connected Refugees' through a Non-Media-Centric and Local Approach." *Communications* 43, no. 1 (March 26): 113–123. https://doi.org/10.1515/commun-2017-0041.

Smith, Linda Tuhiwai. 1999. *Decolonizing Methodologies: Research and Indigenous Peoples*. London: Zed Books and University of Otago Press, distributed in the United States by St. Martin's Press.

Stepan, Nancy. 2001. *Picturing Tropical Nature*. London: Reaktion.

Stepan, Nancy Leys. 2006. "Constructing Tropical Nature." In *Human Impacts on Amazonia: The Role of Traditional Ecological Knowledge in Conservation and Development*, edited by Darrell Addison Posey and Michael J. Balick, 17–32. New York: Columbia University Press.

Strasser, Bruno J., Jérôme Baudry, Dana Mahr, Gabriela Sanchez, and Elise Tancoigne. 2018. "'Citizen Science'? Rethinking Science and Public Participation." *Science & Technology Studies* (October 30): 52–76. https://doi.org/10.23987/sts.60425.

Strate, Lance. 2008. "Studying Media as Media: McLuhan and the Media Ecology Approach." *MediaTropes eJournal* 1: 127–142.

Stuart, Forrest. 2011. "Constructing Police Abuse after Rodney King: How Skid Row Residents and the Los Angeles Police Department Contest Video Evidence." *Law & Social Inquiry* 36, no. 2: 327–353. https://doi.org/10.1111/j.1747-4469.2011.01234.x.

Swann, Patricia. 2014. *Cases in Public Relations Management: The Rise of Social Media and Activism*. 2nd ed. New York: Routledge, Taylor & Francis Group.

Syrian Archive. 2021. "Targeting Health: Attacks against Medical Facilities in Syria. https://medical.syrianarchive.org/assets/pdf_reports/Syrian%20Archive%20-%20Medical%20Facilities%20Findings%20PUBLIC%20-%20FINAL%20FORMATTED.pdf.

Syrian Archive. 2025. "About." https://syrianarchive.org/en/about.

Talking Walls. 2019. "Beirut Walls." https://www.talkingwalls.world/blogs/stories/beirut-walls.

Tas, Sarah. 2020. "Frontex Actions: Out of Control? The Complexity of Composite Decision-Making Procedures." *SSRN Electronic Journal*. https://doi.org/10.2139/ssrn.3632712.

Thatcher, Jim E., and Craig M. Dalton. 2022. *Data Power: Radical Geographies of Control and Resistance*. London: Pluto Press. https://doi.org/10.2307/j.ctv249sg9w.

Thatcher, Jim, Andrew Shears, and Josef Eckert, eds. 2018. *Thinking Big Data in Geography: New Regimes, New Research*. Lincoln: University of Nebraska Press.

Toler, Aric. 2020. "How to Verify and Authenticate User-Generated Content." In *Digital Witness: Using Open Source Information for Human Rights Investigation, Documentation, and Accountability*, edited by Sam Dubberley, Alexa Koenig, and Daragh Murray, 185–227. Oxford: Oxford University Press.

Treré, Emiliano. 2019. *Hybrid Media Activism: Ecologies, Imaginaries, Algorithms*. New York: Routledge.

Trilling, Daniel. 2018. *Lights in the Distance: Exile and Refuge at the Borders of Europe*. London: Picador.

Trimikliniotis, Nicos, D. Parsanoglou, and Vassilis S. Tsianos. 2015. *Mobile Commons, Migrant Digitalities and the Right to the City*. New York: Palgrave Macmillan.

Trouillot, Michel-Rolph, and Hazel V. Carby. 2015. *Silencing the Past: Power and the Production of History*. Boston: Beacon Press.

Tybjerg, Karin. 2017. "Exhibiting Epistemic Objects." *Museum and Society* 15, no. 3: 269–286. https://doi.org/10.29311/mas.v15i3.2540.

United Nations High Commissioner for Refugees. 2021. *Mid-Year Trends 2021*.

United Nations Office of the High Commissioner for Human Rights. 2024. "Peru: Fujimori Government's Forced Sterilisation Policy Violated Women's rights, UN Committee Says in Landmark Ruling." https://www.ohchr.org/en/press-releases/2024/10/peru-fujimori-governments-forced-sterilisation-policy-violated-womens-rights.

United Nations Office of the High Commissioner for Human Rights and Human Rights Center, University of California, Berkeley, School of Law. 2022. *Berkeley Protocol on Digital Open Source Investigations: A Practical Guide on the Effective Use of Digital Open Source Information in Investigating Violations of International Criminal, Human Rights and Humanitarian Law*. Geneva: United Nations Office of the High Commissioner for Human Rights and Human Rights Center, University of California, Berkeley, School of Law.

UNITED. 2024. "Fortress Europe: Death by Policy." https://unitedagainstrefugeedeaths.eu/about-the-campaign/fortress-europe-death-by-policy/.

Vihalem, Margus. 2018. "Everyday Aesthetics and Jacques Rancière: Reconfiguring the Common Field of Aesthetics and Politics." *Journal of Aesthetics & Culture* 10, no. 1 (January): 1506209. https://doi.org/10.1080/20004214.2018.1506209.

Virilio, Paul. 2002. *Desert Screen: War at the Speed of Light*. London: Continuum.

Virilio, Paul, and Bertrand Richard. 2012. *The Administration of Fear*. Los Angeles: Semiotext(e).

Vorobej, Mark. 2008. "Structural Violence." *Peace Research*, 40, no. 2: 84–98. http://www.jstor.org/stable/23607799.

Warren, Jeffrey Yoo. 2010. *Grassroots Mapping: Tools for Participatory and Activist Cartography*. https://dspace.mit.edu/handle/1721.1/65319.

Weizman, Eyal. 2017. *Forensic Architecture: Violence at the Threshold of Detectability*. New York: Zone Books.

Weizman, Eyal. 2019. "Open Verification." *E-Flux Architecture*, June. https://www.e-flux.com/architecture/becoming-digital/248062/open-verification/.

Wiggins, Andrea, and Kevin Crowston. 2011. "From Conservation to Crowdsourcing: A Typology of Citizen Science." In *2011 44th Hawaii International Conference on System Sciences*, 1–10. Kauai, HI: IEEE. https://doi.org/10.1109/HICSS.2011.207.

Wild, Johanna. 2021. "The Exciting Possibilities of New Open Source Tools." Podcast, July 28. https://www.patreon.com/posts/bellingchat-of-54207591.

Wilde, Lawrence. 1998. *Ethical Marxism and Its Radical Critics*. London: Palgrave Macmillan.

World Meteorological Organization. 2017. "Special Clouds." https://cloudatlas.wmo.int/en/clouds-special.html.

Yusoff, Kathryn. 2018. *A Billion Black Anthropocenes or None*. Minneapolis: University of Minnesota Press.

Zook, Matthew A., and Mark Graham. 2007. "Mapping DigiPlace: Geocoded Internet Data and the Representation of Place." *Environment and Planning B: Planning and Design* 34, no. 3 (June): 466–482. https://doi.org/10.1068/b3311.

INDEX

Publisher contact:
The MIT Press
Massachusetts Institute of Technology
77 Massachusetts Avenue, Cambridge, MA 02139
mitpress.mit.edu

EU Authorised Representative:
Easy Access System Europe, Mustamäe tee 50,
10621 Tallinn, Estonia
gpsr.requests@easproject.com

Printed by Integrated Books International,
United States of America